THE NATURAL HISTORY OF GOWER

BY THE SAME AUTHOR

Instructions to Young Ornithologists IV—Sea Birds
1963 Brompton Library Series; Museum Press, London.

A Naturalist in New Zealand
1966 Museum Press, London and Reeds, N.Z.

Sub-Antarctic Sanctuary: Summertime on Macquarie Island
1967 Victor Gollancz Ltd., London and Reeds, N.Z.

November storm clouds over Three Cliffs Bay   *Author*

View from Outer Worm back to mainland   *Author*

The Natural History of Gower

by

Mary E. Gillham, B.SC., PH.D.

D. BROWN AND SONS LIMITED COWBRIDGE

First published 1977

ISBN 0 905928 00 8

DESIGNED AND PRINTED IN WALES BY

D. Brown and Sons Ltd., Cowbridge and Bridgend, South Wales

Colour separations by TPS (Technigraphics) Ltd., Cardiff

Bound by Western Book Company Limited, Maesteg

To the memory of

JO HAMBURY

who did so much for Gower's wildlife

ACKNOWLEDGEMENTS

I am greatly indebted to a number of the local naturalists on Gower for their generous help in the compilation of information for this book. Special thanks go to Mrs. Winnie Weston who gave unstintingly of her wide knowledge of the area and of her hospitality during my spells of field work. Also to Dr. Quentin Kay, Dr. Tony Nelson-Smith and Dr. Derek Thomas who read through the script and gave me the benefit of their deep specialist knowledge. Dr. Bill Kwantes and Mr. David White waded manfully through the first draft and left it much improved by their efforts; as did Professor Geoffrey Asprey in the very early stages.

Dr. T. G. Owen checked geological details and supplied the geological maps; Dr. John Evans inspired the comments and diagram on recent deposits and Dr. Tom Jefferson gave details of cave fauna. Valuable data on the animal life was made available by Dr. June Chatfield, Mr. T. G. Beynon, Dr. P. Niedzwiedzki, Dr. T. J. King, Mr. Syd Johnson, Dr. P. Makings, Mr. E. Scourfield, Mr. Christopher Methuen-Campbell and Mr. R. M. S. Hatton. The index is the work of Mr. Roy Denning.

For a significant proportion of the photographic illustrations I am deeply grateful to have been able to draw on the work of Mr. Keri Williams, Mr. Harold Grenfell, Mr. Arthur Morgan, Dr. Michael Claridge, Dr. Phil King, and the National Museum of Wales for old fishing prints. Mr. Ivor Penberthy supplied the seven landscape sketches, Miss Ruth Eyre the Whiteford lighthouse view and Mr. Rob Hume the recognition plate of gulls. The endpaper map has been done by Mr. Paul Brown.

I have drawn freely from published papers and unpublished reports, as indicated in the Bibliography, and extend sincere thanks to all who have contributed data or criticism in one form or another.

Financial help towards the considerable cost of the illustrations has been generously donated by British Petroleum Ltd., BP Oil and BP Chemicals, (through the good offices of Dr. Brian Sage) and guarantees kindly granted by West Glamorgan County Council.

CONTENTS

CONTENTS

ILLUSTRATIONS

1. COLOUR PLATES

2. MONOCHROME PLATES

3.   LINE DRAWINGS

The ninety-seven line illustrations, maps and scraper-board
drawings in the text are largely by the author.

FOREWORD

By The Marchioness of Anglesey
Vice-Chairman of the Prince of Wales Committee
Chairman of the Welsh Arts Council

GOWER is a small area within easy reach of the whole population of industrial South Wales. It is exceptionally rich in animal and plant life. If this wealth is to survive and flourish, and if we are to continue to enjoy it, we must all come to accept the need for a positive policy of conservation and amenity planning. First we need to know about these riches themselves, and then we need to understand the arguments for their preservation and for the ways by which this can be achieved. Dr. Mary Gillham's book gives us an opportunity to do all this, and with pleasure.

Shirley Anglesey

The spirit of Gower: Cormorants West of Mewslade

PREFACE

IT is tremendous fun to slide down a bald dune and clamber back with the sand cascading away from scrabbling feet. None of us is too old to remember those momentum-gathering sprints and the breathtaking leaps into space from where the tattered marram grass held the remnants of an overworked dune. Many of us recall the springtime posies of primroses and cowslips and autumn baskets of crabapples and chestnuts which we gathered as children. But there were fewer children then on Gower's green acres. Those idyllic days of unfettered freedom have gone—swamped by the size and mobility of our growing population.

Forty years ago the holidaying family threaded its way through tall dune grasses and boiled a tea kettle on the driftwood fire which warmed them after an invigorating frolic in surf which creamed up the wide sweep of Rhossili Bay. The kettle and cups were carried home in the picnic hamper. In the August heatwave of 1976 the equivalent family shuffled through loose sand which is slowly engulfing Llangennith carpark, traversed an outsize dune blowout and emerged onto a beach where they were hard put to it to find an unoccupied patch of sand big enough to sit on. There was neither fuel nor space for a picnic fire and when they bathed they picked their way through tide-drifted belts of discarded beer cans, polythene pop bottles and crumpled cardboard cups left by the misguided multitude which thinks its fellow men *enjoy* sitting among accumulated rubbish—or just doesn't think. Our family, after running the gauntlet of broken glass and crude oil washed in from the Bristol Channel, may have been tempted to think, like the rest, that a few more tins and bottles would make little difference.

Children must always have the opportunity to slide down dunes, and to dig on such broad expanses of tide-washed sand as are denied those who throng the meagre strips of brown bordering the tideless Mediterranean. But sand is all too readily picked up by the wind and deposited somewhere less convenient. If the play is not channelled to selected spots where sand movement can be contained by suitable wind breaks, there may be no more dunes to play on. Nor should children be denied the innocent pleasure of picking flowers, but they should be led to the more prolific growths, as of buttercup and heather. Today's hosts emulating yesterday's few will leave no more primroses and cowslips for the taking and all will be the poorer for not being able to admire these as they grow.

The Gower Peninsula was the first part of Great Britain to be designated as an 'Area of Outstanding Natural Beauty'. It is still very beautiful except in the vicinity of the big beach carparks during high summer. It is up to everyone to sample this beauty wisely rather than exploit it. Nature is very resilient and responds if treated kindly.

In 1976 it is still possible to wade out from Salthouse Point in August to meet the tide racing in over Llanrhidian Sands and be the only swimmer for a couple of miles. The farm boys of Crofty can still gambol out across the saltings after a hot day on the harvest fields and splash in the deep, hard-floored pools with only the marsh ponies for company. There are still lengths of magnificent limestone cliffs where sheep may safely graze and stonechats breed in peace, disturbed only by the more determined long distance walkers.

Choicest of the dune flowers grow in level slacks where sand does not blow away because the water table is near the surface. But the flat firmness of the slacks lures more and more cars and caravans. Bee orchids are among rarities which have almost gone from Llangennith where once they flourished—battered to death by a surfeit of wheels and feet. Others survive, however, in the National Nature Reserves, where farsighted planners have stepped in to save at least some portion of this precious heritage which each generation holds in trust for the next. While there are reservoirs of wildlife preserved for posterity there is always the hope that some of the surplus may spill out to the despoiled areas and repopulate them if prudent land use allows. And is it too much to cherish a hope that the otherwise non-criminal individuals who carry cans of beer to the beach will learn in time to carry the empties back?

Swansea is very close: Cardiff is a mere 60 miles or so away. Holiday makers from southern England come bowling in along the new M4 motorway; those from further north along the new Heads of the Valleys road. They pay Glamorgan a compliment in travelling so far to sample what she has to offer. Those who can partake of Gower's fresh sea air all the year must not grudge them their short few weeks of ecstatic freedom. But neither locals nor visitors must run riot over the whole spectrum and expect it to retain either its rural charm or its wealth of plants and animals —more than a few of which are national rarities and hence held in trust for the nation.

The pressure on Llangennith in the North West is tremendous at the peak of the season, with the visual intrusion of cars, caravans and tents, overloading of sewage schemes and general wear and tear. Rhossili carpark in the south west has a capacity for 2,000 vehicles and is on the coach tour itinerary of Butlin's Holiday Camp at Barry. Quantities of litter are collected daily from the popular beaches of South Gower—litter which should have gone in the way it came, with every user leaving his little patch as he would like to find it on the morrow.

1. The Mumbles from Oystermouth Castle

Untreated sewage pours from Swansea's main sewer outfall at Mumbles and more is spewed from Llanelli into the Burry Inlet. The Pembroke Power Station is upwind, so Gower may lie in the fallout path of its sulphur dioxide effluent emission on a day of low pressure.

The hazards are great indeed, but go to Gower, on a blue day of crisp breeze and scudding white cloud in May or June, when the cliffs and dunes are ablaze with flowers and the birds in full song and you will think you have strayed by chance into a corner of Heaven. No-one who reads this account of the natural wonders to be seen on this small plot can remain in any doubt that we have something rather special here; something which we must conserve at all costs against thoughtless exploitation and pollution. We who inherit such beauty cannot, in all conscience, deprive our children of doing likewise.

There are certain basic rules of countryside behaviour which need to be observed if we are to retain sufficient of our wild and lovely places to serve our psychological and aesthetic needs and keep us sane in these chaotic times. As in all civilised living, consideration for others is the keynote —for our contemporaries, our successors and other forms of life. Only this can bring lasting satisfaction. With the dwindling of our countryside, the country code assumes a greater importance for all who come to recharge their batteries among the real values which have survived through aeons of time, as new life rises eternally young from the withered fragments of the old.

Planners and land developers have the greatest responsibility. Conservation of the Gower heritage is being taken seriously—by the Gower Society, the Swansea District Council, the West Glamorgan County Council, the Glamorgan Naturalists' Trust, the Nature Conservancy Council and the National Trust. 1975 and 1976 were earmarked as 'Swansea

Heritage Years'. Swansea's heritage in the Gower Peninsula must be the envy of thinking people in every other similar sized industrial complex in the land. Let us not squander it. In the end we get the countryside we deserve. Only by aiming high can we hope to succeed in retaining the dignity of our God-given landscape.

MARY E. GILLHAM
Cardiff, 1977

Plate 1 PUBLIC PRESSURE

1. Naturalists on the seaward cliffs of Burryholms
   Author
2. New erosion after fencing of old path (right) on clifftop sand above Three Cliffs Bay *Author*
3. Intersecting paths on the dunes above Pobbles Bay
   Author
4. Rubber carpets help curb sand erosion on Pennard golf course *Author*

5

6

7

8

Plate 2   RECENT GEOLOGICAL DEPOSITS

5. Raised beach East of Langland shows as a pale band between old cliff cut in glacial till above and modern cliff being cut in Carboniferous Limestone below   *Author*

6. Fossil limpet shells in the *Patella* raised beach East of Langland   *Author*

7. Windborne and waterborne deposits of dune and saltmarsh to seaward of limestone cliffs at Oxwich
                                                                            Author

8. Head, a kind of solidified limestone scree. Pennard cliffs   *Author*

2

INTRODUCTION AND GEOLOGY

GOWER is that little scrap of green on the map of Wales which juts untidily from the South Coast, as though the Maker of the mountain block let his finger slip in passing on to the West. Its ragged outline is its chief beauty, the grey bastions of the cliffs cradling broad sandy bays and thrusting seaward again as rugged headlands. It is small wonder that the region bears the distinction of being the first in Great Britain to have been designated an 'Area of Outstanding Natural Beauty' in 1957 by the National Parks Commission.

Stretching along the South coast from the tidal islands of the Mumbles to the tidal island of the Worm, Carboniferous Limestone cliffs rise in blocky magnificence. Their feet are washed by a line of creaming surf, their faces lashed by gales from the Atlantic; but they soak up sunshine where the winds are blocked and reflect an oceanic mildness.

Northward to the tidal island of Burryholms, the coast is gentler. A long sweep of yellow sand lies to seaward of Rhossili Down and Llangennith Burrows, reappearing at Broughton Bay beyond the north western limestone outcrop. At Whiteford Point it reaches further north towards the old Carmarthenshire coast as a jutting sand spit and is backed by some of the finest dunes in Wales—a National Nature Reserve.

Eastwards again along the North coast the cliffs are more subdued and often wooded. They are sheltered from the impact of the Westerlies by their northerly aspect and from the impact of the waves by the broad stretch of sand and alluvium deposited at their base. Towards the head of the Burry Inlet (or Loughor Estuary), they dwindle in height and merge into the loftier Coalfield hills behind Swansea.

A backbone of peaty moorland runs obliquely across the peninsula from Penmaen in the South to Llanmadoc Hill in the North West, where it rises to 609 ft. (185 m.). Gower's loftiest point, the Beacon on Rhossili Down in the South West, is only slightly higher and it is from here that intrepid young men and women launch themselves the 632 ft. (197 m.) to the beach below in the new sport of hang gliding, so popular by the mid seventies.

Cefn Bryn occupies a four mile length of the moorland backbone and commands views which encompass the heights of Somerset and Exmoor across the Bristol Channel, the wind-scourged island of Lundy, the Preseli Hills away to the West and the Carmarthen Fans and Brecon Beacons to the North. More immediately a green and brown patchwork of rich farmland stretches southwards and westwards to the sea, dissected by leafy lanes and sturdy walls.

The undeniable attractiveness of the 15-20 mile long Gower Peninsula reaching westwards from Swansea lies in its diversity. With the exception of high mountains, it has as much to offer scenically and scientifically as Wales itself. Biologically it supplies some extra titbits—boasting flowers and animals which occur in no other British county.

Nor is it just a *Wales* in miniature. Its inner end comprises a South Wales in miniature, but its outer end has been likened to a 'Little England beyond Glamorgan'. This portion has a deal in common with the better known 'Little England beyond Wales' of South Pembrokeshire—the same bed-rock of Devonian and Carboniferous age, the same south-facing limestone cliffs and sandy bays, the same sun-warmed fields of early potatoes and even a major estuary. The division in each case is both structural and cultural.

The sunnier, fertile lands of the South and West have been referred to as Gower Anglicana or Anglica; the rainier, infertile ones of the North and East as Gower Wallicana or Wallica. The dividing line was determined geologically in the first instance and perpetuated by the Normans, who appropriated the more productive limestone country of the West for themselves, leaving the more acid lands of the East to the native Welsh. When coal mining started the 'Bad Lands' turned out to be the more productive of the two, but the Normans were interested only in the agricultural potential. At present arable farming is concentrated in the West and livestock farming in the East.

In the arable countryside of the South West the population is aggregated into villages and speaks a dialectal English with a touch of Devon and Pembrokeshire, Irish and Welsh. Although containing Gower's largest village, Penclawdd, the pastoral countryside of the North East has scattered farms predominating and the people are more likely to speak Welsh. Geographically this is an outlier of the main South Wales Coal-field. In the 1974 reshuffling of political boundaries, the sparseness of population here was reflected in its division into the two 'Communities' of Llanrhidian Higher and Llanrhidian Lower with Gowerton in the East, whereas the similar-sized West is dissected into no less than sixteen 'Communities' based on the old parishes.

The scenery as we see it today is the result of a long sequence of geological events starting before Carboniferous times with the laying down of the Devonian Old Red Sandstone some 350 million years ago.

South West of a line from the Mumbles Peninsula in the East to White-ford in the West most of Gower is composed of blocky Carboniferous Limestone which was thrown into east-west trending folds by intense earth movements around 280 million years ago. Where the limestone strata were bent over the tops of the upfolds or anticlines they were not only structurally weakened by stretching, but were exposed to weathering, so that they were eroded away to reveal the older Old Red Sandstone which lay beneath. Thus it is that all the high ground—of Cefn Bryn, Harding's Down, Ryer's Down and Rhossili Down—consists of these resistant, non-calcareous Devonian rocks poking up from below.

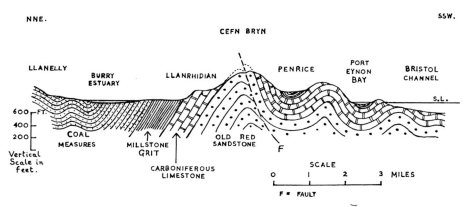

2. Geological section through Cefn Bryn. (After T. R. Owen)

The present coastline does not follow the folding of the limestone beds but cuts across them, giving a variety of cliff formations. Where the strata are practically vertical—as where Cefn Bryn terminates at Great Tor—or where they are inclined to seaward at an angle of about 45° —as East of Pennard—smooth, uncompromising faces are presented for colonisation by plants and animals. Where they are inclined inland —as west of Porteynon—it is their edges, not their surfaces, which form the cliff face, and these weather into a series of sloping steps or ledges retaining more rain and collecting more soil in which vegetation can become established. Westwards at Thurba and the Knave the strata are almost vertical again, resulting in sheer cliffs where kittiwakes and fulmars can nest undisturbed.

In the bottom of the downfolds or synclines some of the Millstone Grit shales overlying the limstones have been retained. These are softer and have been eaten into by the sea at Oystermouth, Oxwich and Porteynon to form bays in which splendid sandy beaches have been deposited.

Moving North-eastwards from 'English Peninsular Gower' to 'Gower Wallica', the Millstone Grit is overlain in parts by Coal Measure shales. Together these form a band of soft rock running East to West from West Cross to Llanrhidian and the sea has encroached at either end to form Swansea Bay and the Burry Inlet.

5

The harder Pennant Sandstone of the Coalfield in the extreme North-east has resisted this attack and forms the ridge of high ground from Town-hill to Penclawdd, where it drops beneath the more recently added tidal muds.

Newer Mesozoic strata have eroded away completely except for a little patch of Triassic rocks near Porteynon. Boulder Clay and Gravel transported by ice has been dumped over much of the Gower Limestone, however, giving poor acid soils quite similar to those of the Coalfield and Millstone Grit shales. This is especially true of the limestone area North of Cefn Bryn.

The Coal Measures lying between Swansea Bay and Wernffrwd on the Burry Inlet have been extensively worked, but no coal has been dug since 1947, Whitewalls being the last of the collieries to close. Old coaltips can be seen on Fairwood Common and the northern mudflats and brick and stone engine houses analagous to those of the North Cornish tin mines by abandoned pits on the hills behind. The taking of the last of the coal from some of the smaller opencast workings revealed clay suitable for brick-making, so employment could continue—the miners' 'Fairwell Rock' becoming the brickmakers' 'Hallo Clay'! An old coal seam and some fossil 'mussels' are recognisable at the Killay Brick Pit in Clyne Woods.

Late Tertiary submergence under the sea caused the tops of what is now the highest land (Cefn Bryn, Llanmadoc Hill and Rhossili Down) to be planed off at about 600 ft. (185 m.) above present sea level. Later, a 200 ft. (62 m.) platform was levelled off by marine erosion. At this time most of Gower was under the sea with the ridges rising as islands. The two main levels can be distinguished from many viewpoints, whether on the lower land of the main area looking to the flat-topped hills, or on the hills looking onto surprisingly even surfaces such as that of Worm's Head. An intervening 400 ft. (124 m.) platform is less well marked but can be recognised on the commons of Fairwood, Clyne and Pengwern.

Later oscillations occurred between the various Ice Ages as the sea level rose and fell with the melting of the ice. These have left raised beaches along the southern cliffs, one of which is particularly well marked. This is of shelly shingle, the limpets, dog whelks, periwinkles and pebbles cemented together into a sort of concrete or conglomerate by stalagmitic calcite or limestone. Because limpets (*Patella*) are the commonest shells, it is called the Patella Beach, and is probably of Ipswichian age. It lies about 30 ft. (9 m.) above sea level and is recognisable at Brandy Cove and a number of other sites, where it rests on a narrow, wave-cut rock platform. At Minchin Hole the Neritoides beach (named after the periwinkles) overlies it, and must therefore be more recent. A still newer one of concreted shelly conglomerate and shingle occurs at Heatherslade below present day high water mark.

Caves around these cliffs often open out onto the Patella beach and concealed the remains of many creatures which roamed through Gower during past centuries. In Pleistocene times the bones of mammoths and soft-nosed rhinoceros were carried into the caves by creatures which ate them—men, hyenas and possibly cave bears. Post-pleistocene inmates included bear, badger, wolf, dog, wild cat and reindeer. Human remains are represented by the Cromagnon 'Red Lady of Paviland', who lived some 18,000 years before our time and turned out to be a young man after all. The coastal caves are not spectacular, but it is interesting to reflect that the few feet of very ordinary earth separating different bone deposits represent a time span which the human mind finds difficult to grasp.

Gower is as rich in natural and human interest as it is in scenery. The predominant limestone nurtures a rich flora with its dependent fauna, whilst the landscape is dotted with relics of the Ancients—barrows, dolmens, menhirs and castles. The old county of Glamorgan, in spite of supporting more than half the population of Wales, possessed until its division in 1974, the most varied flora of any Welsh county and most of its 1,100 species of flowering plants can be found in this delectable small area of the Gower Peninsula.

This natural gem is situated delightfully, but dangerously, near the great conurbation of Swansea and will be more and more subject to invasion from 'over the Border' now that the new trunk roads are pressing steadily westwards.

The Gower Society and Glamorgan Naturalists' Trust are well aware of the threats to both rural charm and wildlife—as are national bodies such as the National Trust, Nature Conservancy and Royal Society for the Protection of Birds—and the future of the Peninsula is in good hands.

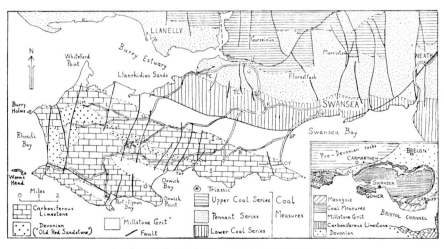

3. The Geology of Gower. (After T. R. Owen)

'Enterprise Neptune' has been at work and a large proportion of the coast is now safeguarded from building development as national and local nature reserves. Inland the county Trust holds a number of smaller areas of woodland, fresh water and rock exposure.

Tourists who like sophistication of the funfair type are not catered for: the more discerning are accommodated mainly in a few large carparks backing fine stretches of sand at Oxwich, Porteynon, Rhossili and Llangennith. At the southern approaches Limeslade, Bracelet, Langland and Caswell Bays filter off a fair proportion of the holiday traffic. For most of the rest Gower remains much as it has always been, offering an unspoiled charm to walkers and naturalists, pony trekkers and fishermen, and boundless opportunities for biological education and scientific investigation.

Part One

The Moors, Woods and Fields

Sparring hares and Molinia

1 THE SHAPE AND COLOUR OF THE MOORLANDS

ONE stretch of brackenny grassland may look much like another, but the limestone grass swards of the South and West differ from the acid grass moors of the East in soil fertility, water retaining capacity and the plants which make up their swards. There are 34 tracts of poor quality common-land on Gower, totalling more than 7,000 acres, and most of these are of moorland type.

These moors have produced mainly meat and wool in the past but the pattern is changing. As Gower takes on its new role of rural playground for an urban hinterland, riding schools and pony trekking centres are springing up to cater for recreational needs. Shaggy Welsh mares convert the coarse grasses into an annual crop of charming long-legged foals and travellers on Fairwood Common may find ponies as well as store cattle sheltering from the rain in roadside bus shelters.

Part of the inherent infertility of the moors is due to the washing down of nutrient material to subsoil layers below the reach of plant roots. Unless land improvement is carried out, these impoverished soils become covered by a layer of peat, which soaks up rain like blotting paper and prevents much of it from reaching the mineral soil below.

Most of North and East Gower is occupied by this type of country, whether underlain by Coal shales, Millstone Grit shales or Boulder Clay. The Old Red Sandstones of the central and western hills yield a similar sort of vegetation characterised by rough grass and bracken with heather chiefly on the crags. The ground here is more varied, however, only the coarser textured sandstones yielding leached soils akin to those of the Coal Measures. The softer marls give higher quality, richer coloured 'brown earths' with properties nearer to those of soils derived directly from the limestones.

The geological map shows two thirds of Gower to be composed of lime-stone, but much of this is lost to sight under infertile glacial deposits dumped by the retreating ice sheets. There is thus more poor quality grassland than might be expected, with snippets of limestone flora only on rock outcrops and steep slopes where the glacial debris has washed away.

Sticky clays hinder drainage and become waterlogged, so that aeration suffers and the ground is slow to warm up in spring. The soil microbes responsible for breaking down the dead remains of plants and animals and recycling them for use by future generations are inhibited on both counts, so that undecayed peat builds up, increasing soil acidity and hindering breakdown yet further.

Much of the peat-blanketted country has smoothly rounded outlines, as where the road through Cilibion and Llethryd undulates over successive hummocks. The rounding off got under way at the end of the Ice Ages when summer warmth was just sufficient to thaw the surface soil but not the subsoil. Sodden with meltwater, the topsoil sludged down over the permanently frozen permafrost layer below in the process known as sollifluction. During the warmer ages which followed, the surface continued to slip imperceptibly downwards under the influence of gravity, wind and rain in the phenomenon known as soil creep.

A lot of the rolling moorland country is covered by purple moor-grass (*Molinia*), with bracken on the deeper untilled soils—so long as these are not waterlogged, as they are on Pengwern Common. Intensive trampling by cattle will damage bracken fronds, but very few animals will eat them. The bracken of Hardings Down is sometimes cut and carted away for stock bedding.

Thin dry soils of the upper slopes may be occupied by bent-fescue grassland (*Agrostis-Festuca*), but mat grass and heath grass (*Nardus* and *Sieglingia*) are also quite common. Bristle bent (*Agrostis setacea*), which is uncommon in many areas, dominates big tracts of Harding's Down, Clyne Common, Cefn Bryn and Oxwich Point, whilst the delicate silky heads of wavy hair-grass (*Deschampsia flexuosa*) cast a purple sheen over the highest tops in summer. Bilberries growing among them are nibbled short by grazing animals and are unable to produce the good fruit crops of plants which escape by growing on the crags. Heath rush, deer-sedge and the rare white beak sedge (*Rhynchospora alba*) add to the upland character of the moors.

Although poor in species compared with the more verdant tracts of limestone country, the moorland commons produce more spectacular seasonal colour changes. Bracken fades from the rich dark green of summer to a tawny brown which becomes deep bronze when sodden by rain, then disappears altogether from the windier areas. Purple moor-grass is purple only in late summer beneath the wispy fruit heads, fading to a whitened winter mass of dead leaves which the new green shoots of late spring pierce only reluctantly.

The white plumes of common and hare's-tail cotton grass transform the buff-coloured quagmires of spring to a sea of breeze-ruffled silk in summer, then fly away or drown to expose the aging orange-red leaves. 'Bog cotton' is a more appropriate name for these, because they are not grasses at all, but sedges.

Cross-leaved heath produces a subtler pink in the wet areas than do the fine-leaved heath and ling of drier ones, but heather moor is well developed only on the east face of Rhossili Down and on parts of Clyne Common. The chief brighteners are the gorse, the European species flowering from October through the milder winters to June and the smaller western species (which is much the commoner on these acid soils) taking over in late summer, to produce a beautiful colour mosaic with the purple of fine-leaved heath and ling. Although often occurring together, the smaller rounder domes of the western gorse are particularly characteristic of the top of Llanmadoc Hill and the other is very much a feature of the clifflands, where it transforms whole areas to gold in the early spring. Broom is confined to old mine spoil and pinpoints the occurrence of this throughout the Morlais Valley Coalfield.

Clumps of downy birch establish themselves in places, the pale gold of their autumn leaves followed by the more subdued crimson of slender winter twigs with stiff terminal catkins. Sometimes durmast oak trees add a deeper tinge of brown in autumn and a soft apricot red as the tender leaves unfold in spring.

All too often the changing colour sequence is transformed abruptly in March to a charred black wilderness. Birch and oak succumb to the flames: bracken, gorse and the coarser grasses sprout again from the scorched earth. The intensity of the annual fires depends on the weather in the early part of the year, being fiercest in the drier springs. Burning may be due to vandalism or carelessness, but is also part and parcel of the system of land management, aimed at getting rid of the trash to enable the young shoots to push through and produce 'early bite' for winter-hungry livestock. It is least harmful when carried out in winter, but is a controversial practice, destroying organic matter and allowing minerals to be washed out by rain, and it may diminish as sheep are gradually replaced by ponies.

All the species mentioned so far are commonplace, but the boggy areas hold many choicer ones. The whiskery white flowers of bogbean flecked with red rise among robust, trefoil-shaped leaves in late May and June. Other rosy tints are supplied by the delicate bog pimpernel and brighter lousewort, with its slightly asymmetrical flowers into which the larger pollinating bumble bees may have to edge sideways. Always delightful are the rich purple marsh orchids and filigree-patterned heath-spotted orchids, which have a white-flowered population on Kennexstone Common.

Flying and crawling insects unfortunate enough to alight on the glistening pin-headed tentacles of sundew leaves are held fast in a tangle of mucilage. Digestive fluids are poured over them and their essential animal proteins are drawn off to nourish the plant's own tissues, leaving the empty chitinous husks to be removed by wind or rain. Gower boasts not only the commoner round-leaved sundew but also the oblong-leaved sundew, which grows on partially bare peats such as are provided by paths

13

4. Moorland grasses. Wavy hair grass, mat grass and bristle bent grass

through the Whitemoor Valley in the West. Rather surprisingly no butterwort occurs on Gower, although there is an old record for Rhossili Down.

An attractive associate of the sundews in the *Sphagnum* moss bogs is the yellow-flowered marsh St. John's wort, on whose downy, unwettable leaves, water beads up into translucent pearls. Bog asphodel contributes patches of gold in summer and rusty red in autumn. West Gower is still the best habitat for the noble royal fern, which grows handsomely tall in hedgelines as well as on the bogs. There is more in open hollows of Fair-wood and Clyne Commons, Cefn Bryn, Rhossili Down and Llangennith Moors, but it is much scarcer than formerly, as, indeed, it is all over Wales.

Whorled caraway rears feathery leaves and wispy white flowers on damp meadows and boggy commons. The red-fruited cranberry of Fairwood Common is at one of its most southerly stations in Britain here, yet it is locally abundant.

Some of the acid valleys are fragrant with bog myrtle or sweet gale in summer, the aromatic leaves falling in winter and the bare, reddish twigs

14

sprouting stiff little catkins, some male and some female. The bushes used to reach ten feet high on Whitemoor, but burning now prevents them from attaining their full potential except in a few wet hollows, such as those west of Broad Pool. Many West Gower quagmires support short nibbled growths of creeping willow, a species which is more often found in dune slacks. Double-flowered lady's smock or cuckoo-flower is common here, with marsh marigolds and lesser spearwort.

2   ANIMALS OF THE MOORLANDS

BROWN hares are perhaps the most characteristic wild mammals of the commonlands, where they can be seen lollopping lazily over the tussocks and nibbling at the tender grasses between. Although reputedly shy, they are in fact quite bold, cantering off in leisurely fashion with black-tipped ears erect when disturbed as though well aware that only a greyhound or a beagle could outpace them. Only when really worried do they go 'flat out', with ears laid back and legs extended as they skim the ground in ten foot leaps. Going uphill they are virtually uncatchable as they push forwards with disproportionately long hind legs. On downhill stretches such a length of leg is an embarrassment and a speeding animal is likely to turn a somersault.

The well-worn tracks stop short of the 'forms' or depressions where they shelter from the sun, wind and predators, these being reached by long bounds which leave little clue as to their whereabouts. Hares are red-brown in summer and smokey grey in winter, when the fur thickens. They tend to avoid rabbit-infested country, just as they avoid most of their own kind, being generally solitary except during the bizarre sparring matches of spring.

Even less shy are the short-tailed field voles which tunnel among the grass in vast numbers, emerging about their business by day as well as by night. Their population is cyclic and in plague years their highways ramify in all directions. These often run above ground and are formed by gnawing through of the grass bases, so that they become marked by sinuous strips of withered leaves cut off from their water supply but still effectively roofing the passages beneath. If an extensive bare patch is to be crossed the tunnels are excavated below ground level.

15

Common lizards bask in the sun, scuttle among the heather shoots and disappear into the labyrinthine moorland 'underground'—as do any number of other 'wee timorous beasties'. Adders, too, like the drier heathery sites and furze-clad knolls rising above the general level of the wetter moorland soils. Grass snakes find seclusion among sedge tufts and are not so averse to water. Palmate newts are the most generally distributed of the three newt species, but smooth newts are more plentiful on Fairwood and a few of the other commons. Toads breed regularly, in big numbers, but frogs have been scarce during the seventies. The sparkling lights of glow worms are a pleasant and frequent sight in season around Llanmorlais.

The cheerful chinking of stonechats on the gorse tips is part and parcel of the Gower scene and whinchats are a recent addition to the list of local breeding birds. On crisp 'peninsula days' when the air is flowing in over the commons from the sea like chilled wine, pushing cotton wool clouds before it, yellow hammers can be watched sunbathing on the rounded bramble tops. Clinging with difficulty to some wind-tossed spray, they droop and spread their wings in response to a burst of sunlight through a hole in the clouds, exposing the rufous rump. The stance is held on the swaying perch until some specially fierce gust blows the wings back into position and only the yellow on the head and breast distinguish the streaky brown morsel from the fuzz of wind-scorched bramble twigs.

Robins and blackbirds do their sunbathing on the roadsides or on bare trampled peat in the lee of the sheltering scrub patches which they frequent. This exercise is very likely indulged in for sheer physical pleasure, as in humans, but it may produce side effects which are beneficial to health. It has been suggested that the ultra-violet rays of the sun cause an essential vitamin to develop in the oil of the feathers,

5. Nightjar and lesser horseshoe bat

small but adequate quantities of this being imbibed by the bird during bouts of preening. On this count the birds of Gower should be fitter than those of the rainier upland part of the Coalfield.

Skylarks tuck their darkly mottled eggs away in grassy cups among the tussocks and rise trilling over the moors on the gloomiest days to give an illusion of spring. Only the nightingale has inspired more poets and this left Gower long since in its general retreat to the East and South. Dunnocks abound, the smallest patches of scrub sufficing for their needs but meadow pipits are sparser than on the Coalfield Commons of 'mainland Glamorgan'. Tree pipits breed on the moorlands, particularly where there are isolated trees, from which they can launch themselves into trilling song flights during courtship. There is a wealth of potential foster parents for young cuckoos, whose legitimate parents are a familiar sight in May, when four of five may be seen together flying over Broad Pool or perching on roadside wires.

Some of the little acid commons north of Gelli Hir are frequented by big flocks of finches during winter. Goldfinches, chaffinches and linnets forage on seeds near ground level and the occasional party of lesser redpolls flies wheezing over the marginal birches. In summer their place is taken by low-flying swifts and swallows snapping midges from the air. Starlings seem always to be pecking and probing in their endless search for provender, gathering into big flocks in the evenings and whirring off to roosts on both sides of the Burry Inlet.

Representatives of the big flocks of lapwing, curlew and redshank which winter on the North Gower Marshes filter inland to the moors to breed in summer. Curlew were not known to do so in Glamorgan at all until the 1920s, but Gower has shared the general extension of their range and they have nested spasmodically on several of the commons since 1945, at least one pair losing its three eggs to carrion crows in 1972. The odd pair of redshank can be found on Welshmoor and Broad Pool and the latter area yielded a green sandpiper on passage in June 1972 and May 1974.

The evocative calling of whimbrel can sometimes be heard at night during the period of their spring passage. Woodcock are quite likely to turn up in winter and the odd few may stay to breed, as do some of the wintering snipe. Nightjars are disappearing, as elsewhere in Glamorgan, and have bred only spasmodically since 1961, but are still present in some localities.

Every now and again a short-eared owl visits in winter, affording opportunity for some daylight owl watching. Among the rarer diurnal birds of prey a few of the formerly scarce hen harriers now put in an appearance in winter on the Gower commons. Montagu's harriers scarcely come at all, the July 1964 record on Rhossili Down and the July 1968 record at Llanmadoc being the most recent for the moorlands. The marsh harrier comes no more often. Clyne Common boasts one of the triple county's only three records of red-footed falcons, but this was back in 1957. The merlin, a rarity on Gower until 1965, is now more likely to be spotted, engaged in an exciting aerial chase of some luckless pipit or lark.

Invertebrates are present in all types of habitat, often in abundance, but there are far fewer on the moorlands than in the more fertile limestone areas or in the humid shelter of the woodlands. The soil fauna is the most prolific and twenty two different kinds of springtails (*Collembola*) alone have been identified from the acid bracken covered moorlands of Gower. Eighty per cent of the total population, however, is accounted for by only four species (*Folsomia quadrioculata, Isotomiella minor, Onychiurus procampatus* and *Tullbergia krausbaueri*). These tiny animals seem to have quite definite preferences as to which of the soil fungi or other microbes they will eat.

Small heaths and meadow browns are commonest of the moorland butterflies in midsummer. Ringlets are also to be seen, the females dropping their eggs haphazardly as they fly instead of selecting a specific food plant for the up and coming brood. Little caterpillars hatch from the broadcast eggs three weeks later and feed on various grasses, continuing to do so on mild days during the winter and through the following spring until they finally pupate in June. The adults which emerge are also pretty hardy weatherwise, flying even in the rain. but are not strong on the wing and tend to seek the shelter of scrub patches.

Marsh fritillaries are fairly frequent on Welshmoor and on Fairwood and Clyne Commons; green hairstreak butterflies less so and quite difficult to see when settled with only the leaf-green underside of the hind wings showing. Their caterpillars feed mainly on gorse before pupating in the ground leaf-litter in August, but they may also be cannibals.

Garden tigers (*Arctia caja*) and elephant hawks (*Deilephila elpenor*) are probably the most spectacular moths on Fairwood Common: the cryptically patterned pink and green angleshades (*Phlogophora meticulosa*) merges inperceptibly into the russet tints of withered leaves and dry bracken.

Butterflies, moths, bumble bees and flies all visit the delicately pencilled flowers of moorland orchids, collecting truncheon-shaped pollinia on their heads in the doing. These sticky pollen masses, erect and greenish at first, become yellower and fluffier while being carried through the air to pollinate another orchid.

Robber flies (*Scopeuma stercoraria*) have more sinister intentions. Although feeding on pollen, they enjoy animal protein as well and will pounce on any other unsuspecting insect which alights on the same flower head, grabbing it with a cluster of bristly legs and killing it instantly with poison injected through the proboscis. Bluebottles and other flies are common victims. Green grasshoppers (*Omocestus viridulus*) and

Plate 3 MOORLAND PLANTS AND ANIMALS

9. Purple moor grass tussocks sprouting in late Spring by a West Gower hedge

Author

10. Royal ferns produce noble growths in damp corners of the moorlands

Author

11. Eyed hawk moth caterpillar with bizarre tail spine, on a grey sallow leaf

Michael Claridge

12. Giant puffball *(Lycoperdon giganteum)* weighing 22½ lbs. found on Reynoldston Common in September 1973 by Mr. T. Thomas

13. Eyed hawk moth *(Smerinthus ocellata)* displays fearsome eye-spots to warn predators

Michael Claridge

19

14

15

16

17

Plate 4 MOORLAND ANIMALS

14. Bank voles base their secretive lives in mossy
banks   *Arthur Morgan*

15. Long-tailed field mice forage busily through
the hours of darkness   *Arthur Morgan*

16. A Skylark removes a faecal sac from a nest
crowded with almost fully fledged young
                                   Arthur Morgan

17. Slow worms shelter under stones in drier
parts of the moorlands   *Arthur Morgan*

lesser marsh grasshoppers (*Chorthippus bicolor*) spurt from underfoot on sultry summer days like animated tiddlywinks.

So many insects spend their early life under water that moorland pools inevitably increase their diversity. No less than five species of damselfly and six of dragonfly have been recorded on Cefn Bryn alone, including the noblest of them all, the golden-ringed dragonfly (*Cordulegaster boltoni*). These become super-active after their long aquatic infancy and the only opportunity to get a really good look at them is when they have newly emerged from the nymphal case and are clinging to some handy stem while fluid is pumped into the veins of their expanding gauzy wings. The great size of the compound eye of the emergent hunter never fails to impress when viewed through a hand lens.

Violet ground beetles (*Carabus violaceus*) scuttle among the grass bases between June and August, doing most of their hunting by night. Under cover of darkness they devour earthworms and many less beneficial creatures, but are also devoured themselves by larger hunters of the night. The readily recognisable purple-bordered wing cases turn up with great regularity in the crop pellets of owls and dung pellets of foxes.

6. Cockchafer or maybug and violet ground beetle

The stouter dor beetles (*Geotrupes stercorarius*) are taken by the hunters over a longer period as they are about well into the winter, but they survive in good numbers. They are not flightless, as are the purple ground beetles, but fly at dusk, sometimes coming to lights. The humming noise generated in the process has given rise to the name of dor beetle, which comes from an old word meaning drone. The undersides of their body and legs shine an iridescent blue, but the external skeletons are sometimes infested with tiny buff-coloured mites (*Parasitus coleoptratorum*) which, in spite of their name, are said not be be parasites, but to be just hitching a ride. Dor beetles dig burrows beneath cow pats and pony dung,

21

carrying some of the excrement underground and laying their eggs in it, so that their offspring can feed on moorland nutrients discarded unused by the livestock.

The related minotaur beetle (*Typhaeus typhoeus*) has similar habits and is often seen wandering the moorland paths in spring and autumn. It derives its name from the male's bull-like horns and lacks the metallic sheen of the dor beetle. These, too, are plagued by louse-like mites (*Gamasus coleopterorum*) which suck body fluids from the beetle through the vulnerably soft skin at the joints in the chitinous armour plating— the exploitation of an Achilles heel indeed! They have caused their host to be dubbed the 'lousy watchman'.

Tunnelling beneath corpses instead of dung are black burying beetles (*Necrophorus humator*) the acuteness of whose sense of smell enables them to home in on any animal that has fallen by the wayside. A pair will dig so vigorously under the carcase that this is let into the soil to make a snug repository for the beetle eggs which are laid on it so that the emerging grubs can feast on the sumptuous meat supply.

Other beetles with characteristic buzzing flight like the dor beetles are cockchafers or maybugs (*Melonotha melonotha*), their gingery wing cases powdered with white at first. These are night fliers and sometimes crash into car windscreens on the common-land roads.

Trichius auratus, a close relative of the bee chafer, is slightly smaller but more colourful, its broad wing cases patterned in orange and black. Exceedingly hairy, it can easily be mistaken for a bee when settled on the massed mauve flowers of thyme and knapweed to which it seems especially attracted. *Trichius* is a rare northern beetle more likely to be found in the uplands of the Glamorgan Coalfield, and is at the southern limit of its geographical range in Gower. The open habitats which it frequents include rough grazings and the old railway line in the North-east.

Wolf spiders scurry between the heather stems carrying spherical white egg cases under the hinder part of the body, while others of their group spin silken threads of gossamer across the autumn landscape. Scintillating nests of minute spiderlets can be persuaded to erupt at a touch into a radiating orb of tiny golden bodies.

3 TREES AND LESSER PLANTS OF THE INLAND WOODS

GOWER, in common with most of Britain, was once largely covered by oakwood, which has since succumbed to felling, burning and grazing. Given the opportunity, this would re-establish itself in the course of a few generations in all but the more inhospitable sites. A few areas are too windy, a few too salty, others too wet. But even the blown sands at Oxwich lend themselves to colonisation by birches, followed by elms and oaks, and the sodden moorland peats to invasion by alders and sallows. Woodland is not an imposing feature of the landscape at present because many of the woods are tucked away in the valleys, but there are quite a number scattered through the peninsula.

The common or pedunculate oak (the one bearing its acorns on slender stalks) is the principal tree of 'Gower Anglica'—often associated with ash or, in Bishopston Valley particularly, with small-leaved lime, a tree which is quite uncommon on a national level. Durmast or sessile oak (the one with the acorns sitting directly on the twigs) is the species of 'Gower Wallica', as it is of the Coalfield generally. It often grows with downy birch, which is much less common on the limestones, but the true silver or white birch with its gracefully pendulous twigs is quite rare in any habitat. The Glamorgan Naturalists' Trust reserve at Gelli Hir north of Ilston is situated where the Millstone Grit abuts onto the Coal Measures and includes oakwoods of both kinds.

Most Gower woodlands apart from the steepest and rockiest show evidence of the hand of man in tree planting and woodland management. The early woodsmen dealt mainly in broad-leaved deciduous trees and intrusive plantations of exotic conifers are a very minor part of the Gower scene. Sufficiently few conifers have been planted for these to remain a novelty and bring added interest in their specialised flora and fauna. Certain birds like coal tit and goldcrest are especially associated with them, as are some of the more colourful woodland fungi. *Spathularia flavida*, an 'earth tongue' whose splaying fans of bright yellow cluster at the feet of larch trees in Green Cwm, above the Megalithic burial site at Parc le Breos, is one of the more attractive fungal novelties.

Because of past planting it is not always clear which trees are native and which not. Some like beech and hornbeam (which is usually a hedge-row tree) and Scots pine, are indigenous to some parts of Britain but not to Gower. Of the elms the big-leaved wych elm is the common native species and is found principally on the limestones. The smaller-leaved English elm is naturalised and produces the finest trees of all, if not pollarded. The Dutch elm of the limestone valleys and villages is a hybrid which has probably risen spontaneously and there are several other more obscure species.

The commonest poplars are the native aspen at Pwlldu and the hybrid Italian black poplar (*Populus serotina*) which is often planted in moist valleys and can attain great size, sometimes persisting from suckers after felling. Black, grey and white poplars are rarer.

Sweet chestnut and horse chestnut grow well where introduced. The alien sycamore, which reached Britain in the fifteenth or sixteenth century, does not need to be planted, shedding copious winged fruits in all directions and covering the ground with veritable swards of seedlings. There are some splendidly tall field maples in North Hill Wood near Pennard—a site also notable for its wealth of butchers-broom. Yew is much planted in churchyards, from where a few have spread to the north-western cliff woods near Llanrhidian, but it is not present as a native of Gower, although so typical of limestone woodlands in South Glamorgan.

Hazel is the commonest of the lime-loving shrubs, with dogwood, spindle and purging buckthorn on the better soils, crab apple and alder-buckthorn on the poorer ones. Holly, blackthorn and elder are fairly evenly distributed on both, the last often associated with disturbance by rabbits, badgers or farm livestock. Wayfaring tree, which is a species of Southern England, reaches its most westerly British station near Mumbles except for a single outlier in Carmarthen. The related and generally more widespread guelder-rose grows principally on non-limey soils and is quite rare in West Gower.

Tapering flask-shaped hips of dog rose and rounder ones of field rose are both common. Other roses, apart from the burnet rose of the dunes, are not, but several other kinds have been identified. Alders and willows clothe the wet valley bottoms, osier, crack willow and grey sallow commonest of the latter. Eared sallow and goat sallow prefer the acid regions: others, apart from creeping willow, are rare.

The understorey of the East Gower birchwoods and durmast oakwoods is essentially heathy, with bilberry, heath bedstraw and wood soft grass in the deeper shade, ling, bell heather and tormentil in sunnier clearings. Wood horsetail and lemon-scented fern occur in Clyne Wood.

In some of the limestone woodlands May and June see the spreading of a white carpet of wild garlic flowers, leaves crushed underfoot emitting an appetising flavour of Italian kitchens. Triquetrous garlic (or three-cornered leek) is established in a woodland near Caswell. The related bluebell, which spreads its blue mantle at the same season, grows larger and flowers more profusely outside the woodlands, where late sprouting bracken fronds supply the necessary summer shade.

An extraordinary member of this same lily family is the butchers-broom, its side branches flattened into rigid, leaf-like appendages and the true leaves reduced to tiny chaffy scales. The greenish flowers and fat scarlet berries arising from them co-exist on the pseudo-leaves for months at a time. Herb Paris is another speciality quite closely related to these, although superficially very different. It is more sombre than the related *Trillium erectum* which has become naturalised in wet woodlands of Central Wales. Lords-and-ladies and early purple orchids are locally frequent and both have forms with and without purple blotches on the leaves. Once in a while a handsome spike of greater butterfly orchid appears.

Moist woodland hollows near Parkmill contain contrasting stands of blue monkshood and golden kingcups and another rare beauty is the purple gromwell whose flowers are actually a rich gentian-blue. Spurge laurel, which is neither a spurge nor a laurel but a *Daphne*, grows slowly, its slender stems rarely reaching more than 3 ft. (1 m.). The green flowers appear in January, the purple fruits in April or May, alongside the green flowers of the true wood spurge.

Primroses are still plentiful in West Gower but have diminished enormously in the South-east during recent years. Pale wood or early dog violets as well as common dog violets grow among the wood anemones, moschatel and wood-sorrel, with marsh violets in wetter, more acid sites. White-flowered sweet violets, probably introduced, spill out of Parkmill Wood to find a niche for themselves on road chippings thrown onto the banks by generations of roadmen and providing the open habitat which they need. These white flowers are confined to the limestone. On the Coal Measures at Clyne the sweet violets are mauve; at West Cross they are blue. Hairy violets stray into some of the coastal woodlands from the grassy cliffs.

Starry swards of lesser celandines and broad sheets of opposite-leaved golden-saxifrage flower alongside unisexual stands of dog's mercury in February and March. These are followed by red campion, sweet woodruff and wood sanicle, leading on to enchanter's nightshade and tutsan when the tree canopy has expanded to exclude most of the sunlight. The Berry Wood nature reserve is notable for the graceful sprays of wood millet (*Milium effusum*) and narrow buckler fern (*Dryopteris carthusiana*), which may be commoner in Glamorgan than has previously been thought.

These western woodlands are full of ferns, broad buckler and soft shield fern, male and lady fern and hart's tongue doing particularly well on the rubbly floors of scree woodlands. Common polypody often perches on the trunks and branches of trees. The rich moss flora reaches its zenith in winter; the fungus flora in autumn. More perennial fruiting bodies of fungi, like the hard 'black potatoes' (*Daldinia concentrica*) growing on fallen ash logs, persist all the year round, along with the

7. Fungi of fallen sticks. *Xylaria hypoxylon* (Candle snuff) and globose *Hypoxylon fragiforme*

ragged black and white prongs of candle snuff fungus (*Xylaria hypoxylon*). If broken open concentric growth rings can be seen inside.

Cathole Cave, above Parc-le-Breos, formerly used by hunting folk of the Late Glacial Era, and now by lesser horseshoe bats, is surrounded by trees festooned with lichens. These include the shaggy old man's beard lichen (*Usnea subfloridana*) and it is reassuring to see such a profusion of a species which is now widely accepted as a sign of unpolluted atmosphere. The relative of the dog's tooth lichen (*Peltigera polydactyla*) which percolates the open sward below is more resistant to pollution and of little service as an indicator of pure air.

4   PLANTS OF COASTAL SCRUB AND WOODLAND

EXPOSURE to sea winds affects Gower's trees as fundamentally as do type of soil and interference by man — sometimes to the point of annihilation. Most of the native species have soft deciduous leaves which are easily damaged when banged repeatedly against the twigs in a stiff breeze so that salt spray is able to enter through the abrasions and cause a local browning. Stems rising above sward level are also affected, the buds to windward drying out, so that only the leeward ones grow on to give a lopsided trunk slanting away from the prevailing winds. Sideshoots sprouting erect from this are each a little bit longer that the one before; pushing up to form a bevelled top to a densely bristling thicket. Sheep and rabbits find cosy lairs under these impenetrable ceilings but too little light penetrates for more than a few kinds of plants to benefit from protection.

Blackthorn and gorse are the commonest thicket formers, their twigs sometimes so closely appressed that flowers, sloes and pods are produced at ground level. Fast growers, like sycamore and elder, may send up brave new shoots during the calm of spring and summer, but these are doomed to die in autumn and winter gales, their brittle substance finally snapping off to add to the woody complexity below.

Juniper manages to hold its own on the southern cliffs, but its evergreen leaves are frequently wind-scorched and the twigs prematurely truncated. Many trees further inland (and far into the hinterland of Swansea) sustained this type of damage during the phenomenal salty gales of May 1973. Even pine needles became browned off at that time, the only species to escape being those coming into leaf later in the season. Beech was one of the worst affected.

'Wind pruning' where each tree as well as each branch is a little taller than the one to windward, is common on Gower and there is a marked contrast in stature on the exposed and protected sides of the southern bays and headlands. The east-facing flank of the broad valley leading down from Parkmill to Three Cliffs Bay is clothed in thick woodland: the slope leading up to the ruins of Pennard Castle opposite is more scantily clad with bramble and a few tattered hollies and sycamores in a sea of bracken and grass, although well in from the open sea.

Oxwich Head forms another striking example. The splendid woodland to seaward of the little church of St. Illtyd's contains some fine oaks, ashes and sycamores with an understorey of hazel and hawthorn. It occupies the slope facing north-east towards the wide sweep of Oxwich Bay. The west-facing side of the Point bears grass heath with dense mixed scrub established only among the blocky scree of the face, where the young bushes are protected during their most vulnerable phase of growth.

Such limestone scrub must have been more widespread on the Gower cliffs before the coming of man and his livestock. Nowadays few of the tender saplings which manage to germinate and grow in summer in the open are likely to survive being nibbled back during the hungry period of winter.

Old sea cliffs in the North show a mosaic of vegetation types depending on soil depth. The deepest soils support oakwood, shallower ones ashwood with some of the constituent species such as dogwood very near the extreme western limit of their geographical range. Still shallower soils show a scrub of blackthorn and hawthorn and the really rocky parts a hotch potch of flowery grass turf and crevice plants. Tor Gro and North Hill stretching from Llanmadoc to Cheriton are good examples of this type of vegetation.

A similar situation can be traced at Nicholaston, but there is the further complication here of sea sand blown up from the dunes. On the shallow soils at the top of the slope ash is the dominant tree, its roots making direct contact with the limestone. Below this comes the main oakwood on a deeper, sandier soil. The sand was originally calcareous, having a high content of limey shell fragments, but it is porous and the slopes are steep, so much of the lime and minerals are washed out by drainage waters, leaving it more acid.

Where the woodland abuts onto dry dunes and the sand is deeper and flatter, the new ecological niche is exploited by the readily distributed sycamore. Where it borders Nicholaston Pill alder is the principal tree in the waterlogged soil, with ivy climbing the oaks but not the alders.

The relative disposition of woodland, scrub and brackenland is less easy to explain in the Bishopston Valley where the patchiness is possibly due to vagaries of past land use. Oxwich Marsh on the wedge of low ground to the West of Nicholaston is part of a natural succession from saltmarsh through fen to waterlogged woodland or 'carr'. Typical shrubs of the nearby dunes are spindle and privet.

Nicholaston Wood on the cliff behind is a fine example of natural woodland of great diversity. The northwestern end lies in the lee of Oxwich Point and is composed of tall pendunculate oak and other trees, beneath which twenty different kinds of flowers can be found blooming in the first week of March and primroses are so robust as to produce the

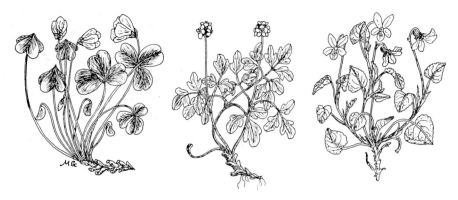

8. Woodland flowers. Wood sorrel, moschatel and wood dog-violet

18

19

Plate 5   BIRDS OF MOOR AND SCRUBLAND

18. Yellow Hammer at its nest in a gorse bush   *Keri Williams*
19. Nightjar alights at its nest among bracken   *Keri Williams*

29

Plate 6   INSECTS OF MOORS AND GRASSY SLOPES

20. White Plume Moth   *Michael Claridge*   23. Minotaur Beetle   *Michael Claridge*
21. Dark Bush Cricket   *Michael Claridge*   24. Marbled White Butterfly   *Author*
22. Angleshades Moth   *Michael Claridge*

25

26

Plate 7 BIRDS OF THE TREES

25. Sparrow Hawk with young   *Keri Williams*
26. Missel Thrush with young   *Keri Williams*

27

28

Plate 8 BIRDS OF WOODLAND UNDERGROWTH

27. Garden Warbler at nest in bramble *Keri Williams*
28. Long Tailed Tit's nest in hawthorn *Keri Williams*

occasional Polyanthus type inflorescence like a large pale oxlip. Yet at its exposed eastern end the stunted oaks are plastered against the limestone faces and typical herbs are rock-rose and madder, as on the open cliffs. Two trees of this wood found almost nowhere else are wild service tree and rock whitebeam (*Sorbus torminalis* and *S. rupicola*).

Leafless, anaemic-flowered toothwort parasitises the roots of hazel and elm—and of cherry laurel, too, at Parkmill; and most of the rarities of the inland woods occur. Both stinking hellebore and green hellebore grew once, the first with glossy evergreen leaves and purple-tinged flowers the second, which has now disappeared, sending up soft new leaves at the first awakening of spring, like the Christmas rose of gardens. Both flower agreeably early in the year. Hellebore, butchers-broom and herb Paris are all plants of South east Britain reaching towards the North-west of their range here.

Tall caper spurge is another Nicholaston speciality with less conservative south-easterly tendencies but thinning out towards the North and West. At the seaward edge of the woodland is orpine or live-long, a tall, red-flowered succulent of the hardy stonecrop fraternity, which also occurs on open cliffs.

5 WOODLAND MAMMALS, BIRDS AND SNAKES

As most of Britain was once wooded most of her animals are geared to life in woodland, which is a complex community, offering all sorts of living quarters, at, above and below ground level. The trees ameliorate the climate, cutting down wind, rain, heat and cold and maintaining a high humidity, Food is likely to be plentiful, the mass of foliage trapping energy from the sun and converting it to more edible form for use by plant feeders, detritus feeders and, ultimately, animal feeders. The potential energy turnover and complexity of plant-animal relationships savours more of a 'food web' than of the 'food chain' traceable in simpler communities.

With the exception of deer, practically all the British mammals are present on Gower, but there is some doubt about the dormouse, a former inhabitant of Berry Wood, west of Penrice and now a Glamorgan Naturalists' Trust Reserve. No dormice have been seen since 1966, but they may still be there pursuing their secretive lives among the old coppiced hazel. A search for the stripped honeysuckle bark of which they build their nests, or for owl pellets, in which their bones sometimes turn up, might provide a clue to their continued existence.

The harvest mouse is unrecorded, but may not be as scarce in South Wales as was previously believed as it has recently been discovered in several sites further East towards Cardiff. Other small rodents, as well as shrews, are to be found quite commonly. Hares and rabbits, although most often spotted in the open, frequent the woodlands quite as much. Red squirrels are thought to have survived competition with the greys in a few parts and other Glamorgan rarities, notably the otter, are still about.

Badgers and foxes are quite abundant and there are badger setts on several county trust reserves. The indigenous polecats died out, but others are filtering back from the Coalfield to join the stoats and weasels and occasionally come to grief on the roads. Pipistrelle and long-eared are the commonest of the bats to be seen flitting round the wood margins

9. Long-eared bat

in summer dusks. The ancient human dwelling of Cathole Caves on the wooded hill north of Parkmill frequented by lesser horseshoe bats may prove to be an important winter roost for hibernating bats.

Two thirds of Britain's breeding birds are associated with trees and a good proportion of these are to be found on Gower. Spotted flycatchers darting from their perches to catch unwary insects on the wing are the epitome of summer, but fewer are nesting now than formerly. Pied flycatchers and ring ouzels linger only briefly as they pass through on their way to and from the Coalfield hills. So too, do common redstarts, but black redstarts are visiting more frequently in winter than hitherto and have been seen in trees at Ilston Cwm and elsewhere.

All the common woodland birds are present and occasionally a few uncommon ones like firecrest, crossbill and lesser spotted woodpecker. There is plenty of old timber to provide breeding sites for hole nesters — and victuals too. Dead and dying wood, which becomes pitted by woodpeckers, harbours as many prey animals as almost any part of the woodland system, nearly a thousand species of invertebrates being associated with it on a national scale. Tree creepers, nuthatches, woodpeckers and tits cash in on this rich food store. Most are omnivorous, feeding on the oily seeds of woodland plants as well as the proteinaceous morsels of wood-boring animals. Hazel nuts are a favourite and it is not uncommon to find the hammered remnants of a nutshell wedged in some crevice of rough bark or splaying fork. Even great tits can tackle these before the green shells become fully hardened.

Green woodpeckers or 'yaffles' forage more frequently in open country than in woodland. The jab marks of their dagger bills in ant-hills — more prominent than those of the turf probing starlings — bear testimony to their partiality for ants. Birds hammering at wooden posts on the Whiteford flats have their nest holes in the hanging oakwood at Cwm Ivy.

Flocks of long-tailed tits are an attractive feature of the woodlands in both winter and summer. As early as the first few days of June big family parties are undulating through the birch twigs to the accompaniment of an insistent squeaky chattering which never lets up—like infants loosed from the sombre confines of the classroom at playtime. And well might the fledgelings exclaim, after being cooped up together in the tiny ball of a nest for their entire short lives. The subtle pinks of their plumage are lacking at this stage, but there are few more charming sights and sounds.

Nest boxes have been introduced among newly planted trees in the Glamorgan Naturalists' Trust reserve of Ridgeway established in the wake of building development at Mayals near Oystermouth. In old established woodlands there is little need for them, particularly where crevices of old walls supplement those of old timber.

The usually pestiferous wood pigeons are less ubiquitous than often, a 1972 bird survey finding them to be present in only seven of the ten woodlands examined. Winter flocks can, nevertheless, number two hundred and fifty or more. Turtle doves are uncommon, but the similar sized collared doves have moved in in a big way since their recent invasion of Britain from the East. They first nested in 1962 and are now quite common, being recorded in five of the ten woods surveyed in 1972. The willow tit is an even newer comer to the list of Gower's nesting birds.

Siskins flock to the small seeds of birch and alder during the colder months, a 1971-72 flock in the Clyne Valley numbering as many as seventy. Redpolls feed on the same trees, but not usually more than thirty together.

Woodcock come to the woods to feed in winter, the odd pair sometimes staying on to breed in Penrice Woods. There is a treetop heronry in Penrice, one of a mere handful in Glamorgan as a whole, and some of Gower's ravens nest in tall trees, though more do so on cliffs. Buzzards are tree nesters too, in Gower, not cliff nesters as in Pembrokeshire, and sparrow hawks, always typical woodland birds, are increasing, but kestrels are commonest of the birds of prey,

An earlier survey of breeding birds was carried out in four woodland sites during the five years from 1966 to 1970 inclusive, and yielded no less than forty different species, though some quite rarely. The woods were in the Bishopston, Ilston and Llethrid Valleys and on the cliff slopes at Nicholaston. Complete counts were not attempted, the purpose being to monitor changes and record relative abundance.

Blackbirds proved to be much the commonest and increased by 50% between 1966 and 1970, when the second most abundant was the robin. Third in order of numbers in 1970 was the song thrush, then chaffinch and then blackcap, with wood pigeon, wren, jackdaw and starling tying for sixth place. Of the other Corvids jays were slightly commoner than magpies and carrion crows than either: commonest of the tits were blue and great tits. Chiff chaffs were slightly more abundant during the years of the census than willow warblers, but this is not always

10. Great tits and alder catkins

so. The only others at all well distributed in 1970 were nuthatch, green woodpecker, dunnock and bullfinch. Bullfinches seem to have partially replaced the formerly more abundant greenfinch, which is tending to become more suburban. Whitethroats dwindled from a fair population in the first three years to none at all by 1970, but were up again to pre-disaster numbers by 1976.

Subsequent counts of nesting birds carried out in 1974 showed wrens to be much the commonest by then — this reflecting the national trend. Goldcrests too, showed the population explosion that has been evident in the country as a whole. These two — the smallest of our winter residents and hence among the most vulnerable to freezing temperatures — completely recovered from their 1962-63 setback in the ensuing decade. A 1974 census in Nicholaston Wood revealed wrens to be far and away the most numerous bird, comprising 17.2% of the breeding population or 33 pairs in 61½ acres. Blackbirds, previously the dominant species, ranked a poor second with only half as many (17 pairs). Goldcrests (16 pairs) and robins (15 pairs) were not far behind. Others averaging more than one pair per 6 acres were wood pigeons (13 pairs), blue tit and chiff chaff (11 pairs each) and chaffinch (10 pairs). It has been suggested that the relative high density of blackcaps (9 pairs) may have caused the displacement of the garden warblers, which have similar ecological requirements and were absent in 1974, although nesting in previous years.

Altogether 31 species were found to be breeding in Nicholaston Wood in 1974, with a density of 623 birds per 100 acres, which is likely to be rather above average for similar mixed woodlands elsewhere in Britain and possibly due to the large amount of 'woodland edge'. Some of the species commonly present, notably sparrow hawk, kestrel and cuckoo, bred outside the wood, the cuckoos parasitising the big reed warbler population of the adjacent marsh.

By the 1970s more and more blackcaps were electing to spend the winter in Gower instead of migrating south with their fellows. During November and December 1974 at least fifteen individuals are believed to have been present in a woodland near Mumbles.

Gower woodlands have their quota of snakes, but lizards and slow worms are more often found in the open, with far more than usual of the blue-spotted variety of slow worm among the males. Adders are quite common at Bishopston and Nicholaston where they can be seen basking in patches of sunshine by the paths from March to September. At the beginning of the season there are likely to be two together, as they pair soon after emerging from hibernation. The sun's warmth evidently aids development of the embryos within the body of the female and the south side of a woodland is a more likely hunting ground than the north. Black or melanistic adders occur around Porteynon, and are smaller than average — up to 18 inches (45 cms.) long.

Grass snakes even more than adders favour moist conditions and grow to a full 3ft. long among the meadowsweet in wet valley woodlands near Burry. They pair in April and do not give birth to live young as does the adder. Their eggs are laid in August or September in the sort of warm place favoured by hibernating hedgehogs or garden tortoises — often a garden compost heap if there is one available. The youngsters rip the papery membranes open with their egg tooth and feed on worms and slugs until they are big enough to cope with frogs, toads, newts and minnows.

6 SMALLER WOODLAND CREATURES

OF native woodland trees oak, birch, hawthorn and willow support the greatest number of butterfly and moth caterpillars. Beech, elm, aspen, hazel, blackthorn and pine support fewer; ash, lime, hornbeam, maple and juniper fewer still and holly and yew fewest. Non native trees like sycamore, holm oak and the chestnuts have less wildlife dependent on them because many small animals can exploit only the one traditional host and cannot make use of such relative newcomers.

Butterflies can be encouraged in woodland nature reserves by opening out glades to give the sunlit space which they need for flighting, and it disrupts the web of life least if the alien trees, on which fewest animals depend are the ones thinned out. A notable exception is the alien Buddleia, which is aptly called the 'butterfly bush' for the hosts of insects which come for its nectar. Speckled woods are the butterflies most commonly found in woodland, but orange-tips are almost everywhere and dark green fritillaries occur at Nicholaston.

Silver-washed fritillaries breed at Parkmill and Gelli Hir, where there is an abundance of the violets needed to fatten their growing caterpillars. Their eggs are not laid on violets but amongst moss shoots on some tree trunk or fence post. On hatching the larvae make a meal of their eggshells and go into hibernation for the winter before setting off from the nursery to look for their food plant in spring. The adults are less choosy, taking their nectar from the flowers of brambles and thistles which are seldom in short supply. The silver-washed fritillary is confined in Britain to the South and West and is decreasing, so it is good to know that it is thriving on Gower.

The holly blue is another of Gelli Hir's less common species, although quite widespread. The eggs of the first brood are laid on the holly or dogwood flowers from which the female feeds; those of the second brood on the late autumn flowers of ivy, which are never far to seek. The little green caterpillars burrow into the flower buds and feed on the developing berries, making themselves quite inconspicuous in the doing by coiling around their food supply and merging into its outline.

The common Vanessids (small tortoiseshells, peacocks and red admirals) are to be seen in the woodlands in spring; meadow browns, gatekeepers and small skippers later on in the summer when the rarer painted ladies and hairstreaks put in an appearance. Commas, formerly rare in West Glamorgan, have been spreading in from the East in recent years and can now be seen in Gelli Hir and elsewhere.

The various wild cresses of moist and marginal habitats nurture the inevitable hosts of large and small white caterpillars and seldom a day passed in the long Summers of 1975 and 1976 but emergent butterflies were on the wing. In winter the pale cocoons are lashed to some cranny in an old tree or wall with a silken safety belt, like that of a pole-scaling telephone engineer.

This is the flighting time of the male winter moths (*Operophtera brumata*) which escaped the sharp eyes of foraging tits when they were dangling on gossamer threads in the springtime woods as juicy green caterpillars. The pallid forms of these and the November moths (*Oporinia dilutata*) flit ghost-like through the beams of car headlights on nights which often seem too chilly for any 'cold-blooded' creature to be abroad. Larger white plume moths (*Pterophorus pentadactyla*) can be seen on the wing in June and July, where greater bindweed scrambles through the woodland edge to nurture the hairy green and white caterpillars.

Many other moths have been identified in the Gower woods, from the dull little brown and white grass moth (*Crambus culmellus*) at Gelli Hir to the cream-spot tiger (*Arctia villica*) flaunting brilliant orange underwings beneath the pines at Whiteford Point. Some of the species have delightful names: 'Mother of Pearl' (*Notarcha ruralis*) 'small fan-footed wave' (*Sterrha biselata*) and 'July high-flier' (*Hydriomena furcata*), with the rather more down to earth 'common carpet' (*Epirrhoe alternata*) and 'straw dot' (*Rivula sericealis*). Others are insufficiently well-known to have been given popular names as yet — e.g. *Eucosma trimaculana* on elm, *Peronea caudana* on sallow and *Eudoria truncicolella* on mossy tree-trunks.

Where there are woodland pools and boggy ground, as at Gelli Hir, marshland moths such as the drinker (*Philudoria potatoria*) and china mark (*Nymphula nymphaeata*) may be found. Sallows and willows of these wet woodlands support three of the handsomest moths of all: the puss moth (*Cerura vinula*), whose shaggy white head resembles that of a Highland terrier more than a puss, the poplar hawk (*Laothoë populi*),

39

which settles with hind wings ahead of the forewings, and the eyed hawk, (*Smerinthus ocellata*) which differs from it mainly in the large eye spots on the hind wings.

Smaller winged creatures find sanctuary in the sheltered microclimate of the woods and venture out above the canopy to tempt the insect eating birds. In late April and early May when late migrants are flighting in over the Channel on the wings of fierce south-westerly winds, these flying morsels of fat and protein prove a great attraction. On such days great clouds of swifts, swallows and martins circle busily on the leeward flank of Oxwich Point, snapping up insects over the newly opened leaf buds of the tall trees but rising only briefly above the skyline into the teeth of the gale which brought them in. Swarms of flying ants on the woodland margins tempt black-headed gulls and jackdaws in August and September.

The effect of birds on lesser life is not always a matter of predator-prey relationships and the raucously cawing inmates of the Oxwich Point rookery are instrumental in increasing the populations of some of the animals below the nesting trees. This they do by killing off some of the herbaceous vegetation and replacing it with a thick litter of dead sticks mislaid or discarded from the homes above. These become covered with invisible films of algae and fungi and marginally overgrown with invasive ivy-leaved speedwell, red campion, nettle and elder saplings and the much enlarged leaves of wild arum and enchanter's nightshade which are stimulated by the nutritious rain of guano from overhead. All in all, this is a rank, fertile micro-habitat offering much to organisms which appreciate such fruity lushness.

Woodlice of several species chomp steadily among the debris alongside millipedes and the occasional predatory centipede cashing in on the surfeit of vegetable and detritus feeders. Chrysalis snails (*Lauria cylindracea*) and garlic snails (*Oxychilus alliarius*) become locally abundant here among ponderously perambulating grey slugs with milk white soles (*Arion circumscriptus* agg.).

Garlic snails are very much a feature of this wood (where the garlic itself is practically confined to a few hollows through which water flushes down to the cliff edge). They do not feed on their name-sake plants but on detritus and its associated fungi, algae and other organisms of breakdown. The name comes from the astonishingly powerful smell of garlic which the snail produces from a gland in its mantle when disturbed; a smell derived from the same sulphur based compounds as the vegetable garlic scent. There would seem to be culinary opportunities here if the penetrating aroma could be captured and preserved.

There are far more species of snail in Oxwich Wood than in acid woodlands of the coalfield, as well as some half dozen species of slug (which are merely snails without shells). They usually live among the debris of

29 30 31

Plate 9   WOODLAND PLANTS

29. Beech leaves burst from within shining bud scales *Harold Grenfell*
30. Hazel leaves expand in response to Spring *Harold Grenfell*
31. Early purple orchids grace the Springtime woodlands *Harold Grenfell*
32. Hart's tongue fern fronds uncoil in the sun *Harold Grenfell*
33. Common violet *Harold Grenfell*
34. Male fern crozier beset with shaggy scales *Harold Grenfell*

32

33 34

41

35   36   37

Plate 10   PLANTS OF SCRUB WOODLAND

35. Sessile oakwood, open-floored: winter time at Nicholaston   *Author*
36. Butcher's broom in Nicholaston Wood   *Author*
37. Herb paris is one of the rarer plants of the limestone woods   *Author*
38. Fly agaric toadstool *(Amanita muscaria)*   *Author*
39. Bird's nest fungus *(Cyathus striatus)*   *Author*
40. Crimson elf cup *(Peziza coccinea)*   *Author*

38

39   40

11. Woodland snails. *Retinella nitidula* (Glass snail), *Carychium tridentatum* (Three-toothed herald snail) and *Clausilia bidentata* (Two-toothed door snail)

fallen leaves, but leaf litter is sparse at Oxwich because of the uniformly steep slopes, so the best places to look for them are under rotting logs and among fallen sticks. When this timber becomes too rotten, with little more than raw cellulose left, snails and slugs tend to desert it, along with the boring and burrowing Isopods, leaving little but the coiled Rotifers and minute water bears or Tardigrades.

Slime fungi may still occur at this stage, but mostly even the fungi die out, leaving the sodden yellow-black mass covered with a felt of creeping mosses sprinkled with the translucent fronds of *Mnium undulatum*. This disintegrated wood is not far removed from soil in texture and black-birds treat it as such, scratching away showers of the loose material in their search for any food items lurking in its protection. The sticks and stumps preferred by snails are those recently dead and characterised by the orange and pink pustules of coral spot fungus (*Nectria cinnabarina*), the black and white prongs of candle snuff fungus (*Xylaria hypoxylon*) and the fleshy lobes of Jew's ear fungus (*Auricularia auricula*), which grows on sycamore here as well as the more usual elder.

Among such sticks slenderly elongated two-toothed door snails (*Clausilia bidentata*) can be found along with plaited door snails (*Marpessa laminata*), which are among the largest of the British door snails and recognisable by their smooth, rather shiny shells. These last occur mainly in old woodland on rich soils and are much more characteristic of South East England than of Wales. The three-toothed herald snail (*Carychium tridentatum*) is small and white, the tawny glass snail (*Euconulus fulvus*) brown, tightly coiled, flat bottomed and pyramid-shaped. The rounded snail (*Discus rotundus*), which is very common, looks like a length of neatly coiled rope in miniature. The glass snail (*Vitrina pellucida*) has a big body whorl to its thin green shell but almost no spire and the soft parts of the animal seem to spill out as though it is not big enough.

The land winkle (*Pomatias elegans*) is one of the larger species. It is rather like an elongated shore winkle having, like it, a lid or operculum at the shell mouth, but this is limey instead of horny as in the true winkle.

43

The shell is very thick so the animal can only grow in places such as Oxwich where there is plenty of lime from which to make it. Britain is on the very northern edge of its range and it escapes the winter cold only by burrowing into the soil and hibernating. Largest of all are the common garden snails (*Helix aspersa*) and the brightly coloured grove snails (*Cepaea nemoralis*).

A big slug to be found lurking under logs is *Limax maximus*. Its striking, black-spotted body is often pinkish. The hedgehog slug (*Arion intermedius*), common in woods, is so called because it bunches itself into the shape of a hedgehog when upset. The common dusky slug (*Arion subfuscus*) can be recognised by the yellow slime which it exudes. Adventuring high up the tree trunks are translucent black-banded tree slugs (*Lehmannia marginata*). These prefer sycamores, beeches and other trees with smooth bark, from which they scrape off the algae and lichen, tending to avoid the rougher mossy patches. In dry weather they hide by day in crevices and feed at night.

The smallest species come to light only when a sample of leaf litter is dried, sieved and the contents examined under a hand lens — an essential piece of equipment for any would-be naturalist. The point snail (*Acme fusca*), with its long, narrow, shiny, red-brown shell is another kind with a hinged operculum or lid and is, like the slippery moss snail (*Cochlicopa lubrica*), a typical denizen of leaf litter. Two more of the glass snails occur with them, *Retinella pura* and *R. nitidula* with a waxier shell. The prickly snail (*Acanthinula aculeata*) has a crest of sharp spines around each whorl of the shell. Fragments of mud and humus get hooked onto these and form an excellent camouflage, so that the snails are very difficult to spot. The white, shiny-shelled *Vitrea contracta* is yet another which is common in the leafy debris of the woodland floor.

This layer is an important habitat within a habitat, making its own special contribution to the diversity of life within the woodland. The whole matrix is alive with springtails, mites and other tiny arthropods, many of which fall prey to the pseudoscorpions (*Chelonethi*), which are themselves only a few millimetres long. The luckless ones are caught and then either paralysed or killed by a dose of venom from poison glands on the predator's pedipalps, which are the equivalent of a crab's pincer-bearing forelegs. *Chthonius dacnodes* and *C. orthodactylus* are two pseudo scorpions which live in Gower's leaf litter. *Neobisium muscorum*, *Roncus lubricus* and *Microcreagris cambridgei* are common under stones, particularly in the woods at Parkmill and Clyne, whereas *Neobisium maritimum* is unusual in that it lives on the upper shore among seaweeds and rocks.

Moss-grown chunks of limestone on the woodland floor afford hiding places for the common woodlice, *Oniscus asellus* and *Trichoniscus pusillus* which also live in leaf litter. The woodlouse capable of rolling itself into a ball when attacked and hence known as the pill bug, is *Armadillidium vulgare* with, much more rarely, *A. album*. The rather similar pill millipede (*Glomeris marginata*) does likewise, but when unrolled shows more than seven pairs of legs and no abdominal section. Both extract lime from their food (as do snails) and deposit it in the cuticle as an added armoury with which to meet potential predators. They occur on the dunes as well as in the wood at Oxwich, being quite tolerant of dry conditions.

In the lighter areas of clearings and rides are sun-loving bush-crickets and grasshoppers. Dark bush crickets (*Pholidoptera griseoaptera*), long-horned and long-legged, chirrup from scrub and hedgerow on warm days and nights in summer and autumn. The 'wings' of the male are reduced to sound-producing flaps: those of the female are even more vestigial.

Woodland beetles have provided some records of great scientific interest. One of the most attractive is the bronzy-green ground beetle *Amara aenea*, the polished wing cases sparkling in the sunlight as it basks or copulates on plants or scuttles across paths.

The bluish oil beetle (*Meloe violaceus*) has a somewhat macabre habit of employing bees to look after its young. Like beetles of the devil's coach-horse group, its bulging body segments are only partially covered by the limply overlapping wing cases. Unlike them, it exudes a pungent blood-coloured fluid from behind the head in a most off-putting manner if handled roughly. Although quite local in Britain the bluish oil beetle can often be found from March onwards among nettles at wood margins of South and Central Gower.

The adults are vegetarian, the growing young, with their greater need of protein have a more novel way of feeding. Gravid females appear outrageously big until they have deposited their load of eggs in the soil —

12. Spider spinning web

in batches of several thousands each — and no wonder. As soon as they hatch the gingery youngsters climb up anything which comes handy. If lucky in their choice, they find themselves on a flower head where they are able to grab hold of an individual from a species of solitary bee visiting for nectar and pollen. The bee's covering of forked hairs make this easy; the smoother ones of flies offer no hold. Safely attached, the beetle grub is air lifted to its host's nest where it makes short work of the bee's egg and then scoffs the food prepared for the bee which should have hatched from it. Dramatic change in shape fits the growing beetle to its new habitat until it eventually pupates to emerge from the soil as an adult oil beetle the following March. Slade near Oxwich is a good place to find these — also near Rhossili and Mumbles.

Another Gower beetle, rare in Britain as a whole, which adopts the same ploy is *Metoecus paradoxus*, which spends its youth in the nest of the common wasp, *Vespa vulgaris*. Britain's biggest beetle, the giant stag beetle, has not been found on Gower, but the lesser stag beetle (*Dorcas parallelipipedus*), another southern species, occurs in ashwoods at Pennard and Oxwich. Shiny black rhinocerous beetles (*Sinodendron cylindricum*) blunder round beneath the beeches at Parkmill, the males flaunting the curved 'horn' which gives them their name.

A quite unusual millipede, *Schizophyllum sabulosum* is to be found in sandy-floored woods at Oxwich and Nicholaston, identifiable by the two orange red stripes along its back. The centipede, *Geophilus osquidatus*, recorded in 1961 from Bishop's Wood at Caswell, is a new species for Britain. *Chordana proximum* from the same wood is a second record for Britain. Another notable rarity is the yellow-brown striped Nemertine or ribbon worm, *Geonemertes dendyi*, a terrestrial member of a group which occurs mainly on the seashore. The first British specimen was found in the Clyne Valley in 1935, since when it has turned up in the Llethrid Caves and in the neighbourhood of Swansea. It often occurs with the commoner grey-brown land Planarian or flat worm, *Microplana terrestris*. The possibilities of new species turning up are far from exhausted, much of Gower being relatively unworked by zoologists and always likely to yield something of special interest.

7 THE FARMLANDS

ALL the more fertile parts of Gower which would normally bear a 'climatic climax vegetation' of oakwood have been annexed for agriculture, so the region's principal natural plant community is now fragmentary. To the naturalist this is regrettable in some ways, but the farmlands have much to offer aesthetically and biologically apart from the very necessary food which they produce.

Because of the wide range of habitats, biological diversity on the marginal land goes hand in hand with the most intensive farming in Glamorgan. All categories of farmland occur in the transition from one extreme of fertility to the other, so that there is agricultural as well as natural diversity.

Peninsular Gower is one of the few parts of the three counties of Glamorgan and adjacent parts of Dyfed to possess any of the most productive farmland categorised as Grade I in the Ministry of Agriculture's 1968 classification system. Some is Grade II, a type found in the Vale of Glamorgan but practically nowhere in the Coalfield. All lies below about 300 ft. and produces profitable cash crops. The Grade III lowlands of North Gower are more suited to livestock rearing but there are, in fact, quite a lot of sheep reared in the South—choosy Downland sheep rather than the rough and tumble Mountain sheep which survive the rigours of the cliffs and moors.

The Gower Commons of the 'Welshry' are classified as Grade V farmland, which is the poorest of all agriculturally. The successful maintenance of the turf on Clyne Golf Course, however, shows that they need not be so, but that they will respond to modern methods of land improvement and management. There is further evidence for this in the vicinity of Cilibion, where a sharp contrast exists between the boggy moorland around Broad Pool and the enclosed land to the East.

The Commonlands were left originally as such around the parish margins because they yielded too poorly to merit enclosure. With proper management of the grazing regime, they could be a lot more productive. Overgrazing has resulted in the present steady encroachment of bracken, bramble, gorse and rushes over the more palatable grasses. But under-grazing, too, brings its problems by allowing scrub birch and oak to grow up, along with attractive, low-growing patches of petty whin. Oak seedlings are quite common on both the acid peats of the moorlands and the calcareous sands and clifftops, but pony grazing or fires usually put paid to these.

The best farming soils are on the limestones and are classified as 'Brown Earths'. They are loamy, sometimes gravelly and can be 3 ft. (1 m.) deep, sometimes with a clay horizon above the underlying limestone helping to retain surface water.

The pattern of farming remained virtually unchanged for a very long period up to the early 1920s. Livestock was its mainstay, the product trudging 'on the hoof' to Swansea Market at winter weekends. Crops grown were for home consumption as winter feed. Cash crops became profitable only as transport improved, brassicas, swedes and potatoes being sold to the urban areas.

13. Rooks and jackdaws

Early potatoes, favoured by the mild climate, came to popularity at the beginning of the thirties. Freedom from frost is the important factor here and the best areas are situated where cold air drains down slopes to the cliff edge instead of collecting in frost pockets. Even a short distance inland from the traditional south-facing potato fields, the prevalence of late frosts in the depression around Scurlage and Llandewi precludes the successful growing of earlies. Other vegetables are produced on the same land in rotation, the spring cauliflower harvest overlapping with the early growth of young cabbage, and broad beans coming to fruition in midsummer.

Between the two wars, when much of Britain's agriculture was reverting to grass farming, the demand for early potatoes maintained the arable acreage on Gower and with it the arable weeds. Some of these, such as sun spurge, corn spurrey, field madder, and ramping fumitory, are more at home in the Mediterranean region, where the bare soil which they need is produced by sun-scorching instead of ploughing. Another bright Mediterranean touch is afforded by the corn marigold which persists in fields near Stembridge which are kept in permanent arable rotation.

Machine hoeing clears most of the weeds from between the rows of the crop but not from within them. Spreading out of these refuges over the bared soil are delicate flower-trails of black-bindweed and pink trumpets of field bindweed mingling with the fragile blue flowers of Buxbaum's or common field speedwell. Cut-leaved and doves-foot cranesbills flower on the furrows, but the more striking bloody cranesbill is usually confined to field banks around Rhossili, in areas where the odd clump of thrift or sea pink gets established among the crops and stands of slender thistle rise among bizarre sprouts of moribund and unmarketable cauliflowers.

Bright yellow strips of charlock against ancient walled banks show where headlands have been left unhoed or unsprayed. Fields due for ploughing may disappear under a sea of groundsel in spring—to the satisfaction of crowds of goldfinches and linnets which move in to feed on the seeds. This groundsel is an important food source at a time of year when their more traditional food plants are in the vegetative or flowering phase. The bumper crops of pineapple-weed seeds, added to those of grasses which escape the mowing machine, tide the flocks of seed-eaters over to the main thistle seed harvest of late summer.

They are joined then by house sparrows from the farmsteads and hamlets, reverting to their usual vegetable diet after the weeks of collecting more proteinaceous morsels for their growing broods. Later in the autumn the flocks adjourn to the hedgerows to tweak the nutty fruitlets from the feathery styles of wild Clematis—allowing the fluff of 'old man's beard' to drift away on the breeze. The little double-winged seeds are picked delicately from August birch catkins, leaving the denuded stalks intact.

Herbicides which are selective against broad-leaved plants can be used in corn crops as they cannot in root crops, so the wheat and barley fields are cleaner and their weed flora sometimes restricted to narrow-leaved species such as annual meadow grass.

Milk production began in earnest in the late thirties but was hindered by the sparsity of surface water for the cows to drink, many of the streams and ditches disappearing underground into the soluble limestone in summer. By 1974 corn was paying better than milk and the acreage devoted to it was increasing, with the inevitable enlargement of fields by the destruction of old banks and hedges to accommodate increased mechanisation. Most of the grassland for the milch cows takes the form of highly productive short term 'leys' or specially sown grasses and clovers which are ploughed up after a year or two. Nevertheless, some of the old permanent pasture remains, the richness of its flora commensurate with its age.

Typical flowers in the ancient turf are yellow rattle, red bartsia, eyebright, cowslip and bird's-foot trefoil, with cuckoo-flower and silverweed in moist depressions. The newly sown leys, whether mown or grazed, have many years of leeway to make up before they become as botanically and zoologically interesting, and this they will almost certainly not be allowed to do unless agriculture goes into a decline. Some of the older pastures are reverting to open scrubland, with gorse, bracken, hawthorn, rose and bramble gradually taking over.

In spite of planning protection against the inroads of building development seeping westwards from Swansea, Bishopston is fast becoming a dormitory suburb. It nevertheless retains some of the tiny farms and fields which are a survival from the old strip system of agriculture. These, and the handiness of the urban consumers, have led to a preponderence of market gardening and horticulture, providing a multiplicity of restricted niches for wildlife. Evidence of the old enclosures can be seen behind Rhossili, where the vile affords a good example of communal strip cultivation.

In the South-west cornfields and potato fields alternate with rough grazing on the poorly drained patches. Here the store cattle, ponies and even sheep nibble back the tussocks of purple moor-grass and rushes, making room for yellow tormentil, silverweed and creeping buttercup among the disk leaves of marsh pennywort.

Hares may be seen frisking over arable and pasture alike, their black-tipped ears held high. Only when they are badly scared are the ears flattened, as when hiding in the form, and the animal streaking off into the distance appears oddly cat-like. Rabbits remain locally abundant as Myxomatosis waxes and wanes, sheltering in the thick hedge bottoms or digging out complicated fortresses in the old field banks and mowing the young corn and grass crops to a height commensurate with the distance from the burrow mouth. Molehills are common on the better limestone fields and are indicators of fertile land. The moles come for the earthworms and worms cannot thrive in infertile, acid or waterlogged soils.

Foxes, said to have been introduced to Gower at one time for fox hunting, are also doing well. They are a familiar sight on the farmlands and come into the villages to forage at night. Although helping to keep the rabbits in check, they feed on almost anything which comes their way, including earthworms and windfall fruit. Badgers cross farmlands but are more often domiciled in woodlands.

Weasels and stoats encountered on grassy farm tracks are not so anxious to escape that they deny themselves the satisfaction of craning upwards

14. Weasel and stoat

Plate 11 WOODLAND FLOWERS

41. Red Campion	*Harold Grenfell*	**43.** Ramsons or Wild Garlic	*Harold Grenfell*
42. Wood Spurge	*Harold Grenfell*	**44.** Greater Butterfly Orchid	*Harold Grenfell*

51

Plate 12   MORE WOODLAND BIRDS

45. Green Woodpecker or Yaffle   *Keri Williams*
46. Jackdaw   *Keri Williams*
47. Little Owl with vole   *Arthur Morgan*

52

Plate 13   SMALL ANIMALS OF DRY STONE WALLS

48. Two Craneflies mating on wall surface   **49.** Chrysalids of Yellow Underwing Moth from soil   *Both Author*
50. Male Thick-legged Flower Beetle on daisy   *Author*
51. Black-banded Moth merges with lichens   *Michael Claridge*
52. Dry Stone Wall above Fall Bay in the South-west   *Author*

53

53

54

55

Plate 14   SOME OF GOWER'S OUTSTANDING ANIMALS

53. Female Grey Heron with chicks at Penrice   *Harold Grenfell*
54. Badger emerges from sett in Cheriton Woods   *Harold Grenfell*
55. Lesser Horseshoe Bat in flight   *Arthur Morgan*

to ascertain the nature of the intruder. Stoats seem to be getting commoner since the upsurge of rabbits following the initial Myxomatosis check. Sometimes jackdaws take exception to them, mobbing an individual relentlessly as it scuttles from the safety of one gorse bush to the next, to gain breath before running the gauntlet of another chattering swoop.

In September 1971 a stoat was observed on top of a telegraph pole at Kennexstone, Llangennith, clearly trying to catch a young stonechat sitting on the wire a few feet away. The parent stonechat, on seeing the stoat, attacked furiously, and the marauder ran quickly down the pole and melted into its own element.

Other mobbing incidents can be witnessed between bird and bird. Corvids will often harry buzzards, which seem sublimely indifferent, treating the vulgar attacks with the contempt they deserve. Cuckoos, too, are molested, possibly for their resemblance to birds of prey, rather than their unfair habit of 'brood parasitism' in the employment of foster parents for their young. Where woodland abuts onto the little cowslip field behind Overton Mere, a chaffinch was watched attacking a perched cuckoo. The object of its attention sat disdainfully while the chaffinch flew up repeatedly, twittering and fluttering, but sheering away at the last minute, like an excitable terrier worrying a placid retriever.

Scattered pairs of ravens build their bulky nests of sticks high up in hedgerow elms or oaks, and are a fine sight in February, wheeling and tumbling overhead in their courtship flights. While the voracious young are growing to maturity, the appearance of a human figure a field or two away triggers off repeated raucously noisy circlings, while the youngsters remain mute in the nest. The more sociable rooks keep company in rookeries and probe the turf busily with stout, white-sheathed dagger bills. Carrion crows are everywhere, overflowing from the farmlands to join more maritime species on the shores and saltings.

Shoreline waders which reciprocate by coming inland to the fields are lapwing and golden plover, which flock in from the North in late summer and autumn. With them later on are visitors of the thrush family—field-fares and redwings from Scandinavia—and continental flocks of finches, come to seek a Winter haven in the balmier West.

Their summer counterparts in the farmlands are the warblers, pursuing their secretive lives in the dense hedgerows with the resident wrens, and the swifts and hirundines hawking for prey in the upper air. Sand martins flight in across the cliffs with the others in spring and were found nesting for the first time in 1957-58 —inside drainage holes of a wall near Dunvant.

Partridges are essentially birds of the fields and pheasants stray in from neighbouring coverts to feed. Birds are part and parcel of the ecology, whether the farmer likes it or not. The fat, vegetarian wood pigeons which descend in their hundreds to gorge themselves are always unwelcome. Considerably more than half the food of the lapwing flocks, on

55

the other hand, consists of harmful insect pests. Although their greatest services are rendered in winter, the farmer who disturbs their clutches of tapered, blotched eggs during spring harrowings and cultivations, does himself a dis-service.

A farmland bird survey carried out during the sixties in the Hardings Down area of North-west Gower showed a significant difference between the bird life there and that revealed by a similar survey in the Pancross area of the eastern Vale of Glamorgan. At Hardingsdown the commonest species in 1968 were blackbird, dunnock, whitethroat, skylark, robin and yellowhammer in that order, with chaffinch ranking seventh. In the Vale area (which was fairly exposed to sea winds, though boasting taller hedges) chaffinches ranked first, with blackbird and skylark not far behind. Of next average abundance there over the years were whitethroats, dunnocks, robins and yellowhammers.

In 1967 whitethroats tied with blackbirds for first place at Hardings Down, with skylark as runner up, dunnock fourth and chaffinch, rather more typically, in fifth place, followed by yellowhammer and robin. 1968 was a fairly ordinary year, except for the absence of blue tits and scarcity of other tits.

15. Partridges

Whitethroat numbers on the 200 acres covered by the survey were up to 23 pairs in 1968—from 21 and 19 pairs in the two previous years. This was just before the sharp, countrywide decline which resulted in Hardings Down counts of only 6 pairs in 1970 and 5 pairs in 1971. The decline in numbers coincided with the start of the disastrous five year drought in the Sahel Zone of the Sahara where the Gower birds spend their winters. Unable to put on enough fat for the return flight in spring, few of the little warblers were able to return to breed in Europe from the stricken lands of the South.

The population had started to recover slightly on Gower's coastal farmlands by 1974 and the prospect was brighter on a wider front by 1975, after life-giving rains in the desert, brighter still in 1976. But the African rain belt is moving away to the South and this may be only a temporary alleviation, with Gower, in common with the rest of Britain, having to settle for the white-throat as a rare bird in future. Only time will tell.

The movement of the African rain belt is also affecting the swallows of Gower's barns and outhouses. Birds formerly wintering in the Transvaal are now having to follow the rains across the Karoo Desert to further lands in the South and West. Parochialism has never been a character of our far-flying migrants: they have been subject to happenings in the world's other hemisphere through centuries when the folk of Gower believed, like Gilbert White, that their swallows hibernated in the mud of pond-beds during winter. Only today's ringing programmes can start to unravel the adventures of the individual birds which return predictably each spring to their own special corner of the back yard.

Chiff chaffs are seldom recorded on the Gower farmlands but willow warblers are quite abundant. Collared doves arrived in the western farm-lands in 1968 and bred at Llangennith, after doing so in the Swansea area for some six years. By 1974 they were nesting in seven different Gower localities, sometimes converging into flocks, with no less than seventy two seen together at Middleton on 7th February.

8   WALLS AND HEDGEBANKS

THE squat, sturdy hedges of Gower are mostly about a century old, but the stone faced banks which they top are much more ancient. Both were designed to ward off Atlantic gales, many being as broad as they are high. Traditional hedge-laying or pleaching methods in Gower have largely lapsed, but had more in common with those of Pembrokeshire than with methods employed in the rest of Glamorgan. The component hawthorn, blackthorn and hazel are encouraged to branch from the base to leave no loopholes and the resulting hedge is usually quite impregnable.

Spindle, dogwood and other lime-loving shrubs are frequent, but the wayfaring tree, so common in the Vale of Glamorgan hedges, is missing. Sallows occur on the damper soil and oak, ash, elm, beech and hornbeam left to grow into the standards give a typically English character to the landscape. Gorse, although so effective a barrier against wind, livestock and would-be trespassers, is seldom more than incidental.

Honeysuckle is particularly floriferous, as in counties to the North and West, but bird cherry (*Prunus padus*), which is such a feature of Brecknock and Carmarthenshire hedges, is absent. Dwarf cherry (*P. cerasus*) is the wild cherry of the hedgerows in Gower, great cherry or gean (*P. avium*) being mainly a woodland tree.

Field banks provide a sanctuary for flowers surviving from periods of less intense agriculture. On them crosswort and lady's bedstraw from the downlands mingle with bluebell and red campion from the woodlands. Primroses and cowslips growing side by side produce fine hybrid swarms of false oxlips. These, regrettably, are rare now on the roadsides, due partly to plundering by so-called flower lovers, but more obviously to council roadmen who set the cutting blades of their machines disastrously low, ripping out many of the shallow-rooted species.

Colour is still provided locally by marjoram, centaury and St. John's wort. Dame's violet gives a brave roadside show of mauve near Burry as does the bluish purple of introduced meadow cranesbill on the grassy bank outside Penrice Church. Handsome plants of elecampane were eliminated in the early seventies by layby widening near Nicholaston, but still persist in a few places.

The mass invasion of clifftop field banks by thrift, sea campion and other plants of the rock faces below is not a feature of Gower as it is of Pembrokeshire. This is partly because of the more sheltered situation within the Bristol Channel and partly because of the use of dry stone walls instead of rock-faced banks in the more exposed sites,

Cliff plants find sparse roothold on the walls of the Rhossili Mewslade cliffs, but thrift, thyme, biting stonecrop and bird's foot trefoil grow on the more windswept stretches, with navelwort or wall pennywort, wall pellitory, field bindweed and bristly ox-tongue where there is some shelter from gorse scrub. Closely gnawed hawthorns lean against the stones in places and red fescue and cocksfoot grass creep up from the turf below. Sea storksbill affords a maritime flavour to walls on the seaward face of Rhossili Down.

Lichens grow particularly well on the exposed stones here because the wind-blown seaspray contains potash and some of the necessary micronutrients as well as common salt. They also benefit from the unrestricted sunshine, oceanic moistness and clean air.

Orange patches of *Xanthoria parietina* are brightest where gulls perch along the walls, adding a modicum of nitrogen and phosphate in their

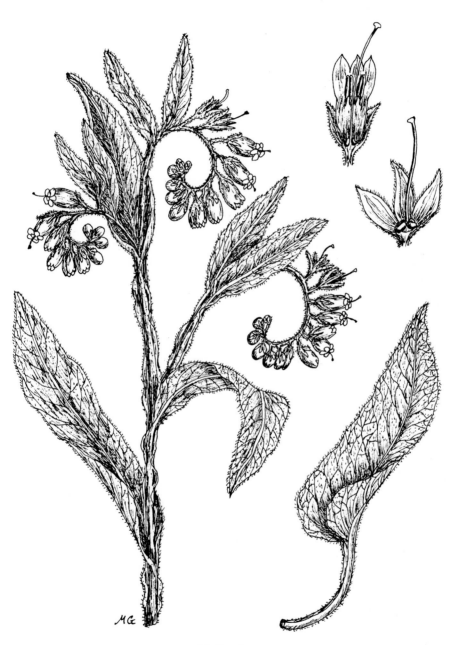

16. Comfrey

59

droppings. Other orange species favouring these seaside walls are *Caloplaca heppiana* and the more lightly adherent *Lecanora marina*. Brown *Anaptychia fusca*, clings to the rock face with closely packed, strap-shaped fronds.

The contrasting yellow green growths of *Rhizocarpon geographicum* with their 'map' of intersecting black lines, are as likely to be found on the coast as the mountains and are world wide in their distribution. There are inumerable greyish white growths of *Lecanora*, *Lecidea* and *Parmelia* and occasionally, overtopping all else, bushily branched growths of *Ramalina siliquosa*, which thrive on the excrement of perching birds.

Of the smaller passerines, yellowhammers are most prone to use the walls as song posts, whilst the less melodious stonechats utilise protruding sprigs of wind-tossed bramble or gorse. Dunnocks and whitethroats seek protection among the low scrub and nettles to leeward: wren and robin come to pick off the herbivorous woodlice and millipedes and the carnivorous spiders and centipedes which harry them.

Flora and fauna of the walls backing the Cheriton-Llanmadoc saltings are more maritime because the saline influence here is water seeping up from the base at high tide instead of wind-blown spray. Walls stabilised with crumbling mortar into which roots can penetrate and backed by soil in which they can spread out behind the stones, supply the best plant habitats.

Such walls show a plant zonation from top to bottom based on increasing salinity instead of the more usual increasing humidity. Grazing and breakage by livestock also limit free growth, causing larger plants like marsh mallow to be squeezed back into crevices during their seedling phase. Creeping aloft from the salt marsh turf below are sea wormwood, spear-leaved orache and common sea lavender. Of the true salt marsh plants only red fescue, sea pink, sea plantain and buck's horn plantain extend more than half way up.

Plants of the upper wall are mostly small but very numerous and belong more properly to the cliffs and dunes, Such are darnel poa (*Catapodium marinum*), sea mayweed and wild carrot. There is a strong annual element of dune and arable weeds including field madder, slender trefoil, thyme-leaved sandwort, field speedwell and cut-leaved cranesbill. Ferns are represented by dwarf maidenhair spleenwort and wall rue, with stunted tough-leaved polypody and hart's tongue.

On taller walls well above the marsh at Cwm Ivy tiny rue-leaved saxifrage shares the crevices with wall pennywort and shining cranesbill. The still loftier walls of Weobley Castle ruins on these same north facing cliffs, support some thirty species of flowering plants, including wallflowers, calamint and ploughman's spikenard, as well as a wealth of rusty back fern and a few sycamore saplings.

60

The wall leading out along the sheltered face of Oxwich Point from the village to the church supports most of the expected wall plants plus a few unexpected ones. Most individual is Gower's own special rarity the yellow whitlow grass (*Draba aizoides*). It may possibly have been planted here but the crumbling bastions of Pennard Castle further east are one of its traditional and best known localities. The cushions of golden flowers appear early in the year and the fruits are well formed by May, splitting open in early July to reveal the silvery internal partitions, like miniature honesty 'pennies',

White stonecrop is another attractive introduction to walls hereabouts. It is found principally in Western Britain and grows at few other places in Glamorgan. Even before the upstanding white flower clusters arise, the plump leaves have matured through shades of apricot and flame to a deep crimson behind the green shoot tips. Tucked away in crevices are the mauve flowers of corn salad or lamb's lettuce and the paler ones of ivy-leaved speedwell.

The rock snail (*Pyramidula rupestris*) is to be found on little ledges formed by the walling stones. The shell of this is flatly coiled like the ramshorn snails' of ponds, and is a deep violet brown, the top often bleached almost white.

The strawberry snail (*Hygromia striolata*) finds sanctuary in wall crevices, although possibly more contented when wreaking havoc in garden strawberry beds. The latter part of the scientific name refers to the striations on the whorls of the shell. Young specimens are slightly hairy, but the hairy snail (*H. hispida*), to be found with it, retains the hairiness throughout life. The little curved white bristles coating the shell are just visible to the naked eye and appear most impressive under a hand lens, when the snail's softly horned head shows a faint resemblance to a gelatinised rhino.

Common or garden snails (*Helix aspersa*) come to the walls to hibernate, little ones sometimes using the discarded shells of big ones in which to do so.

17. Cuckoos

Few grow as large in the wild as they do in gardens, the rate of infant mortality being evidently higher, or the quality of the food lower. Song thrushes need no special anvils on which to bang their snails when there is a wall top handy.

In May and June, when the shell has been growing rapidly, the band of newly formed material around the rim is still quite soft and different in colour from older parts of the shell. Its breadth and thickness depends on the amount of lime which reaches it from the soil via the food plants—as regulated by drought and type of substrate, be it rock, soil or mortar.

Many of the woodland snails are to be found in the walls, where the humid woodland microclimate is simulated in a small way in the crevices. Among these are the aromatic garlic snail, the transparent slippery moss snail, the inadequately contained glass snail, the elongated chrysalis snail and the two-toothed door snail. Large black slugs (*Arion ater*), their ruddy counterparts (*A. rufus*) and tubercled hedgehog slugs (*A. intermedium*) seep smoothly from cracks in wet weather when the basking lizards have retired to await the next burst of sunshine.

Millipedes, beetles and spiders are an integral part of this busy hidden world which so often passes un-noticed, but perhaps the most remarkable creatures of the walls are the minute 'water bears' or Tardigrades. Mostly less than a millimetre long, these are among the smallest multicellular animals to occur anywhere. And they *do* occur anywhere—in soil and organic debris of field and woodland, in fresh water (to depths of 150 metres) and in the sea.

Those living in moss and lichen tufts are the most noteworthy because they have an astonishing capacity to dry out with the mosses and lichens to a state of extreme desiccation and yet take no harm. In this state they consume very little oxygen and no food, but can withstand freezing temperatures to survive to the ripe old age of six years. With such a tenacity for life, they may have things to teach the human race about how to survive in adversity. The commonest of the moss-living species on Gower bear names quite disproportionate to their size: *Macrobiotus hufelandi*, *Echiniscus granulatus* and *Hypsibius tetradactyloides*.

Walls alongside some of the ancient woodland tracks threading the seclusion of the valleys of Burry Pill and Bishopston Pill are so grown into their environment that wall species have given way to woodland ones. Trees and bushes meet overhead, conserving moisture and excluding light, so that typical wall plants become attenuated or die out. The leaves of navelwort wax exceedingly large to compensate for lack of light but, in spite of this adaptation, the species cannot penetrate far into the gloom.

Maidenhair spleenwort occurs as a lax, soft-leaved shade form contrasting markedly with the smaller tougher one of sunny walls, while other wall ferns increase in size and are joined by soft shield fern. Vertical sheets of liverwort border patches of lesser celandine and moschatel—*Conocephalum*

56

57

Plate 15   WOODLAND FAUNA

58

56. A great tit on Pengwern Common collects
caterpillars for its brood   *Harold Grenfell*

57. Spotted flycatchers deliver flies to their young
Arthur Morgan

58. Puss moth caterpillar *(Cerura vinula)* in defensive
posture   *Michael Claridge*

59. Puss moth caterpillar's inverted head, warning off
predators   *Michael Claridge*

60. Puss moth: shaggy head and feathery antennae of
male   *Michael Claridge*

59

60

Plate 16   WOODLAND INSECTS

61. Eggs of Green Lacewing *(Chrysopa)* dangling on slender threads   *Michael Claridge*

62. Larva of Green Lacewing *(Chrysopa)* which, like the adult, feeds on aphids   *Michael Claridge*

63. Adult Brown Lacewing *(Hemerobius)* inhabits woodlands   *Michael Claridge*

64. Snakefly *(Raphidia)* gets its name from the elongated pro-thorax which resembles a striking cobra   *Michael Claridge*

65. Seven-spot ladybirds *(Coccinella 7-punctata)* waxed very abundant during 1976   *Author*

66. Long-horned bush cricket *(Meconema thalassinum)* on hazel leaf   *Michael Claridge*

conicum, its surface pocked by openings into internal air chambers, and *Lunularia cruciata* with crescentic gemmae cups releasing discoid green reproductive bodies to perennate its kind.

Wren, robin and dunnock nest against the wall surfaces, blackbirds, song thrushes and chaffinches in the shrubs which sprout from their summits. Blue and great tits 'post' themselves into slit-like orifices which seem far too small for them. Tunnels of wood mouse and bank vole are marked by caches of hazel nut shells and haw stones, each with a neat round hole through which the kernel has been extracted, and the occasional battered nutshell may be found wedged in a crevice which has been used by woodpecker or nuthatch as an anvil.

Ruined cottages in the Bishopston Valley have passed beyond the herbaceous phase of plant succession to the shrub phase, their crumbling walls supporting hazel, hawthorn and ash, with bird-sown gooseberry bushes draped with honeysuckle and black bryony.

Walls bordering rivers, as below the waterworks at Parkmill, give root-hold to hemlock water-dropwort and alder, whose roots thread crevices to the water table below, whilst aquatic mosses and liverworts plaster the wall faces, enabling moisture to seep upwards among their shoots and nurture shallow-rooting flowers.

9   NATURE RESERVES IN OLD QUARRIES

In Glamorgan as a whole the extraction of limestone is an important and expanding industry, but the only limestone quarry still worked on Gower is at Bishopston in the South-east. A threat to start quarrying on the west side of the famous cave system at Llethrid Cwm in 1961 was contested by the Glamorgan Naturalists' Trust and other interested bodies and the proposal was rejected. Nevertheless, small quarries have been opened in the past, both inland and on the cliffs. Some of these are now County Trust Nature reserves, representing different phases of the succession of plants and animals colonising bare rock faces.

Only a specialised flora of bluff and crevice plants can survive on newly exposed rock until such time as a modicum of soil has built up from dead remains and dust particles. Observations of changes over the years can make a fascinating study, but it would need a century or so to get the whole story from a single site.

Ilston Quarry north of Parkmill was regarded as too forbiddingly bare when acquired by the Glamorgan Naturalists' Trust as a nature reserve in 1968 and the local naturalists decided to speed things up by planting. This would not affect the chief scientific interest, which is geological and a unique feature of the Carboniferous Limestones in South Wales. The quarry cliff exposes alternating bands of limestone containing fossil sea lilies with lead ore and clays associated with lens shaped coal seams. The different layers deposited under different conditions illustrate the successive rising and falling of the land in relation to sea level at the time of their formation.

Many of the plants introduced would probably have arrived eventually by natural means, but hurrying things along will provide earlier cover for birds spreading in from adjacent woods of Ilston Cwm. A pair of kestrels had already taken up residence on the cliff by the early part of the seventies.

A spinney has been initiated around the pool which forms the central feature. Other saplings introduced to the spoil tips will eventually shade out the fine crops of wild strawberries which were among the first of the spontaneous arrivals to form a more or less complete cover and scree woodland will become established in their stead.

Introductions to the pool include greater water-plantain and creeping Jenny. Islets of spoil have been banked around with rocks and drain-pipes have been partially buried to tempt burrow-dwelling water fowl. The resulting verdure and consequent colonisation by small water creatures over the years, coupled with introductions of fish, have persuaded the grey wagtails, dippers and kingfishers of the nearby stream to come and investigate. Even green sandpipers have dropped in on migration.

A central concrete monstrosity has resisted all attempts to blow it up and it is hoped that this may eventually become covered with creepers. Who knows but that barn owls, jackdaws or pied wagtails might not then be cajoled into nesting there? Such species have 'adopted' some of the unlovely relics of the industrial revolution elsewhere in East Glamorgan. Wildlife is very resilient, and Time a great healer.

Clements Quarry below Oystermouth Castle near Mumbles reveals an important exposure of so-called "Black Lias" rocks belonging to the D3 zone of the Carboniferous Limestone. The black limestone shales, where wall butterflies bask in the sunshine, yield interesting fossils and are the 'type locality' for *Spirifer oystermouthensis* and other species — that is the site from which these were first described. Fine stands of red valerian act as a foil to the gold of bird's-foot trefoil, sending white roots into crevices and plumping their upper parts into fleshy stores of food and water, against summer drought. In warm years their massed flowers attract humming bird hawk moths and silver Ys, which hover on rapidly vibrating wings as they probe down for nectar. The inevitable

18. Kestrels

nettles provide nurseries for peacock and small tortoiseshell caterpillars and the stillness of the enclosed atmosphere attracts a wealth of smaller insects.

Clements Quarry, although designated as a Site of Special Scientific Interest by the Nature Conservancy Council, was not acquired as a nature reserve and is now, alas, a carpark and base for refuse lorries. The urban influence is apparent in its plants, several of which must have arrived in dumps of garden refuse. Garden escapes among the shrubs are Duke of Argyll's tea-tree, raspberry canes, lilac and the related privet. 'Strangers' among the herbs are montbretia, garden mint and creeping speedwell.

The plant succession in the Llanrhidian Quarry nature reserve on the old sea cliff overlooking the northern mudflats, has already progressed to natural limestone grassland and is now moving into a shrub phase en route for woodland. The end point in years to come is likely to be steep, dense woodland of oak and ash, as on the old sea cliffs at Cwm Ivy.

Tiny ferns find roothold in rock crevices—wall rue, maidenhair spleenwort and rusty-back—lichens cling to unfissured surfaces and ivy creeps across from above and below. Flowers among the dew-retaining Yorkshire fog grass of less precipitous parts include fairy flax, eye-bright, red bartsia and bulbous buttercup.

Hawthorns are the first of the shrubs to appear in profusion among the bramble and some of these are quite big towards the West, where ash and sycamore saplings are springing up. Blackbirds and dunnocks are already moving in to join the jackdaws and starlings and the light bush cover and grassy slopes make an admirable playground for butterflies. Meadow browns, wall browns, small heaths and large skippers can be very active here on mild summer days.

Callencroft Quarry at Oystermouth is sunk deep in mature woodland so that plant succession had a running start on Llanrhidian, with plenty of woodland species round about to act as parents for the pioneers of the young community. The most open area where lorries turned is still largely grassed, but lack of grazing has enabled this sward to grow tall and lush, with larger components such as meadow-sweet and red campion already squeezing out the lowlier primroses and cowslips.

Elsewhere the quarry floor is partially whitened by sheets of aromatic ramsons in spring. These follow an attractive assemblage of naturalised beauties — daffodil, narcissus and Solomon's seal. Soft shield-fern is common here, splaying upwards from the carpet in elegant profusion, with hart's-tongue fern where the garlic peters out among the talus at the foot of the ivy-draped cliff. Saplings of hawthorn, elder and sycamore are pushing up among the bluebells, wild arum and dog's mercury, as leaf mould builds up on the old working surfaces.

The local birds have included this man-made scar as an integral part of their territorial system and any of the common woodland species may be seen. Collared doves have moved in during the course of their population explosion and grey squirrels scamper round the cliff and squat on boulders to split their nuts open. One of the most characteristic butterflies of this more secluded site is the speckled wood.

Part Two

Wetlands: The Pools, Fens and Streams

Damselfly, dragonfly and fringed water lily

AT THE time of writing, in 1976, 'European Wetlands Year' is in full swing, with nations taking stock of their dwindling assets of submerged and marshy habitats. It seems appropriate, therefore to take a look at Gower's wetland heritage in the national context. So long as planners live by slogans such as 'wetlands are wastelands' and believe the wetlands ripe for damming, dumping, draining and development — as holes to be filled in and flats to be tipped on — these most valuable of wildlife habitats are doomed to become forever fewer.

The Oxwich-Penrice complex of lakes and fens on Gower rivals in quality the best of East Anglia and is the more precious for being sited in the West. Gower's rivers are small, but rather special with their swallet holes and impressive underground cave systems. Perhaps best of all are the wide acres of creeks and saltings flanking the Burry Inlet all along the northern shore. Here are extra riches, additional to the craggy limestone and rolling sandhills for which the peninsula is so justly famed.

European governments have come together in 1976 in the Ramsar Convention to promote wetland conservation and designate wetlands of international importance, and little Gower is in the forefront of this recuperative movement, with two wetland national nature reserves already declared in Oxwich and Whiteford—as well as the County Trust's first ever reserve at Broad Pool.

10 THE SMALLER PONDS

WITH the advent of piped water and galvanised troughs, the little ponds of field and farmland are among the dwindling wetland assets on a national scale, but Gower retains a fair quota of these.

There is something darkly sinister about her woodland pools and wildlife tends to avoid them. Dead leaves accumulate on their floors, giving off acid compounds as they decay and making life difficult for both animals and plants. The meagre light penetrating a summer tree canopy is enough for few plants other than wispy strands of water starwort, but slightly less shaded, peat-stained waters may support the green ribbon leaves of flotegrass and bronze ellipses of broad-leaved pondweed. Fragile shoots of marsh bedstraw wander up through tufts of remote sedge and soft rush. As the irises open, the reddish fruit clusters of marsh marigolds become overshadowed by orbicular leaves which expand to compensate for the diminishing light as the tree foliage unfurls overhead.

An open woodland pool can be more interesting. One such, in the fifty acre nature reserve at Gelli Hir, was brought into being as a fish pond by damming the stream which fed it, but in course of time it became silted with woodland debris and overgrown with willows. Volunteers from the County Trust got busy clearing it out in the sixties—by sheer muscle power, but with much muddy satisfaction. During the seventies the lopped sallows began to sprout from islets surrounded by clear water and now afford adequate cover for woodland birds coming to drink.

Kingfishers perch decoratively on the sawn-off branches as they scan the waters for fish and grey wagtails bob and curtsey on favoured posts. Willow warblers utilise the willows and blackcaps trill musically from alders and birches which shed their little fruits into the pool as additional duck food. Both mallard and teal nest at the water's edge and moorhens skulk among the bulrushes. The occasional wood sandpiper drops in and can be watched from the sturdy wooden hide above.

Delicate flowers of greater water-plantain sprout from the shallows while angelica and purple loosestrife brighten the more sombre marginal growths of tussock sedge and branching bur-reed. Over the quagmire below the dam grow spring carpets of golden-saxifrage peppered with lady's-smock and merging into a summer froth of meadowsweet and lady fern in an atmosphere fragrant with bruised water mint. Frogs and toads bred in the smaller pools find sanctuary here in adulthood.

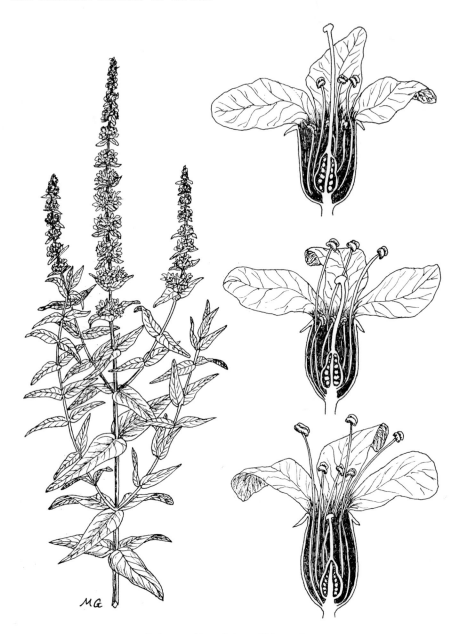

19. Purple loosestrife and three different flower types

Flowers appear earlier in ponds which dry out in summer, the fine show of bog-bean flowers by the roadside at Gelli Hir fading by the end of May when those of permanent pools on Fairwood Common are only just coming into bud. Marsh cinquefoil is an attractive plant of moorland pools, pink-flowered like the closely related water avens. Both are plants of North and West Britain, but cinquefoil is the species of South Glamorgan and avens that of North Glamorgan, particularly along the limestone streams.

Special rarities of Gower pools are lesser water-plantain and insectivorous lesser bladderwort, which gulps water fleas and other unwary passers-by into transparent lidded bladders on its feathery leaves. These are digested and the trigger mechanism re-set in readiness for the next victim.

The old duck decoy pool with its four curved arms in the woodland east of Broad Pool was re-excavated in the mid seventies and promises to be an exciting area for water fowl if it ever comes into commission again as a decoy—the catch to be ringed and released instead of eaten as in years gone by.

The caterpillars of a rare species of china mark moth (*Cataclysta lemnata*) have been found in ponds at Pennard and Fairwood. Representing the two-shelled bivalves in the Fairwood pond are the big swan mussel (*Anodonta cygnaea*) and either the tiny orb mussel (*Sphaerium*) or the very similar pea mussel (*Pisidium*). Lake limpets (*Ancylus lacustris*) cling to stones. Commonest of the browsing snails is the wandering snail (*Limnaea pereger*); others are the ear pond snail (*L. auricularia*), the bog or marsh snail (*L. palustris*) and the white ramshorn snail (*Planorbis alba*). Flattened water scorpions (*Nepa cinerea*) occur in pools on Cefn Bryn and various beetles adapted to life under water scud around, using flattened, hair-fringed legs as paddles. Some carry the necessary air with them as a trapped bubble, others as a silvery surface film. Largest and most predatory are the great diving beetles (*Dytiscus marginalis*).

An attractive set of ponds exists on rough grazings of the Rhossili-Pitton-Scurlage area of South-west Gower. These are the haunt of mallard and other wildfowl, which are none too plentiful, but which suffer at the hands of so-called sportsmen with guns.

Spring-flowering gorse supplies spiky cover where their banks are eroding back into the grassy heath, with its nibbled mounds of creeping willow and pink flecks of lousewort. Water crowfoot and water starwort form an underwater thicket beneath a leaf raft of broad-leaved pondweed and flote grass. Fine clumps of great water dock, branching bur-reed and soft rush fringe the shallows, with yellow iris and lady's-smock behind. One of the larger islands is skirted with a floating sward of bogbean and satiny green wefts of blanket weed cluster about the forget-me-not, mint and spearwort.

Field ponds on the better farmland are more trampled and less interesting. Fertilisers drain into them, nurturing lesser duckweed and common farm weeds at the expense of the rarer bog plants. Great water dock is

73

replaced by curled dock, which is not eaten by grazing animals but is stimulated by their dung. Hemlock water-dropwort is loaded with poisons and avoided by most stock. Creeping buttercup, silverweed and sorrel escape breakage under trampling hooves by growing flush with the ground, but the deep swards of flowering spike-rush (*Eleocharis*) are often eaten back to a height of a few inches.

Unless dredged occasionally, ponds such as these become silted with mud displaced by animals coming to drink. The seeds of animal-tolerant plants such as water pepper germinate in profusion among the spike rush and there is an increase in marshland species, particularly the mints, which are left alone by most animals because of their powerfully aromatic oils. As soil and debris accumulate, the hollow-stemmed grey club-rush and bur-reed may persist for some time, rooting through to the water table below, but starwort changes from the loosely ascending water form to the tightly prostrate land form, whilst creeping buttercup and silverweed take over more and more of the former pond bed.

Further north at Burry Green grazing is less concentrated, although ponies and sheep roam freely and churn up the pond margins. The northern pond has silted up, the previously floating flote-grass now a lawn-like sward and the yellow iris clumps protecting the few remaining kingcups and cuckooflowers from questing noses. Fool's watercress occupied much of the southern pond in 1973, broad-leaved pondweed in 1974, with common duckweed and a large-flowered water crowfoot growing below the summer margin. Above this is a colony of ivy-leaved crowfoot bearing smaller flowers and none of the feathery underwater leaves of the down-shore species. More plants grow round about than in the fertilised fields, among them winter-cress, bog stitchwort, water blinks, marsh bird's-foot trefoil, marsh bedstraw, brooklime, thyme-leaved speed-well and fleabane.

By mid May most of the Burry Green tadpoles have waxed fat and blotchy and are sprouting hind legs. The entire bed of rock, silt and clay is thickly sprinkled with Jenkin's spire shell snails and among them some larger wandering snails. Slender pond skaters and rotund whirligig beetles scud across the surface; water beetles in a variety of sizes and tiny red water mites rove the miniature submerged forest below. Predatory water boatmen row from plant to plant, sometimes with inch-long worms pro-truding from their mouths.

It is these small fry which bring pied wagtails and moorhens to forage, but there is too little cover to tempt the water rails domiciled near-by. Fly 'hatches' bring swallows and house martins to swoop and wheel on summer days and collared doves have recently moved into gardens round the village green.

Further west towards Llanmadoc Down a roadside pool affords an apt illustration of the effects of grazing animals on pond plants. A fence

20. Water rails

across the middle excludes free range livestock from the hinder portion but the protective hawthorn hedge at the back is now breached so that this part may be grazed too if the field behind carries stock rather than an arable crop. In such years the differences between the two halves are masked, but reappear again when stock are once more excluded.

The roadside half is more open and dominated by large-flowered water crowfoot in spring and greater water-plantain in summer. The other half is occupied by taller growths of soft rush and spike-rush, among which the water-plantain struggles through with difficulty and the water crowfoot is practically excluded, along with the open water. The crowfoot may have been pushed out during the normal course of plant succession, a lowly water species over-run by tall marsh species, but survives outside the fence because the distasteful alkaloid so prevalent in its family enables it to survive grazing better than those others.

Puddling by livestock is helping to keep the water from getting over-grown and replaced by invading vegetation; so, although the pond plants suffer some damage from the livestock, they may have these to thank for their very existence.

Tall grey clubrush is confined to the ungrazed side whilst soft rush and spike rush get severely trimmed back where they push through the fence. 'Lady's-smock' grows larger on the ungrazed side, as does silverweed, but the latter is much commoner on the grazed side, where its stunted leaves occupy more than half of the grassy sward to roadward of the pond. Marsh bedstraw and water forget-me-not are dwarfed here too. Duck-weed stimulated by pony dung, drifts through the fence to occur on both sides. A pond of this sort is likely to support a rich fauna and plenty of undisturbed cover for moorhens and warblers.

75

11 THE SAGA OF BROAD POOL, CILIBION

BROAD POOL near Cilibion became the Glamorgan Naturalists' Trust's first nature reserve in 1962. It is interesting in its own right as a bog pool in the pitted Boulder Clay overlying the limestone, but the real reason for its acquisition was the attractive small stand of fringed water lily. This is rare in Wales, being indigenous to the Mediterranean and South-east England, but having retreated from its most south-westerly sites in the Hereford-Gloucester area some time prior to 1930.

By 1963 a patch of the 'lily' which had occupied one square yard the year before was occupying 110 square yards and a continuing spread was forecast. It happened! By 1968 the Trust was moving heaven and earth to curb the plants' exuberance—and encountering more of earth than heaven in the doing—and very muddy earth at that. This must be an almost unique conservation case history, of the turning of the tables by a cherished rarity! Conservation is never simple once man has waded in and upset the status quo.

The pool occupies 2.83 acres of moorland and is nowhere more than four feet deep. It is sited on a small raised plateau sloping down to the West, so there is a negligible catchment area, drainage being away from it rather than into it. Nor has any spring been seen to enter. Yet the pool has only been known to dry out twice, once in 1897 and once in the 1920s.

The water is neutral in reaction, suggesting that it cannot come primarily either from the alkaline limestone below or the acid peat round about. If from a mixture of both, the one would serve to neutralise the other.

Nearly three acres of water surface is sufficient for waves to build up, cutting back the leeward shore, while there is a silting to windward which, perhaps fortunately, has partially blocked the only outflow. The ultimate end of this gradual migration towards the North-east is not just that the pool will move off the edge of its plateau and drain away downhill, but that water loss will be more catastrophic, directly into caverns of the underlying limestone by way of a swallet hole sited in its course less than 20 yd. (18 m.) away. But this is not imminent.

The pool itself occupies a sink hole, plugged up by impermeable Boulder Clay, so that water cannot escape into the hollows dissolved out beneath. There are many such holes visible on the North-facing hillside south of the pool, some of them overgrown with bracken, some containing stands of the rare bog myrtle.

76

21. Moorhen

The pool is on commonland, and therefore does not appear in old manorial records, so is not well documented, but was probably in existence 330 years ago, around 1645. It is on record that stray livestock on Cefn Bryn were at that time driven by way of 'The Great Pool' to the top of the hill about 12 to 15 days before midsummer.

The adjective 'great' suggests that Broad Pool was as broad then as now and did not takes its name from the area as a whole which was known as Broad Moor. There is no evidence that peat was ever cut or that the pool was worked for gravel, clay or stone to enlarge or maintain it, but licences were issued for commoners to dig mud out of it. This they mixed with lime and used as a fertiliser on their fields. It may have been this practice which preserved the smaller 'Horse Pool' on Fairwood Common as a pool, for this has been more or less swallowed up by the surrounding moorland since digging ceased.

Rudd can sometimes be seen leaping from open stretches of water on the north side of the pool and three-spined sticklebacks are abundant. Frogs, newts and toads deposit their spawn here each spring and no less than 230 toads, mostly male, were counted during the first week of February in 1972. By the end of that week both spawn and tadpoles were in evidence, although at the beginning of the century when winters were cold and summers hot, toad spawn was not expected until the first week in April.

By mid May in the seventies veritable regiments of well grown tadpoles followed each other on a broad front, thousands strong, in a clockwise migration around the pool, peppering the pale clay of the eroded north-east margin like animated currants. Others huddled in amorphous masses on the water plants, nibbling the algae from their surfaces. Sleek yellow frogs and warty red-brown toads hopped and heaved through the sedges above.

Freshwater limpets (*Ancylus lacustris*) clamp on to lily stems and leaves. Pond snails (*Limnaea auricularia* var. *acuta* and *L. stagnalis*) ooze ponderously over sludge and weed and are preyed upon by big black horse leeches (*Haemopsis sanguisuga*), which have extraordinary powers of contraction and expansion, enabling them to halve or double their length in the twinkling of an eye. These feed on insects and carrion too, not horses as their names suggests, although there are plenty of paddling equine fetlocks onto which they could clamp if so inclined. Other snail-sucking leeches cohabiting with these 5-10 inch monsters are *Glossiphonia complanata*, *Erpobdella atomaria* and *Protoclepsis tesselata*.

This is a particularly good habitat for dragonflies, which zoom purposefully and lethally among their winged prey after emergence from their prolonged nymphal stage in the pool. That is if not previously eaten by heron, duck, rudd, stickleback or predatory beetle. Fourteen of the twenty four species recorded in the three counties of Glamorgan have been seen at Broad Pool.

Dragonflies proper are divided into the hawkers and the darters. Two of the pool's three hawkers have a wing span of more than 4 inches (up to 11 cm.) and a body length of up to $3\frac{1}{2}$ inches, and can be ranked among Britain's largest insects, although some beetles are heavier. They patrol regular beats, hawking back and forth for flies and moths, which they catch in the 'baskets' of their pronged, forwardly projecting legs. Largest of the three is the golden-ringed dragonfly (*Cordulegaster boltoni*), second the emperor (*Anax imperator*), the male azure-blue and the female grassgreen. The female of the common Aeshna (*Aeshna juncea*) retains the yellow and green colours of the newly emerged adult but the male changes to blue as he matures.

The darters rest more frequently on the ground or on plants between short sharp spurts in pursuit of prey or intruding members of their own kind. Broad Pool has four species, including the common, the red-veined and the black Sympetrums. *Sympetrum striolatum* is red or yellow; *S. danae* is smaller, with the males all black and the females and immatures black and gold. The larvae of *S. fonscolombii* cannot survive here but a few adults pass through on migration.

The remaining darter is the four-spotted Libellula (*Libellula quadrimaculata*) largest of the four, with a $3\frac{1}{2}$ inch (9 cm.) wingspan and a fat hairy body. Easily recognisable by the black spots on the wings, the adults are very abundant in mid June, when one is likely to be seen every five to six yards along the bank. This is the time when the broods of reed buntings and meadow pipits are fledging and the parent birds take a heavy toll of the young adults as they emerge, rather stupefied, from their pupal cases to dry out on the marginal sedges or make their first halting flights over the fringed water lily. The birds do not collect the less easily caught adults, even when these alight nearby.

Five species of smaller damselflies have been seen at Broad Pool, the two blue ones difficult to distinguish in flight. These are the common blue and the common Coenagrion (*Enallagma cyathigerum* and *Coenagrion puella*). Colour on the slender body of the common Ishnura (*Ishnura elegans*) is confined to the electric blue spot on the third segment from the rear. In the green Lestes (*Lestes sponsa*) of the rush patches both sexes are an iridescent green, though the adult males become dusted with powder blue. Unmistakeable, by virtue of its colour, is the large red damselfly (*Pyrrhosoma nymphula*) which shows off its crimson body to advantage by settling frequently on the short green turf of the northern shore.

Alder flies (*Sialis*) and mayflies (including *Cloeon*) 'hatch' in summer, tempting no trout. Caddis fly larvae, large ones with protective tubes and small ones without, amble round the pool floor and water bugs are plentiful. Scooting across the water surface (such as is left of it) are water boatmen (*Corixa scottii* and *Notonecta*), pond skaters (*Gerris*) and water measurers (*Hydrometra stagnorum*). Seeking their prey of small animals on the bottom are plump saucer bugs (*Ilyocoris cimicoides*) and the tiny *Plea leachi* which feeds on water fleas and their ilk. Gnats (*Culex*), biting midges (*Ceratopogon*) and non-biting midges (*Chironomus*) emerge in clouds and bring flocks of Hirundines to feed over the water. Other flies such as *Corethra* and *Cyclorrhephan* also spend their larval phases in the pool.

Great diving beetles (*Dytiscus marginalis*) prey ferociously on lesser life, both as larvae and adults. Hydrobe larvae (*Hydrobius*) hold their prey out of the water to eat it. Silvered whirligig beetles (*Gyrinus*) scud dizzily around on the surface and the common underwater beetle, *Agabus bipustulatus*, pupates in mudcells at the water's edge.

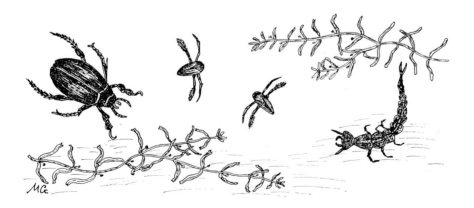

22. Great diving beetle and larva with two water boatmen, among flowering water starwort

The water spider (*Argyroneta aquatica*) collects bubbles of air to fill its underwater net and there are many species of *Hydracarina*. Copepods, *Cladocera* and the water hog louse (*Asellus*) are small Crustaceans providing food for some of the more aggressive creatures.

Many species of Rotifers can be collected in plankton nets. Minute, many-celled Polyzoa are represented by one of the few freshwater Bryozoons or moss animals, *Cristatella mucedo;* single-celled Protozoa by *Arcella*, an almost globose, 'root-footed' Rhizopod, *Carchesium* and spherical *Radiolaria* with their beautifully sculptured skeletons. Many-celled spheres of the colonial green alga, *Volvox*, bowl round among these animals.

Hydra, well known to schoolboys, waves questing tentacles from its firmly anchored base and many species of primitive worms or Nematodes have been found but not identified. Flat worms (*Platyhelminths*) are represented by the Turbellarian, *Polycelis nigra*, which is more characteristic of acid soft water ponds, but is abundant here, sheltering under stones and leaves. Tiny, black and many eyed, these little flat worms possess extraordinary powers of regeneration, new parts being generally paler in colour than the original. *Polycelis tenuis* is another species common both here and in the neighbouring ponds.

So much small life attracts larger life to poke and probe, as well as to snap it from the air in the manner of swifts, swallows and martins. Black-headed gulls and redshank feed here with a few oyster catchers strayed up from the coastal flocks and herons drop in from time to time. Snipe may be flushed from the undergrowth, or the rarer green sandpiper on passage. In some summers a coot will bring off a pair of young in June and the occasional Bewick swan drops in from Northern Russia in winter. Little brown birds among the poolside sallows are mostly reed buntings.

Pool vegetation in danger of being engulfed by the invasive fringed water lily includes a few species seldom found elsewhere. One of these is the elegantly feathery stonewort (*Nitella? flexilis*) which forms dense masses in the North-west and is associated with floating club-rush (*Scirpus fluitans*). The similarly feathery creeping marshwort is well distributed and rose to dominance near the road in 1974 where the lily had been raked out by Trust members and school children and heaped on the roadside bank. Chief underwater associate of the lily in the East is the alternate-flowered water milfoil.

Unbranched bur-reed, which is a much less common plant than branched bur-reed, rears out of the raft of fringed water-lily and broad-leaved pondweed in the North west, near the white water-lily plants. This is an interesting corner, the less overgrown parts showing ivy-leaved crowfoot, water purslane and marsh St. John's wort in deeper water, marsh violet, water blinks and marsh pennywort in the shallows.

To windward, where the peaty swamp is encroaching into the pool, common cotton-grass is the most conspicuous invader in the South,

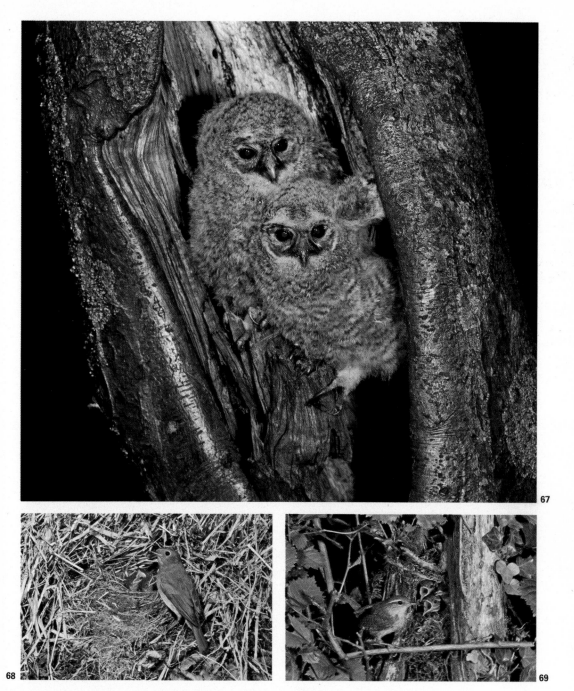

Plate 17 BIRDS OF WOODED HEDGEROWS

67. Young Tawny Owls wait patiently for their returning parents   *Keri Williams*

68. Robins tuck their nests into the rough grass of wooded banks   *Arthur Morgan*

69. Wrens insert their mossy homes into ivy-draped stumps   *Arthur Morgan*

70   71

72

Plate 18   FARMLAND AND QUARRY

70. False oxlips growing with one of the parent species on a West Gower field bank   *Author*

71. Ilston Quarry; the newly constructed pool as it was in 1972   *Author*

72. Meadow Pipits nest in rough grazing land   *Keri Williams*

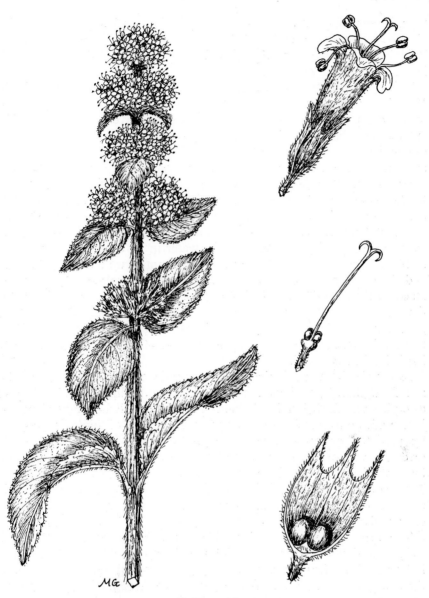

23. Water mint

bog-bean in the North. There are some fine moss swards here composed
not only of the water-absorbent *Sphagnum*, but of smooth pale mats of
Aulacomium palustre and loose dark cushions of *Polytrichum commune*.
An attractive fungus resembling little orange-headed drumsticks which
appears among the *Sphagnum* in May and June is *Mitrula paludosa*.
Spike-rush and true rushes were still marginally abundant in the West in

83

the mid seventies, but the general plant distribution had altered considerably from that shown in the 1963 map published in the Glamorgan Trust Bulletin at the time when the fringed water-lily occupied only a discrete hemisphere by the roadside.

This notorious 'rarity' was first recorded in Broad Pool in 1952. By 1969 there was estimated to be 230 tons of it! If life in the pool was not to be completely engulfed something would have to be done. The experimental hand clearing of plants from 30 square yards led to the calculation that to clear the whole would occupy some 3,000 man hours and leave a liberal sprinkling of unseen fragments in the suspended mud to start off another vigorous lily crop. And what else might be happening to the ecology of the pool in the doing, how many animals would be dragged out and stranded on the bank?

In fact, fewer than anticipated, most of them sluicing back into the pool as the weed was dragged through the water in an experiment conducted in 1968. The only ones removed in large quantity were the pond limpets and the china mark moth caterpillars (*Nymphula nympheata*), which live glued to their food plants in little cases. The upheaval caused some of the water spiders to get trapped in their own nets and hauled out with the general mass. Fly larvae, too, tended to come out with the weed. Water bugs, alder fly larvae and the aquatic phases of damsel flies were mostly left behind in the mud.

Although a 'stranger' in the area the fringed water-lily had been accepted as a food plant by various animals and several million china mark moth caterpillars made their living from it. But several million pairs of chomping jaws made no impression on the mass, and the idea of 'biological control' by predator or parasite was shelved as merely academic until the seventies, when everything short of hippos and sea cows was considered by the scientific committee of the Glamorgan Trust. The Wildfowl Trust could suggest no likely candidate among the water fowl and the potential of Chinese grass carp or white amurs (*Ctenopharyngodon idella*) came under discussion.

These are very voracious fish, able to eat more than their own body weight per day and to reach to 100 pounds in weight and 4 ft. (120 cm.) in length after a few years. Having a gut only one fifth as long as that of the average herbivore, half their food passes through them un-digested, so that they need to eat twice as much, A good point, but the faeces are that much richer in nutrients and are an excellent manure for boosting growth of the unwanted plant pest.

The possibility of them breeding and overunning the area is remote: they need higher temperatures than Gower can provide (except in 1976) and running water. But even a few hundred pounds of fish eating a few hundred pounds of vegetation daily could wreck havoc, and their effectiveness is open to doubt.

They are selective feeders, going preferentially for soft wefts of green algae and then delicate species such as water milfoil, Canadian pondweed and duckweed. Under cold conditions they eat only the most tender plants, becoming less selective as it gets hotter. The fringed water lily is among the tougher plants and it seems likely that the marshwort and stonewort, purslane and milfoil, which the lily is threatening to swamp, will be consumed before the aggressor. But it might still be worth trying if the carp were confined in a wire netting cage (and the necessary licence to risk keeping them could be obtained from the Fishery authorities.)

The idea of using herbicides has been rejected because of the undesirable side effects; that of mechanical removal by heavy machines because of the danger of damaging the pool floor and letting the water out. A steam generator was sought, unsuccessfully and could scarcely be expected to do more than kill surface growths.

There is always the hope that the story of the Canadian pondweed in Britain will be repeated and that the rampageous newcomers will starve themselves of the necessary nutrients and fade back to reasonable proportions alongside the natives. The idea of waiting for a self-defeating 'sick monoculture' after all else has died commends itself as offering the naturalists a campaign of masterly inactivity, but the ponies and cattle which come to drink continue to deliver a daily quota of manure in a most uncooperative fashion. Any attempt to drag the stuff out, however, must inevitably result in a stirring of the bottom sufficient to release yet more plant foods from the ooze of the bed, so there is a strong temptation to 'let Nature take her course'.

At the time of going to press the possibility of starvation seems as remote as ever and it looks as though this alluringly handsome yellow pest will be part of the Gower scene for a long time yet. It is already becoming entrenched in pools on the flanks of Cefn Bryn and elsewhere. It must be conceded that the massed golden flowers of late summer are a sight well worth seeing and it may still be many years before they completely block the pool and cause the last of the water to overflow from the little plateau. Or it may never happen.

Normally the upper part of the outlet stream carries water only during rainy spells, but its course downhill to the big grassy swallet into which it finally disappears to underground caverns through a series of rocky orifices is marked by a line of rushes. Before tumbling out of sight it nurtures one of the finest stands of bog myrtle on Gower and provides sustenance for a lively population of eels and amphibians. This hidden cavity in the level surface of the moorland is much frequented by ponies, which find the short turf more to their liking than the coarse tufts of purple moor-grass on the windy flats above—or the succulently tempting fringed water-lily of the pool!

12 PENRICE LAKES

A vast amount of alluvium, blown sand and peat has accumulated in Oxwich Bay, so the former shoreline is now deeply recessed. Nicholaston Pill cuts into the old land surface to form a broad, smooth-sided valley debouching onto the new land of the low-lying flats from the North-west. It flows vigorously down from the 200 ft. land platform until well below Penrice Castle, which is the largest in Gower, with a keep dating from 1240 and a stone pigeon house from about 1500.

In the lower valley the speed of flow has been reduced by a series of locks and spillways and the course much widened to form a large fish pond and a lower jack pond. These are on private land and are overlooked by the modern 'castle', built about 1775 by Thomas Mansell Talbot and now occupied by an ex-president of the Glamorgan Naturalists' Trust, Christopher Methuen Campbell. Landscaping of the surrounding parklands was tackled in the late eighteenth century, but the colourful banks of *Rhododendron ponticum* mirrored in the idling waters came later, in Victorian times—as cover for pheasants. Goldcrests are particularly fond of their dark seclusion and have increased of late, as have the similarly tiny wrens.

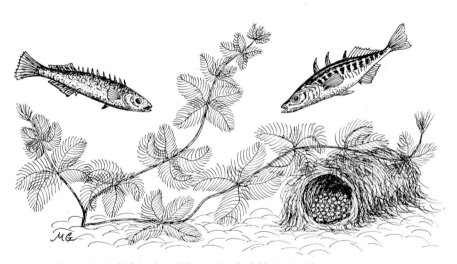

24. Ten-spined stickleback and three-spined stickleback with nest among water milfoil

86

The upper lake is partially silted and Nicholaston stream enters it across an extensive headwater marsh at the western end. Surplus water gushes through a sluice from the southern arm or slides over a spillway to the jack pond. The ample waters have been stocked with brown trout and rudd, which were formerly preyed on by pike (*Esox lucius*). Trout (*Salmo trutta*) feed on small animals, mostly underwater ones, in seasonal sequence, depending on what is available. Rudd (*Scardinius erythrophthalmus*) are partly plant browsers and partly animal hunters after a spell of concentrating on Crustacea as juveniles.

Eels (*Anguilla anguilla*) find their way up from the sea and grow to large size and there are fish-eating perch (*Perca fluviatilis*) in the lower pond and marsh. Ten-spined sticklebacks (*Pungitius pungitius*) occur in the upper lake, three-spined sticklebacks (*Gasterosteus aculeatus*) in the jack pond and swamp as well, where there may be a trace of brackishness. In both species the male fish builds a nest in which to care for the eggs but that of the wholly freshwater species is made among dense vegetation instead of in the open. It is more timid than the other and its ten spines less fearsome, but sufficient to protect it against predatious perch and pike. Sticklebacks are themselves predatory, swallowing their prey whole and living principally on small Crustaceans.

White water-lily is established in the lower pond; yellow water-lily or brandy bottle in the upper, where it is 'taking over' almost as surely as the fringed water-lily is in Broad Pool, curtailing the area of open water. It was introduced originally for the attractive underwater foliage, which is crisply curled and delicate, like lettuce. By 1974 this was partially obscured by the raft of tougher floating leaves, their blades forced erect by mutual crowding.

Other aquatic plants include some extensive stands of a large-flowered water crowfoot with circular lobed leaves at the water surface and neatly dissected ones below. Lesser duck-weed is sparse; there are far more of the fragile, tri-partite fronds of ivy duckweed suspended below the surface. The water bistort is mostly marginal and of the erect land form rather than the floating water one.

Spiked water-milfoil is abundant, filling the water with suspended leaves and piercing the surface with pinkish flower spikes in mid-summer. Much rarer is the marestail, which grows well in the upper lake, its thick white stems beset with whorls of strap-shaped leaves bearing minute flowers or fruits in their axils. There are two kinds of pondweed which seldom break surface—the fennel pondweed, *Potamogeton pectinatus* and the curled *P. crispus*, whose appeal lies in the delicate, wavy-edged leaves rather than the dull flower spikes.

Reeds skirt a central island and meet across the lake below it, in conjunction with a robust growth of great bulrush or cat's-tail. Reed-canary-grass is more marginal and is sometimes associated with big tussocks

87

of greater tussock sedge (*Carex paniculata*). Great pond-sedge (*C. riparia*) and grey club-rush (*Schoenoplectus tabernaemontani*) line the lower end of the fish pond with a little remote sedge (*C. remota*).

Woodland shores are fringed with water mint, water forget-me-not and woody nightshade, grading back into meadowsweet, soft rush and feathery growths of giant horsetail. Shores bordering pasture are badly poached by cattle (and donkeys?) and the plants are lowlier. Brooklime (*Veronica beccabunga*) grows alongside the much rarer water speedwell (*V. catenata*) with water-cress, lesser spearwort, water pepper, bog stitchwort, jointed rush and others of the field ponds.

Thousands of small water boatmen (*Notonecta*) scud among the water starwort and whirligig beetles have their own private pool in a waterlogged iron boat.

Water snails of various kinds browse among the pondweeds. The common ramshorn and white ramshorn (*Planorbis planorbis* and *P. albus*) occur in both lakes, *P. crista*, apparently, only in the lower one. Wandering snails (*Limnaea pereger*) have been found in both, the eared pond snail (*L. auricularia*) only in the Jack Pond. The shiny snail (*Zonitoides nitidus*) is really a marshland species but is not averse to water and often joins the pond snails in the upper pool. Local blackbirds feed quite sizable water snails to their young—whole—with no attempt to smash the shells, as song thrushes do!

The lake limpet (*Ancylus lacustris*) occurs in both lakes, the river limpet (*A. fluviatilis*) only in the upper one, possibly brought in by Nicholaston Pill. There it cohabits with the abundant Jenkin's spire shells (*Hydrobia* or *Pomatopyrgus jenkinsi*), which have not been found in the lakes nor in the streams leading away into the marsh below. Big swan mussels are numerous in the bottom deposits, where dead shells gape to expose their pearly interiors and a close search may reveal tiny pea or orb shells lurking in the mud.

Dragonflies and damselflies, red, blue and green, are a conspicuous part of the summer scene. Vari-coloured females of the damselfly *Ischnura elegans* are not accompanied by the males when laying eggs, but make solo flights, alighting on the pink tips of the water milfoil spikes to curve their slender bodies round and deposit the eggs on the stem just below water level. The males, black with powder blue thorax and penultimate band, are everywhere along the shore, alighting on rush, reed and sedge, with wings held obliquely at first, then sunk to the sides. This stance is commonly adopted by the similar *Lestes sponsa;* most kinds of damselflies fold their wings down very soon after alighting. The greenish brown nymphs of *Ischnura elegans* are as slender as the adults and take two years to mature.

Bumble bees of various kinds thread in and out of the yellow iris flowers, the sensitive stigmatic hinge bending to accommodate them and scrape off life-giving pollen grains brought from other flowers. In 1972 fifty two different species of moth were caught by the lake on a single night, one of them a very rare wainscot.

A tiny grey gall fly (*Chirosia parvicornis*) produces crisply knotted tips to the fronds of waterside lady ferns. The fly inserts her egg into the leaf and the larva which hatches mines into the green tissue, initiating a coiling and entwining by causing the death of some cells and the proliferation of others.

Another parasite is one which infects no less than three hosts—warm and cold-blooded vertebrates and an invertebrate. This is a Trematode worm or fluke (*Posthodiplosoma cuticola*) which causes black spot disease of fish in the local rudd and lives on in the herons which eat infected fish. The remaining part of its life cycle is passed within the tissues of water snails, whose identities have not yet been determined.

The heronry is situated on the central islet, birds using the exotic copper beech for their bulky nests as freely as the native trees. They have been increasing over the years with a few minor fluctuations, from a total of 18 broods successfully reared in 1967 to 29 broods in 1971 and 1972. In 1973 there were 32 occupied nests, in 1974 only 24 but they increased again in the next two years to 34 nests in 1976. They are noble birds, in spite of the gawky scramblings and throaty squawks of the youngsters at

25. Grey herons

the nest. Adults rising with a clatter of wings from the treetops to circle with the same majestic sweeps as the local buzzards in the same thermal, lose nothing by comparison.

They stay around for most of the year except for a few weeks after Christmas, reappearing by St. Valentine's day, the traditional day for pairing. Like otters, they prefer eels to other fish and may be seen doing battle with these in the shallows before swallowing them. Every now and again a passing spoonbill arrives to roost with them—enjoying the social clamour of its closest relatives in a strange land.

Mallard lead their fluffy broods of ducklings out among the lily pads in June and July, alternately upending to feed and standing on their tails to flap. Coot and moorhen tuck their big egg clutches away among reeds and reedmace and disport themselves dipping, splashing and preening, along the inner vegetation margin. Every year a pair of dabchicks nests on each of the lakes. Big flocks of mallard and teal arrive in October and consort with smaller parties of shoveller on the jack pond. As the weather gets colder little groups of pochard, goldeneye and tufted duck fly in. Their animal prey has benefitted by the recent dredging of two parts of the lake and more diving duck came to visit after this operation.

The big jackdaw flock milling round the castle ruins on the hill above spills untidily out over the dreaming lakes at intervals, side-slipping down the wind, inter-weaving with their fellows and 'chacking' fractiously as others cross their flight path. Both jays and magpies have increased in the last decade and there has also been a welcome upsurge in the birds of prey—kestrels and buzzards, sparrow hawks and merlins. A pale, softly feathered barn owl hunts regularly along the sleepy shoreline in the evenings, and brown owls break the stillness with their eerie hooting.

Scratchy songs of reed and sedge warblers emanate from the reed beds to mingle with the sibilant piping of blackcap or willow warbler from the sallows and bisyllabic monotones of chiff chaffs in the rhododendrons. Dippers dip and bob beside the pill which feeds the lakes. An old game book of 1790 records the shooting of large numbers of red kite—as well as 'hawks' and 'wild cats', which may have been feral or gone-wild domestic ones. Today one has to travel to Mid Wales to see the Welsh national bird.

But otters are still about, leaving tell-tale signs in the form of pad marks and half eaten fish. Adults have been seen and heard among the reeds on occasion, particularly around the jack pond and may even have bred in 1973. (There is a tale still told of a 95-year-old in the village who was chased by three otters when riding his bicycle.)

Stoats are less common than formerly, their numbers having fallen with those of the rabbits, but weasels are still abundant, feeding on beetles and other large invertebrates as well as small mammals. Badgers breed in the woods about two miles higher up the valley and bachelor badgers travel from there to share an earth in the copse south-west of the lake with the resident foxes. The rightful owners pad regularly along the edge of the lake and keep the occupants of Penrice House awake in February and March when the mating urge incites them to vocal display.

Silting at the head of the upper lake has given rise to a marshy woodland or carr through which the inlet stream has carved a meandering, earth-floored channel. The dominant grey sallow and crack willow are fully grown trees, their narrow greyish leaves, when silhouetted aloft against a blue sky, looking for all the world like those of a grove of stringy-bark Eucalypts. Their boughs and those of the associated alders are thickly hung with old-man's-beard lichen (*Usnea subfloridana*). Polypody ferns extend well into the tree crowns, with a wealth of epiphytic mosses.

The ground is sodden, even in summer, when it supports high growths of greater willow-herb, hemlock, water-dropwort and yellow flags, with gipsy-wort and fool's watercress. In deeper shade enchanter's nightshade and woodland loosestrife predominate in summer, but carpets of golden-saxifrage flecked with the deeper gold of kingcups exploit the lighter phase of early spring, when the willows and alders are clothed only with catkins.

This rich fen carr merges sideways into marsh dominated by soft rush and iris with ragged-robin and fleabane. Stools of tussock sedge in the transitional zone provide a roothold for nettle and lady fern on their skirted sides. A similar wooded swamp occurs below the main lake to the South and East, but the land rises to the North. The parkland there supports good crops of fungi most years, including ceps (*Boletus edulis*) as big as dinner plates, which make delicious eating, whether fried or casseroled. 1975 and 1976 were bumper years for fungus forays, as autumn's moistness permeated a cooperative soil warmed by the suns of the two long summers.

13 OXWICH LAKES AND FENS

BOTH routes to the car park at Oxwich Bay descend steeply from the 200 ft. plateau but the main ingress road from the North continues for another mile at something very near sea level. Much of the level expanse crossed is under water—very obviously so in February 1974, when flood water from phenomenal rains was backed up by especially high tides and spread across the tarmac, lapping against walls and obscuring the position of deep roadside ditches.

Nowhere do the Millstone Grit shales which occupy the Oxwich syncline come to the surface. Soil borings have shown them to be overlain by alternating layers of water-borne alluvium and wind-borne sand, with a rich fen peat of slightly alkaline reaction building up at the surface.

The steep land face curving round for three miles behind the marshes from Oxwich in the South West to Crawley Top and Little Tor in the North East is an old sea cliff. It is probable that the inshore waters were gradually converted to a saline or brackish lagoon as sand began to accumulate across the mouth of the bay, this drying out progressively to form a saltmarsh behind the restrictive sand bar. When the sea was finally excluded, drainage water flowed in to wash out the salt and convert it to a freshwater marsh with flashes of open water.

In the Middle Ages the area was shared between four manors and was used for grazing and haymaking. A survey in 1632 recorded that of 200 acres of fresh and salt water marsh 71 acres was meadowland and 9 acres of the salt marsh were grazed. Productivity has been intermittent since then.

A period of deteriorating land use terminated in 1770 when Thomas Mansell Talbot built the eight feet high sea wall which finally excluded the sea from the inner marsh. He constructed ditches to lead off surplus water and landscaped the area by construction of the Serpentine Pool or Broad as well as the Penrice Lakes. Two hundred acres of land were thus improved, and continued to be grazed by sheep and cattle until early in the twentieth century, cattle utilising one of the currently flooded areas as recently as 1945.

The region is no longer grazed and part of it is maintained as a private rough shoot and fishing beat. Biologically it is an extremely valuable area and 542 acres are managed as a National Nature Reserve by the Nature Conservancy Council. It embraces freshwater lakes, swamps and marshes, salt marshes, sand dunes, cliffs and woodlands and contains over 400 species of flowering plants and ferns. 624 species of flowering plants alone have been found since 1970 in the 10 km. grid square of which it is part, this representing a third of all the British flora. Perhaps an even greater measure of its wealth of life is the recording of no less than 603 different species of Diptera or two-winged flies within the reserve—a Herculean task undertaken by Mr. Fonseca over the twenty years from 1952 to 1972. Also on record are 35 species of bees and wasps. No doubt other groups would prove as numerous if field scientists with the necessary expertise were available to find out.

The marsh at present receives the run-off from about four square miles of hinterland. Nicholaston Pill is the largest of five streams flowing in from the North and West and subsidiary springs occur along the peripheral seepage line. Other brooks enter from the South and East. The old natural drainage pattern of meandering water courses can be distinguished now only from the air, but the original sinuous course of Nicholaston Pill is remembered in the parish boundary. Oxwich stream seems to flow contrary to expectations, rising quite close to the sea near Oxwich village but flowing North to join the Nicholaston stream where the road crosses the long Serpentine Pool.

The arcuate segments of partially blocked saltmarsh gutters can be made out among the all enveloping growth of reeds on aerial photographs. Dominant drainage of the marsh at present is to a semi-circular channel passing from Oxwich village along the boundary of the reserve to the eastern sluice gate where the Nicholaston Pill makes its exit through the sea wall—a wall that was breached by the army during the war and by floods in February 1974, enabling high tides to seep through into the lake behind. Sea-going flounders sometimes find their way into the lake system, a fish as much as 10 inches (25 cm.) long being caught 30 ft. (9 m.) from the lower end of the lake in 1975.

Straight ditches mark former field boundaries and it seems likely that the cruciform, reed-lined ditch system dissecting the four flashes in the North West was constructed to allow boat-borne wildfowlers a view of the four pools whilst remaining hidden themselves. These flashes are accessible only by boat, which has to be portaged through thickets of reed growing in deep sloppy peat, so the wildlife is seldom disturbed.

The wetlands occupy 150 acres and lie about twenty feet above Ordnance datum level. Largest of the stretches of open water is the Serpentine Broad covering eighteen acres in all. The entire system, however, is choked by silt and weeds, making boat access generally as tedious or

26. Pike and rudd among hornwort

impossible as access on foot. Fertility is high throughout, with plentiful mineral nutrients and organic matter in a fen peat akin to that of East Anglia.

Water movement between the various pools is restricted by peat banks or reed beds which act as giant strainers, so that plant fragments do not pass through easily and aquatic flora varies widely from one to another. It is worth, therefore, considering some of them individually, starting with the four flashes in the North West.

Although immediately adjacent to the Serpentine Broad, the murky brown water of the most north westerly flash contains none of the suspended mass of feathery hornwort (*Ceratophyllum submersum*) so abundant there. The fronds seem unable to penetrate the floating mat of reed, reedmace, branched bur-reed and yellow flag which separates them. Water is stagnant and possibly deficient in oxygen, with small fish leaping frequently into the air.

Sympetrum striolatum dragonflies, which are abundant, make good use of the root mat. They fly in tandem, the crimson male whipping the yellow female's tail sharply down onto the sodden black bur-reed rhizomes just above summer water level. At each jerk she deposits an egg, which will hatch into an ugly, predatory youngster to harass the freshwater shrimps and midge larvae of the bottom muds. A larger hawker dragonfly which has been seen here is the Southern Aeshna (*Aeshna cyanea*), which is less general in the West than the common Aeshna (*A. juncea*), but which prefers this type of non-acid water. The male is handsomely striped with blue and yellow, the female more greenish. A familiar damselfly here is the black and blue *Coenagrion puella*. Pond skaters scud across the opaque water surface and there are hosts of spiders among the reeds. An islet favoured by the dragonflies is used by roosting mallard and nesting coot.

The North East flash has more diversity in the marginal flora with great pond-sedge, willow herb, mint and gipsywort among the abundant bur-reed. A reminder of the nearness of the coast is given by stands of sea sedge and glaucous bulrush or grey club-rush, which last also appears inland, replacing the common bulrush (*Scripus lacustris*) throughout Gower.

The South West flash is notable for marestail, which is always a local plant. No flowers are borne on the softly feathery underwater shoots, which have the same flexuous habit as the still absent hornwort except that their air-filled stems are stouter and whiter.

The sedge fen adjacent to the South East flash is dominated by a floating mass of iris, bur-reed and bulrush penetrated by the creeping stems of water horsetail, which reach out into the water to throw up their primitive-looking aerial shoots. There are more short-stemmed flowers here than among the reeds, including marsh bedstraw, lesser water-parsnip, blue skullcap, soft rush and the attractive Cyperus sedge (*Carex pseudocyperus*), with its nodding flower spikes.

Forked fronds of the aquatic liverwort, *Riccia fluitans* are massed in the open water channels with a little water starwort and lesser duckweed. Water voles come here to feed, leaving neat piles of oval dung pellets on the root mat and the gnawed stubs of succulent food plants. These hidden channels make ideal highways for otters, better, perhaps, than any in Glamorgan, and these mammals are thought to visit the area quite frequently, although always elusive and seldom seen.

The northern end of the Serpentine Pool becomes choked with horn-wort in some summers, particularly to the West of the road. This is a species of southern affinities which seldom flowers and fruits in Britain but which does so prolifically here in warm summers such as those of 1973, 1975 and 1976. Shoots remain green beneath the water but change to a deep bronze colour at the surface by September. Towards the end of the season they are encrusted with lime, some of the older leaves getting cemented together by the crisp deposit and breaking surface as white wisps. The floating mass around a bird-roosting raft becomes spattered with white guano and moulted feathers.

The vertical banks, as excavated, are still distinguishable, but the reeds have advanced well beyond them. Associated species must be large to survive and include great water dock, great willow-herb, bittersweet, branched bur-reed and yellow iris. In its middle and southern reaches the Broad opens out and the water is much clearer. Ivy duckweed and *Riccia fluitans* compete effectively with the hornwort and soft strands of the water moss (*Fontinalis antipyretica*) provide cover for a host of small fish, water beetles and dragonfly nymphs.

Most remarkable of the rootless submerged plants is the greater bladder-wort (*Utricularia vulgaris*) which sends yellow pea-like flowers above the surface in late summer, these being succeeded when the petals fall by squat, flask-shaped seed capsules nestled between two brownish sepals. Like hornwort, this is a southern species and performs best in warm sum-mers. Plants are much bigger than the lesser bladderwort of more acid moorland pools. Their long shoots and narrowly dissected leaves produce an underwater filigree of lace-like consistency and are beset with delicately transparent insect-catching bladders.

Most attractive of the plants with floating leaves are the white water lilies with broad-leaved pondweed reaching out among them from con-siderable depths. Very occasionally the rare and beautiful flowering rush (*Butomus*) can be found. Marginal colour starts with the kingcups of early spring and ends with the bur-marigold of late autumn. Rafts of vegetation support sizable alders and apparently stable islands rock if these are climbed. There is a lot of epiphytism, even water plants like gipsywort getting an adequate living perched on alder stumps. Yellow

27. Broad-leaved pondweed with linear, under-water leaves

sedge (*Carex serotina*), which is rare in most of South Wales, occurs both here and in dune slacks. Common sedge (*Carex nigra*) occupies broad peripheral belts.

96

The most striking feature of the fringe vegetation on the Broad is the replacement of much of the common greater bulrush by the uncommon lesser bulrush. The latter grows only on rich fen peats of sites like this and Crymlyn Bog east of Swansea. Greater bulrush is an efficient trapper of inorganic silt and builds itself a slightly raised rim in places, with free water before and behind. Grey club-rushes spread into the water and splashes of pink are provided by marsh cinquefoil, bogbean and greater water-plantain, with ragged-robin, red rattle and hemp agrimony further back. The reedswamp grades outwards through marsh to wet woodland or carr dominated by alder or any one of grey, goat, white, or crack willows, ash being the principal tree to appear as the carr dries out.

Oxwich affords an admirable illustration of the dynamism of plant succession—both forwards and backwards. The forward succession from open water through plant-clogged water to reedswamp, sedge marsh and willow carr is actively progressing through the 1970s, helped by man-made drainage schemes, The reverse succession from dry pasture and meadowland through sodden quagmire to reedswamp with flashes of clear water is sufficiently recent for some of the locals to remember the close-cropped grazing lands of the early part of the century. These two modern successions are part of the larger whole which has taken place over the course of many centuries. The long term sequence started with open sea and progressed through saline lagoon and saltmarsh to brackish and then freshwater marsh—silty at first, then peaty—with subsequent drying out to give productive farmland.

Noisiest and most conspicuous of the breeding birds are the black-headed gulls of Gullery Flash—a stretch of open water behind the sea wall where the reedswamp narrows in the East. Once abundant, their numbers dwindled from about eighty pairs to forty-five pairs in 1961, when rats were blamed, rightly or wrongly, for eating nearly all the eggs. The water level probably then rose too high for comfort and there were none by the late sixties, but birds were showing an interest in the pool again by the early seventies. Eggs were laid in two nests in 1972 but may not have hatched, as the eggshells were found on the pool floor. Six pairs bred in 1973 and 1974. By the end of May 1975 twenty-six occupied nests held a total of seventy eggs, but by the 9th of June only fourteen eggs remained and four of the five chicks which had hatched were dead. The culprits were clearly herring gulls and not rats. Only four of the twenty to thirty pairs building in 1976 were still around by mid July, but two fledgelings on the beach showed that at least some had bred successfully.

Grey herons feed in the flashes and very rarely a purple heron, night heron, little egret or little bittern is spotted. A purple heron stayed around the marsh for a full three months in the summer of 1976. 'Common' bitterns, formerly confined to East Anglia, although breeding at Oxwich during the nineteenth century, are now seen increasingly often in late winter and early spring. Their characteristic booming has been heard during April and May and it is possible that the odd pair now stays to breed.

East Anglia's other speciality, the bearded reedling, turned up during its population 'eruption' in the 1972-73 winter, after an earlier sampling of the less extensive reedbeds further East at Kenfig. All had left by April, but 1974 saw some of them nesting. Young birds with black eye patch but no 'moustache' were caught in mist nets and ringed during 1976. These so-called bearded 'tits', with their striking gingery brown and slaty blue plumage and dark moustache, are as exciting an acquisition as the bitterns and are, in truth, bringing the best of the East to the West.

The insistent calling of water rails resembles the squealing of a posse of disrupted piglets and there could have been as many as fifty rails about, grazing the grassy road verges by the Serpentine Lake during early summer mornings in 1976. These halcyon hours belong to the birds, which must later retreat to the secret fastnesses of the reedbeds as the waves of breakfast-satiated holidaymakers surge down to the beach. Only at the dawning of these long hot days can the solitary birdwatcher appreciate how much life must gain a living from this reedy paradise where most see only coot, moorhen and dabchick, or the odd cormorant flying in to fish and roost in the trees, like its arboreal cousins of the Southern Hemisphere.

Ducks flight onto the lakes mainly in winter, but flocks seldom exceed a hundred birds. They also use the area as a retreat in August and September when considerable numbers are out gleaning on the barley stubbles round about. It is in this season that adults incapacitated by the moult are skulking among the reeds. Mallard, teal, shoveller and probably tufted duck build their nests here. Garganey are rare spring migrants; wigeon, pintail and golden-eye are winter visitors.

28. Mallard

The terrain is too overgrown to attract large numbers of waders, but a flock of thirty-three snipe was observed in the early part of 1974. Jack snipe drop in occasionally, also common sandpiper, green sandpiper and woodcock. Waders spending the winter at Oxwich include curlew, oyster

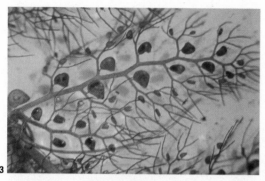

73

74

75

76

Plate 19   FRESHWATER PLANTS

73. Greater bladderwort: insect-catching bladders on
feathery leaves in Oxwich Serpentine Lake   *Author*

74. Double Cuckoo-flowers among sallow fruits by
the River Burry at Cheriton   *Author*

75. Fringed water lily flowering on Broad Pool in
July, 1966   *Author*

76. Oxwich reedswamp drains seaward into
Nicholaston Pill   *Author*

77. Red rattle: semi-parasite of swampy places   *Author*

77

99

Plate 20 FRESHWATER ANIMALS

78. Common toad *(Bufo bufo)*   *Arthur Morgan*

79. Common frog *(Rana temporaria)*   *Arthur Morgan*

80. Common sympetrum dragonfly *(Sympetrum striolatum):* a crimson-bodied male   *Author*

81. Golden-ringed dragonfly *(Cordulegaster boltoni):* newly emerged from nymph; one wing still crumpled   *Author*

82. Galls of bean gall sawfly *(Pontania viminalis)* on osier   *Author*

83. Galls of bean gall sawfly *(Pontania proxima)* on grey sallow   *Author*

catcher, dunlin, ringed plover, sanderling and turnstone. Whimbrel are common on both spring and autumn passage and greenshank may be seen in autumn. An osprey turned up in 1965 and marsh harriers are not much more frequent. Reed buntings are commonplace, both in and out of the reeds, and pied wagtails are always around. The willow spinneys are full of willow warblers, blackcaps, robins, blackbirds and tits, including marsh and willow tits. Even marsh warbler and aquatic warbler have turned up on occasion.

Because reeds are essentially eastern in their distribution, becoming more maritime in the West, the reed warbler, too, fades out westwards. Oxwich was its most westerly breeding site in South Wales for many years but this is no longer true. There has been a rapid spread of birds to the North and West lately and they have now reached several sites to the West of Oxwich. Over recent years it has been estimated that it is probably the commonest bird on the Oxwich Marshes, numbering around seven hundred pairs in 1975 and possibly up to a thousand pairs in 1976. As many as twenty or thirty birds can be seen to the acre of reedbed and it is thought that the breeding density could be up to ten pairs per acre. But these are not the easiest of birds to count, in spite of their continuous scratchy singing.

Although traditionally preferring to nest exclusively in reeds, some of the big concourses of reed warblers at Oxwich now choose other types of vegetation, which do not necessarily even grow in water. It is only on the higher, drier ground, however, that they overlap with the locally less common but generally more widespread sedge warblers, which opt mostly for clumps of brambles in the sparser reedbeds which dry out in summer. Of the eighty-eight pairs of sedge warblers nesting in 1975, seventy chose the West Marsh, congregating mainly towards its southern end. It is because they are more adaptable in choice of site that they are so much more numerous in Glamorgan as a whole, and only in vast reedswamps such as Oxwich do the reed warblers have the advantage. But maybe they, too, are becoming more adaptable with increasing pressure of numbers.

There is a good chance of seeing one of the resident kingfishers perched on a stump or sluice gate in the non-breeding season, but they seem to go elsewhere to nest. The short piercing whistle repeated six or seven times as the bird shoots jewel-like over the water to the shelter of reeds or overarching trees is an evocative sound. Spotted flycatchers, swifts and Hirundines, including sand martins, cash in on the big fly 'hatches' from the vast complex of sheltered waters.

Swallows roost among the reeds in large numbers in autumn and martins as well as wagtails are regular passage migrants. Pied wagtails flock to temporary night roosts in the reedbeds when passing through and may sometimes continue to use them for more permanent winter roosts, as did a hundred and fifty birds in December 1961. Starlings, too, sleep among the reeds on autumn nights, but start moving in October and November to the old established winter roost in the Pembrey Forest across the Burry Inlet. Over a hundred and thirty different bird species have been recorded in the Oxwich reserve, although only about forty-four species are known to have bred there recently—not all in the wetlands. Nightjars were regular nesters until the middle fifties but the last breeding record is for 1961 and they are rarely seen in summer now.

Water voles pursue their hidden lives in the seclusion of the reedbeds, which harbour infestations of brown rats locally. Bank voles, wood mice and common shrews are all abundant in the damp alderwoods. Stoats and weasels are present and foxes and badgers are thought to visit the reserve quite frequently. The possibility of the taking of a reed harvest in future years inevitably poses the question of how this will impinge on the wildlife.

Pond snails of at least three genera (*Planorbis*, *Limnaea* and *Bithynia*) are present in the pools, along with *Hydra*. Among the damsel flies likely to be seen are the large red *Pyrrhosoma nymphula*, the common *Ischnura elegans* and the blue *Coenagrion puella*.

The larvae of several of the fruit flies or gall flies (*Trypetidae*) develop in the fruiting heads of marsh thistles, among them *Urophora stylata*, *Trypeta ruficauda* and *Chaetostomella onotrophes*. Other pest flies of the family Ephydridae utilise aquatic plants during their larval phase and the related *Anthomyza gracilis* spends its youth within the upper leaf sheaths of the reeds themselves.

In fact the fenlands are extremely rich in Diptera generally, these including several first records for Glamorgan. The two craneflies, *Limnophila ferruginea* and *L. scutellata* of the reedbeds are both 'new' for the three counties and a third cranefly, *Erioptera stictica*, strays into the reeds sometimes from the saltmarsh. Another Dipteron more usually associated with salt marshes and also an only record for Glamorgan is the parasitic Braconid, *Rogas punctipes*, which is a close relative of the Ichneumons. The squash bug, *Corizus hyoscyami*, occasionally visits the reedbeds at the back of the dunes, deserting its more usual host plants of rest harrow and storksbill.

Theobaldia annulata, another denizen of the reeds behind the dunes, is one of the fiercest of all mosquitoes, with spots on the wings and rings on the legs and body, and the female is always ready to help herself to a blood meal from visiting naturalists.

14 STREAMS OF WEST GOWER

NICHOLASTON PILL in the South and Llanrhidian and Morlais Brooks in the North are the only streams of any size in Mid Gower. West of this drainage is to the North and West by streams rising mostly on the Old Red Sandstone hills and flowing across the limestone to Rhossili Bay or the Burry Inlet. East of it drainage is to the South by streams rising on the Millstone Grits and flowing across the limestone to Three Cliffs Bay and Pwll Du Bay.

Gower's main water supply came from local resurgences until recently and all the old cottages were built near springs. The little rivers were harnessed to water wheels to supply power for corn grinding from earliest times and there are historical references to grist mills, dating back to the early thirteenth century. The first millstones came from the Old Red Sandstones of Rhossili and Ryers Downs and Cefn Bryn—not from the more appropriately named Millstone Grits, which are represented in Gower only by soft shales.

An Elizabethan survey of 1583 tells of four mills built between then and 1543, the only one now identifiable being at Penrice on the Nicholaston Pill. No less than seven of West Gower's thirteen grist mills were on the River Burry and one of the finest views in North Gower embraces the still extant millpond and three storey Nether (or Lower) Mill built at Llanrhidian in 1803. This was still operational into the 1950s, but the old water wheel has now gone. No river is shown here on the map, the water disappearing into a sink hole in a blind valley near Stonyford away to the South, to reappear at the base of the old wooded cliffline near Llanrhidian Church.

Gower's western watersheds are Llanmadoc Hill and the ridge of high ground connecting the inner face of Rhossili Down with Hardings Down. Drainage waters gather on the north side of this to flow out across Llangennith Moors to 'Diles Lake' on Rhossili Bay, but this 'lake' remained dry throughout much of 1975 and 1976. The upper stream courses of the West are brightened by the pinks of lesser skullcap, bog pimpernel, lousewort and cross-leaved heath and the yellows of lesser spearwort and marsh bird's-foot-trefoil. Humbler components of the flora are marsh pennywort, knotted pearlwort, slender club-rush (*Isolepis cernua*) and the yellow, star, carnation and flea sedges (*Carex demissa*, *C. echinata*, *C. flacca* and *C. pulicaris*).

Lower down the hill soil acidity is mitigated by accumulated sand and flying sea spray and the vegetation becomes lusher. Yellow iris, hemlock

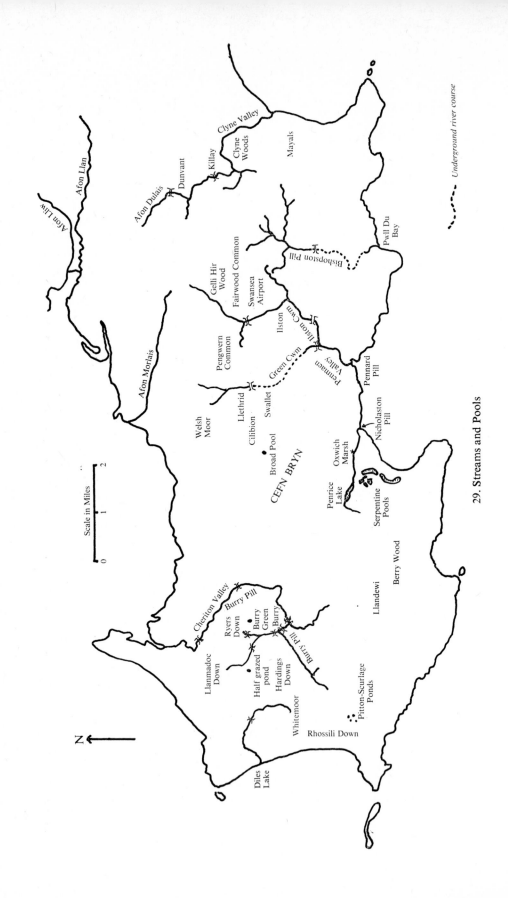

Afon Llan

Afon Lliw

Afon Dulais

Dunvant

Killay

Clyne Valley

Clyne Woods

Mayals

Pwll Du Bay

Gelli Hir Wood

Fairwood Common

Swansea Airport

Ilston

Ilston Cwm

Bishopston Pill

Underground river course

Pengwern Common

Welsh Moor

Llethrid

Cilibion

Swallet

Broad Pool

Green Cwm

Pennard Valley

Pennard Pill

Scale in Miles

0   1   2

CEFN BRYN

Oxwich Marsh

Nicholaston Pill

Penrice Lake

Serpentine Pools

Afon Morlais

Berry Wood

Llandewi

Cheriton Valley

Burry Pill

Ryers Down

Burry Green

Burry

Llanmadoc Down

Half grazed pond

Hardings Down

Burry Pill

Pitton-Scurlage Ponds

Whitemoor

Rhossili Down

Diles Lake

N

29. **Streams and Pools**

water-dropwort and fool's watercress are characteristic, with water mint, water forget-me-not (*Myosotis scorpioides*), fleabane and hard rush. Delicate liverworts finding protection in the water trickling beneath these include the transparent leafy *Chiloscyphus polyanthus* and chunkier *Pellia epiphylla*.

The Burry River—only major watercourse of the West—has four main branches. The two longest rise only 1½ and 3½ miles respectively from the mouth, but double back on themselves to give a course some 7-8 miles long. Branches from the Old Red Sandstone of Ryers Down and Llanmadoc Hill combine before joining the main branch, which comes from the same rock type at the southern end of Rhossili Down. Their confluence with the fourth branch from the limestone around Llandewi is near the village of Burry, whence the united waters wind northwards through Fairy Hill, Stembridge and Cheriton to reach the Burry 'Estuary' between Whiteford Point and Llandimore Marsh. In geological times when Lake Loughor was shut off behind the Pencaerfenni—Machynys moraine, the inlet could well have been regarded as the Burry Estuary, but the term used now seems incongruous for so small a river and so large a tidal inlet.

Moorland sections of the main Rhossili Down branch resemble those beyond the watershed already referred to. Occasionally the brook cuts deeply into a wooded cwm, as at Talgarth Well behind Pitton Cross, flowing swiftly over clean gravel and overarched with fern and bramble. Greenfinch, chiff-chaff and blackbird come to drink and collared doves visit from nearby farmyards.

Through cultivated land the current is confined in man-made channels beside solid earth banks topped by hedges. It is diverted occasionally to loop into a neighbouring field to form a drinking place for stock, or allowed to linger as a pool in the angle of a wall: but not for sufficiently long to deposit silt. The water is clear and slightly peat-stained, the pool floors gravelly. Only the banks and islets are of stock-trampled mud alternating with tough clumps of jointed rush, meadowsweet, angelica and sorrel. The streaming raft of flote-grass leaves is pierced by the spears of iris and bur-reed. Fool's watercress and hemlock water-dropwort eke out a disturbed existence between the hoofprints which provide moist micro-habitats for mini versions of water starwort and bog stitchwort.

In stiller pools where the flow is checked, the entire bed may be covered by conical Jenkin's spire shells and whirligig beetles circle on cloud-reflecting surfaces. St. Mark's flies (*Bibio marci*) are on the wing by late April—droves of hairy black males with trailing legs, dawdling in the lower air layers waiting expectantly for a female to rise from the grass below. When she does she is grabbed and mating takes place during flight. Peacock and other butterflies favour the waterside thistles for feeding and resting; bumble bees the water mint flowers.

The rushy pastures and rough grazings through which the stream passes on its way to the lowlands, provide nesting sites for lapwing, curlew, meadow pipit and skylark, and hunting territory for buzzard, kestrel and raven. Magpie and wood pigeon share the hedges with yellow hammer and chaffinch—massive unkempt hedges into which whole posses of steers or ponies can disappear in search of shade or shelter. The valley deepens and becomes more wooded as it progresses North to the confluence west of Burry village.

Certain stretches of the limestone tributary from the South are normally dry between May and October, though not in the wet midsummer of 1972. As the stream vanishes with the falling water table, the leaves of watercress and willow-herb become a deep purple; those of water star-wort wither to be replaced by miniature replicas of themselves. Cuckoo flowers, like those of the limestone reaches in the Cheriton area, may be double and sterile, their male and female parts distorted and petal-like, but not, apparently, without nectar, as they still attract the usual green-veined white and orange-tip butterflies.

As the water disappears, seedlings of field bindweed, silverweed and broad dock sprout between man-made banks coated with the gemmae-rich liverwort, *Lunularia*. Feathery water-crowfoot lingers on in shallow pools where the tadpole population becomes highly concentrated by May —for want of anywhere else to go—and no doubt provides succulent feeding for hungry birds—along with the equally abundant spire shells. Formerly most were gobbled up by domestic ducks.

A sizable spring bubbles up by the derelict farm at Burry Head and a colourful marsh occupies the valley bottom. There is a seasonal sequence of yellow here, from kingcup through iris to monkey-flower offset by the rich red-purple of greater willow-herb and the water-dropwort of late May is replaced by meadowsweet. Early-flowering golden-saxifrage, which cannot normally compete in such a press of vegetation, comes into its own where the dead trash is burned off in autumn. By May it is smothered. Osiers and other kinds of willow are scattered through the marsh and the rare almond willow (*Salix triandra*) grew here formerly.

Small fish, abound, along with freshwater shrimps, water snails and leeches. The kaleidoscope of flowers attracts nectar feeders and sultry summer days are filled with the hum of insects and the more vulgar bumbling of bees.

Good watercress beds occur in the now fast-flowing river by Burry Dairy Farm and *Fontinalis* moss streams out with the current. Bulging green clouds of water starwort a yard or so across are peppered with yellow stamens in spring, as though stuck with a shower of tiny pins. Waterside neighbours are bittersweet, brooklime and reed canary-grass.

Several pairs of moorhens frequent this stretch, laying clutches of fawn eggs in conspicuous nests of green iris leaves. Water rails skulk among the rank stems and sedge warblers churr contentedly from the iris-reed-grass water meadows leading back to a steep bank of bluebells. This is a delectable bathing place for smutty house sparrows from the adjacent farmyard and they are joined in their splashings by dunnock and song thrush. There are cuckoos and chiff chaffs in spring, wrens and blue tits in winter and tree creepers working systematically over the ash trunks.

Downstream drifts of yellow crosswort succeed the golden-saxifrage and the tall dame's violet shows occasional fasciation or fusing of stems to give a compound 'cockscomb' form. Purple loosestrife, mint and large-flowered forget-me-not (*Myosotis scorpioides*) give summer colour in the stands of branched bur-reed. The deep leaf mould of the bordering quagmires supports wood speedwell and wood bittercress, leading back to hazel coppice speckled with primroses.

Myriads of Jenkin's spire shells scrape a living from the bed. They are everywhere, from source to sea, in their thousands—a food potential for more wagtails than ever sought sustenance on the Gower streams.

30. Grey wagtail and heath speedwell

From Stembridge to Cheriton the river flows North West along soft shales at the base of the Carboniferous Limestone. This stretch is heavily wooded, with little iris-quilted water meadows dipping down between the trees. The air is full of floating fluff from the sallow catkins in May and the water becomes scummy with countless windborne seeds, only a fraction of which will germinate.

The footpath crossing the river by the three-arched stone bridge South of Landimore is a fine spot for a little quiet contemplation of the intricate life-web of woodland and water. Freshwater shrimps thread their way between the snails and wriggle over the lobed green swards of *Pellia* which grow under several inches of water, beneath the *Lunularia* and *Conocephalum* of the banks. Flattened submerged shoots of the moss,

Eurhynchium riparioides, provide cover for mayfly nymphs, whose shed skins drift over the surface among the billowing willow down. Stonefly nymphs cling to every other stone and pond skaters search the slack water under ferny banks. Caddis larvae build short protective cases of sand grains—multi-coloured mosaics of translucent quartz, rose-tinted Old Red Sandstone, white limestone and black shale, which are a delight to view under a hand lens.

Painted ladies may appear in clearings which are alive with brimstones, orange tips, and green-veined whites, whilst spiders scuttle in hordes among pond-sedge and iris. Riverside trees stabilise undercut banks with a veritable trellis of woody roots and the 'mangrove swamp' atmosphere is accentuated by the prodigious length of the polypody fronds and the fuzz of roots produced all round the ivy stems instead of just towards the moistness of the supporting treetrunk.

Three feet high clumps of pick-a-back plants (*Tolmeia menziesii*) established at the riverside have the capacity to produce well-formed plantlets on their leaves, begonia style. Their flowers bear wispy appendages and are veined a darker red, the protuberant pinky-yellow stamens flecking them with star dust.

During the high tides of January and February 1974 the water backed up under Cheriton Bridge so that the broad silt-laden flood swirled about the alder trunks. In calmer times the sunlit stretch above the bridge is visited by moorhen, swallow and green woodpecker and the grey stones and discarded debris of the river bed are strewn with the sand-grain tubes of *Agapetus* caddis larvae, as though bushels of gritty sultanas had been tipped in. The tree-shaded stretch below the bridge is different; the birds more secretive and the stones moss-covered.

Below Glebe Farm the Burry winds in tight loops over stock-puddled pastures where milch cows have chomped back the taller waterside plants leaving space for smaller ones like winter cress. The first true reeds come in at this level, building up to a dryish reedbed on the undergrazed, western side, with a peripheral understorey of Jack-by-the-hedge, hemlock water-dropwort, fool's watercress and curled dock.

The river narrows and deepens, cutting into the reedbed to expose a mesh of rhizomes, and the floor is of mud, but still speckled with spire shells. Swift-moving, dark-freckled trout begin to give way to fledgeling flat fish some four inches long and three inches wide. These sand coloured infants flecked with brown are mostly flounders (*Platychthis flesus*) but are joined by dabs (*Limanda limanda*) in July. They dart rapidly from place to place, seeking no cover but merging invisibly with the clay bottom as soon as movement stops. Sedentary Crustaceans, Molluscs and worms supply the bulk of their food. All the large fish live in deeper water offshore and these youngsters exploring so far above the tide will have to return to the sea when their time comes for breeding.

Plate 21 FRESHWATER PLANTS AND ANIMALS

84. Adult Mayfly in typical stance   *Michael Claridge*
85. Male blue and yellow banded *Aeschna Juncea* Dragonfly   *Michael Claridge*
86. Flower of Fringed Water Lily from Broad Pool   *Author*
87. Canadian Pondweed can be invasive   *Author*
88. Marsh Cinquefoil grows in acid pools   *Author*

109

89

90

Plate 22 BIRDS OF THE OXWICH MARSHES

89. Reed Warbler at nest in reeds *Keri Williams*
90. Black-headed Gull at nest in 'Gullery Flash' *Harold Grenfell*

110

Plate 23 FLOWERS OF THE LIMESTONE CLIFFS

91. Chunky, maritime Ox-eye Daisies on cliff face   *Author*
92. Slender Thistle on overgrazed cliff edge   *Author*
93. Hoary Rock Rose and Basil Thyme   *Author*
94. Common Rock Rose   *Author*
95. Cemented, Breccia-like Head over Fall Bay limestone   *Author*

97

96

98

99

Plate 24   SEA-BIRDS AND THE WORM

96. Adult Gannet in flight   *Harold Grenfell*
97. Little Gull in first Autumn Plumage, North side of Mumbles   *Harold Grenfell*
98. Worm's Head from near Rhossili   *Author*
99. Fulmar Petrel in soaring flight   *Harold Grenfell*

112

Mullet (*Crenimugil labrosus*) come into the mouth of the pill from the estuary and sewin run up from the sea in autumn. The name of sewin, which is that commonly used for sea trout in Wales, will be found in few of the standard fish books. These fish belong to the same species as the common brown trout (*Salmo trutta*), but they have held on to the ancestral migratory habit which the brown trout of the rivers and pools have almost lost. They move to and from the sea, returning to the rivers to breed in successive or alternate years, the mortality rate being much lower than in the related salmon. More silvery than their darkly speckled cousins of the streams, the richer feeding of their sojourns in the sea can be detected in the sudden expansion of the growth rays on their scales.

Plants are less mobile, but show some interesting overlaps of maritime and inland species at river mouths. Brookweed (*Salmolus valerandi*) is one of the first brackish water plants to come in on the riverside mud of Burry Pill, followed by sea aster and scurvy grass (*Cochlearia anglica*). First of the salt lovers higher up the banks is marsh mallow, growing upstream among the feathery parsley water-dropwort and downstream in a sward of pasture grasses silvered with sea wormwood, silverweed and spurrey (*Spergularia rubra*).

For the rest of its journey Burry Pill loops to and fro across the saltings —separating an eastern sward of fescue, thrift and sea plantain from a western one flushed mauve with the flowers of sea lavender in late summer.

15 STREAMS OF EAST GOWER

THE three river systems of East Gower all flow to the South coast. Most westerly are the Llethrid and Ilston streams which unite at Parkmill and empty into Three Cliffs Bay as Pennard Pill. East of these are the moorland streams from Fairwood and Clyne Commons which converge on Barland Common to flow to Pwll Du Bay as Bishopston Pill. Further East again and marginal to Gower proper is the Afon Dulais draining the Coal Measures with the same general southerly trend—from Dunvant and Killay down the Clyne Valley to Blackpill on Swansea Bay, where sewin can be watched swimming up under the little so-called "Roman" bridge.

The Llethrid, Ilston and Bishopston have underground sections in the limestone karst country, the first and last tumbling by swallet holes into extensive cave systems, the Ilston just seeping away with the water table, like the southern branch of the Burry. On the interfluve between the Ilston and Bishopston Valleys is an old dry river bed carved when there was a lot of meltwater about after glaciation.

The water of the Llethrid rising on Welshmoor and Pengwern Common derives a fair degree of hardness from the Millstone Grit and Glacial Drift before it crosses the limestone. It flows crystal clear over pebbles through the ash-elm wood near Cilibion, with hemlock water dropwort along the bed, primroses, bluebells and red campion on the banks. Shingle beds downstream of the road are brightened seasonally by lesser spearwort, winter-cress, bog stitchwort, angelica, bittersweet and brooklime.

The waters are crammed with small animals. Gossamer-light flies idling among the more animated pond skaters are preyed on by spiders, their infinitesimal weight spread over an octet of feet which scarcely dents the surface film. Crowds of freshwater shrimps sidle sideways among the pebbles or venture forth to swim upright in the open. River limpets without the suction powers of their marine namesakes, cling to the stones, lest they be washed downstream to the caves. Jenkin's spire shells and wandering snails share the invisible goodies of the sand-banks.

The nets of caddis larvae are stretched between holdfasts on the bed, getting progressively more silted with age, like soiled cobwebs, as they

31. Stonefly, adult and larva ready to emerge from water containing the moss *Fontinalis*

strain particles, useful and otherwise, from the sliding water mass. They come in two patterns, one funnel-shaped, like that of a trap-door spider or fisherman's trawl net, the other more like the fisherman's seine. The 'seine' is more vulnerable to damage and tends to be in slacker water behind obstacles, though never in completely still water, where it would be ineffective as a food trap.

Beds of hard water streams such as this are peppered with the short sand grain tubes of *Agapetus* caddis larvae. These are cemented to the stones—a precaution against getting dislodged—*Agapetus* being a non-mobile, sedentary organism. The owners never emerge from their sand castles, the algae on which they feed growing within them. (Pebble surfaces outside are silvered in summer with tiny bubbles emitted from an actively growing felt of green algae and there is likely to be no shortage). If the young caddis run out of food, they build a new gallery for themselves and harvest another self-sown crop. When they have had enough, they go torpid in a pupal case resembling the larval case in all but the lack of entrance holes with their border of finer grains.

Species which amble around carrying their homes on their backs prefer slightly more peaceful surroundings. One such here is *Limnephilus*, which builds tubes 2 - 3 cm. long, in contrast to the chunkier *Agapetus*, tubes which are seldom more than 1 cm. with the component yellow, white and black sand grains fitted fastidiously into a neater jigsaw. Brown-winged adults or sedge flies, as the fishermen call them, fly by day and settle on the water as bait for hungry fish in the evenings.

Squat mayfly nymphs crawl around on the stones, their three tail prongs spread and feathery gills undulating softly as they imbibe the necessary oxygen. The rudimentary wings are stubby until they climb to the surface, where they cast the final larval skin and emerge as weakly flying 'duns'. But this is not the end. Unlike any other insect, they moult again, from an immature adult or sub-imago stage to the mature adult or imago which fishermen call a 'spinner'. The shimmering swarms of males performing their courtship dance epitomise the quiet of summer evenings in Gower's less frequented corners.

A freshwater marsh alongside this stretch of the Llethrid nourishes watercress beds, confusingly mixed with round-leaved brooklime and fool's watercress, with greater water-plantain, kingcup and many another. This provides a refuge for amphibians, but the palmate is the only one of the three newts which is at all common on Gower.

Above the famous cavers' haunt of Llethrid Swallet, the stream lies in a broad partially wooded valley where swifts and swallows take their toll of flying insects and pied wagtails have a regular feeding beat along the pebbles. The water disappears with an impressive roar after rain, but the entrance to the swallow hole itself is unimpressive and partially obscured by treetrunks and branches brought down during freshets. There is a gated cave entrance higher up on the West side and the valley continues with its floor about 8 ft. above the level of the sink hole.

It runs for 1-1¼ miles as Green Cwm, which contains the ancient Parc le Breos Burial Chambers North of Parkmill—fault-guided and innocent of the river which carved it when water levels were higher after the Ice Age.

Having tumbled noisily down its two sink holes, the water traverses a bedding plane cave system extending 200 ft. into the hill and opening out into an 80 ft. high chamber decorated with pleated calcite curtains and pendant stalactites extending down to meet the growing stalagmites below. This is known to cavers as the Great Hall and is probably the most spectacular and dangerous place in the fantastic rockscape of subterranean Gower. Tooth Cave downstream has important archaeological interest as well as fine limestone formations and is much the longest known cave system in Gower.

A number of invertebrates have been recorded within the Llethrid Caverns, but their occurence there is mostly accidental, none being of species which are confined to caves. Living in the subterranean darkness are mayfly nymphs (*Habrophleba fusca*), *Dixa* midge larvae and *Tachydroma* which will never fly in the sunlight unless washed right through. Water beetles are represented by *Hydraena gracilis*, *Atheta* and the tiny *Helophorus brevipalpes* and *H. laticollis*.

Pergamasus crassipes is one of the litter mites which are usually found in soil, but is large and predatory, an active hunter of smaller mites, springtails and nematode worms. Among its prey in the Llethrid Caves may be numbered the non-parasitic mite, *Parasitus* and the two springtails, *Isotoma notabilis* and *Anurida granaria*, particularly, perhaps, the latter, which has lost its bounce, having none of the usual springtail springing organs. Minute Copepods are *Acanthocyclops viridis* and *A. nemalis*, relatives of the better known *Cyclops*.

The rare land Nemertine, *Geonemertes dendyi*, has been found in the swallet, also the more mundane earthworm, *Hemlea nasuta,* and the ubiquitous freshwater shrimp (*Gammarus pulex*). The even more ubiquitous spire shell (*Pomatopyrgus jenkinsi*) occurs in Tooth Cave lower down.

The water resurgence at the bottom of Green Cwm was harnessed by the Water Board and much of the outflow pumped back up to an underground reservoir on Cefn Bryn, to give it sufficient head to flow freely from the taps of South West Gower when South East Gower was supplied from a reservoir at Clyne. Depending on the state of the river, the water takes 12 - 20 hours to complete the mile or so through the cave system. Its temperature varies between freezing point and 70°F (21°C) on entering, but is constant on emergence, after being cooled underground and fed by innumerable trickles seeping down through joints and cracks.

It is much harder by this time, having dissolved calcium and magnesium salts on its way through. There is little solution going on in the open cave system, but a great deal where a little water is in contact with a lot of rock, percolating slowly down through cracks in the roof and walls. One of the nine springs supplying the pumping station sometimes runs muddy, entailing filtration. The sediment is derived from glacial drift deposited in the cave and banking up behind a weir.

Genuine and fools watercress and water starwort grow in the rock pool at the resurgence, and almost as much compensation water flows on down the eastern side of the valley as entered at the top—indicating a much bigger contribution from underground than from direct surface drainage. The valley floor is grassed, the sides and stream course wooded. There is a diversity of waterside plants, particularly near the water-splash at the bottom; common valerian and monkey-flower among the more showy. Brashings lopped from waterside trees form miniature beaver dams between the bright orange cross sections of sawn off alder trunks and the white ones of willow.

32. Swifts

A leat has been cut just above the stream to the East, this now sup-plying water to the mill below only in winter when there is water to spare. Clouds of alder flies (*Sialas*) swarm over stream and leat alike in May and June or rest on waterside vegetation. About the size of houseflies (though the aquatic larvae are twice as long) they have opaque brownish wings. Their flight is weak and very erratic on gusty days, when a whole mob undulating gently forwards will suddenly be blown back like a gossamer curtain. Mayflies rest momentarily among the pond skaters and most of the faunal types from above the swallet can be found.

Ilston Stream rises near Whitewalls on the Millstone Grit and flows down through the peaty quagmires of Gelli Hir Woodland Nature Reserve to the limestone. During one section the East side of the valley is a gentle shaly slope and the West side a craggy Carboniferous Limestone cliff—mostly of the *Seminula* zone which was quarried at Ilston first for building stone and then for roadstone. Again part of its course follows a fault leading down to the Gower Inn at Parkmill. For most of the year the stream flows on the surface, sinking only gradually into the stream bed in summer with no dramatic swallet-resurgence system. An impoundent pond at Parkmill was used for the corn grinding mill.

Where the North Gower road crosses it at Cartersford and where the South Gower road crosses it at Parkmill, *Baetis* and *Ecdynuris* are the most abundant mayfly genera, with *Perla* less common. There are stone-flies here, *Agapetus*, the little sand-cased caddis, in abundance, mosquito larvae and *Vellea*, the water cricket, along with the usual wandering and spire-shelled snails and river limpets.

Most interesting of the animals are the larvae of the river lamprey (*Lampetra fluviatilis*). This genus is classified with the hagfish as the most primitive of all vertebrates. The young stages remain in the riverine habitat for about five years, filtering food particles from the water. When about four inches long, they metamorphose to the adult form, but spend another six to eight foodless months in the river before migrating to sea in autumn and winter.

During their year in coastal waters, part of their food is obtained by clamping onto sea fish such as shad (*Clupea alosa*) and salmon (*Salmo salar*) with their suctorial mouth. This stage, which develops eyes and is silvery below, has been taken in tow nets off the Gower coast by the R.V. "Ocean Crest". At sea the lampreys may grow to a foot (30 cm.) long before returning to the river in autumn to spawn, after which they die of exhaustion. River lampreys used to be caught in large numbers in the Severn Estuary for human food and bait.

After flowing down through the Parkmill woodland as Pennard Pill the united rivers wind picturesquely across the sand flats of Three Cliffs Bay, between Great Tor to the West and the sandy slopes crowned by Pennard Castle to the East. There is a gradual transition from fresh to brackish to salt loving species, with the marsh arrow grass of the inland and the sea arrow grass of the saltings (*Triglochin palustre* and *T. maritimum*) growing side by side.

Bishopston Pill rises as a multiplicity of mint-scented trickles in rushy furrows scored in the surface of the moorland and brightened by lesser spearwort and forget-me-not. Where the main North-western arm emerges from beneath the airfield on Fairwood Common the moss, *Eurhynchium riparioides*, extends well up the pipe into the sort of gloom beloved by woodlice. The turbulent stream below the pipe has cut a winding course into the glacial deposits, stony-floored and clay-sided. Water figwort is unusually abundant alongside: marsh violet and marsh willow-herb testify to the acidity of these moorland stretches. Water voles plop in to the stream from capacious burrow complexes, the insulating air within their fur changing them to little silvered submarines.

Plunging downwards into sheltered valleys where brackenny bluebell slopes fend off the worst of the wind, the marginal rushes make way for little clumps of bitter vetch. Yellow shell moths (*Euphyia bilineata*) share the banks with heathland butterflies and teetering craneflies, whose legs seem too long for functional convenience.

Grey sallows dominate the quagmires of the valley bottoms, where the streams get slower and muddier and the tributaries are orange with ferric hydroxide or bog iron ore. The Yorkshire fog grass (*Holcus lanatus*) of the open moorland gives way to wood soft grass (*H. mollis*) in the shady carr, and choice flowers find sanctuary from hungry herbivores and winds more rapacious than any livestock. Lesser celandines and king cups spread a cloth of gold beneath crimson-tipped crabapple blossoms: cuckooflower and bogbean share the clearings between the tussock sedge and reedmace with marsh pennywort. The water figwort is joined by the pink of marsh cinquefoil and ragged robin under sweet scented honey-suckle whilst green-winged and spotted orchids throw up delicately pencilled flower spikes. Water hog lice (*Asellus aquaticus*) live in an aqueous world below those inhabited by pond skaters and St. Mark's flies, whilst stoneflies and mayflies graduate from one to the other.

The streams gather force as they come together, hurrying down through wet woodlands of alder and birch. Woody nitrogen-fixing root nodules of the former get washed free of soil by the tumbling waters. Woodland plants and marsh plants are all mixed up, with subtle changes where live stock come to drink. Leggy sawfly larvae and arch-backed shrimps join the wandering snails in shadowy recesses among water-rounded pebbles.

Emerging onto the Namurian limestone shales, the young river is 6-8 ft. wide and running about a foot deep before being swallowed up by the roadside quarry. Shoals of darkly speckled trout flit through gloomy shallows from rock to rock, as fast as the eye can follow, sucking unwary caddis from their tubes and snapping at becalmed mayflies on the surface or dullard Chironomid larvae on the bottom. Little holes above and below water level probably house water shrews. They are too small for water voles and too wet for other burrow dwellers. Drifts of empty cockle shells on the streambed are a legacy of decades of cockle boiling at Bishopston.

A dry cave system in the cliff above the road to Swansea had its water supply cut off when the Bishopston quarry was opened. Blasting has weakened the rocks and filled some of the caverns with quarry waste. The underground course of Bishopston Pill starts here at the junction of the Upper Limestone shales and the blockier limestone beneath, but subterranean passages cannot accommodate all the water when the river is in spate. It is then that the colonising coltsfoot, silverweed and Jack-by-the-hedge get washed away and the pill flows briefly at the surface. The dusky cranesbill has so far survived.

Collared doves cooing and creaking in St. Teilo's churchyard are more querulously insistent than the longer established wood pigeons, with their recriminatory "You two fools, you two", or, in Wales, "Take two cows, Taffy".

The lower valley follows a fault to Pwll Du Bay. Stones on the dry river bed are scarcely waterworn at first—more like jagged quarry chippings—and the shiny crisped fronds of *Pellia fabbroniana* are confined to the cliffy banks where bank voles or wood mice burrow among polypody fern and dog's mercury, leaving little piles of nibbled hazel nuts lying around. There are a few permanent pools in the river course, and a distant entrance to the underground caves, draped with golden saxifrage and ivy.

The dry valley becomes more deeply incised and boulder-strewn, as though formed in part from collapsed caverns, then plunges into a great amphitheatre under cliffs of 60ft. and more. That water sometimes cascades into this over massive limestone blocks, is shown by the big tree trunks lodged across the lip of the fossil waterfall. Chunks of woodland vegetation—wild garlic and celandines—still cling to fallen boulders: wrens and dunnocks creep mouse-like among the tumbled debris of the swallet floor.

The only exit for flood water is underground, but the valley floor continues at a much higher level, the old river bed utilised as a rocky footpath. Ash, elm and sycamore protect the gorge from the elements above and the trees are full of bird song. It is well to listen carefully to this if the scarce willow tit is to be distinguished from the commoner marsh tit, for the two are very similar in other ways. If light and circumstance permit a visual comparison, the willow tit may be seen to have less gloss on the black cap, a pale patch on the wing and a 'bunchier' appearance arising from the more muscular neck—result, no doubt, of its ability to excavate its own nest hole in rotting tree trunks instead of occupying a ready made one in the fashion of most tits.

Not far beneath the big swallow hole is a cavern from which the roar of unseen waters disturbs the tranquillity of the world they have vacated. But after another spell below ground, they surface again for a last lap on the peaty alluvium which has accumulated in the lower valley since the river was backed up by the shingle bar across its mouth.

Osiers and alders dominate the lower wood on a base-rich fen peat carpeted with ramsons and little clumps of yellow archangel in Spring. The river meanders, deep and broad, across the valley floor, seemingly dark and bottomless beneath overarching trees—then slinks away through reedbed and sedge-fen where the trees open out.

The reeds are to the West: to the East is a thicket of meadowsweet pocked with tussocks of common sedge skirted with their own dead leaves. Patches of water pepper seedlings establish themselves under iris,

Plate 25   KINGFISHER

100. 101. 102. A Kingfisher catches and delivers a fish to the family, then rights itself after somersaulting backwards into the open   *Keri Williams*

Plate 26   FLOWERS OF THE CLIFFS

103. Slender St. John's Wort grows on the more acid cliff soils   *Author*

104. Spiked speedwell may be Gower's rarest flower, as well as being very
   rare on a national scale   *Author*

105. Yellow whitlow grass grows nowhere in Britain other than the South
   Gower cliffs   *Author*

106. Orpine or Live-long occurs rarely in inaccessible cliff crevices   *Author*

107. Clary or wild sage occurs rarely on dry clifftops, where it is often
   grazed off   *Author*

108. Eyebright survives well in closely grazed turf   *Author*

122

33. Water bistort. Land form left; water form right

123

angelica and hemp-agrimony. The mud-floored river is sluggish here and 3-4 ft. deep, with stands of great pond-sedge and woody nightshade alongside.

Trout leap from the near stagnant surface into clouds of alder flies: eels and stone loach lurk beneath rocks or glide sinuously through dappled shadows. Flounders often get trapped behind the shingle bank and the occasional spates which give these a freeway to the sea allow sea trout to enter. Swifts and swallows dip to drink, battalions of jackdaws sweep croaking from the cliffs and hedgehogs prod for worms along the banks.

A final thicket of willow, a footbridge and a ford, and the river has only the three-ranked storm beach to hinder it on its way to its destination. Reed canary-grass and greater willow-herb of an islet yield to spike-rush and flote-grass at the ford and these to scummy *Enteromorpha* or 'green strings' alga with bordering bur-reed.

There is no saltmarsh here as at the mouths of other rivers—just the silent entry of false fox-sedge and sea sedge before the water seeps into the back of the great boulder beach and is lost to sight again as it tackles the final hazard on its arduous obstacle race to the sea.

124

Part Three

The Sea Cliffs

Windswept Gower

16 SUN-LOVERS FROM THE SOUTH

Most Englishmen carry in their minds a picture of Wales as mountainous and boggy, with sodden acres of peat, but nothing could be further from this conception than the Gower coast. With its long hours of sunshine, porous rocks and dry shallow soils, this coast can seem more English than England itself, and is every bit as good to look at.

It was largely because of the spectacle of the southern cliffs that Gower became Britain's first "area of outstanding natural beauty", but the cliffs are more than just beautiful. They and the dunes which they encompass contain some dozen national rarities among the flowering plants alone, along with many which are rare on a more local scale or on the fringe of populations centred further South in Europe. Then, too, there are beetles, spiders and flies which occur nowhere else in Britain—and outlying colonies of some of South-west England's special animals such as sand lizards, marbled white butterflies and southern acorn barnacles.

Botanically the limestone cliffs constitute one of the most interesting of British habitats, parallelled only in the Great Orme of North Wales and Humphrey Head in Lancashire. For the most part the freely draining soils are quick to warm up in spring; aided by their predominantly southerly aspect with an angle of slope which intercepts the sun's rays more or less at right angles, and so receives a maximum intensity of radiation. Rainclouds coming from the West do not always rise to cool and shed their rain until forced to do so over the hills behind Swansea, so rainfall is less than in most of the county. This continental style summer drought was very apparent in late June 1975, when only a few dry weeks after a phenomenally wet summer, winter and spring, turf of the scanty cliff soils was parched and brown: as it was again by early May 1976, and on through the long hot weeks of June, July and August.

It is the summer growing season which is important to plants and certain mid-continental species which are geared to cold winters and hot summers can survive the oceanic mildness of the Gower winter to benefit from the continental light regime and soil drought of summer. The Mediterranean species present need the mild winters as well, because only thus can they escape frosts which they are not physiologically fitted to survive.

British botanists have tended to overlook these climatic niceties in the past, becoming too obsessed with the presence or absence of lime in the soil, and producing a system of plant classification dividing the calcicole

34. Archway at Three Cliffs Bay

or lime-loving plants from the calcifuge or lime-avoiding ones. Continental botanists scarcely notice any such division—their warm dry soils supplying for them what we, in our drizzly island, could find only on the limestones.

The bloody cranesbill/rock rose community of so much of Gower's cliffs, laced with marjoram and a soupcon of spiked speedwell, has always been the epitome of a limestone flora. Yet the same community can be found on the freely draining, acid soils derived from the basic igneous Dolerite of the Breidden Hills on the Welsh Border. These plants, along with ash and whitebeam, are base-lovers rather than lime-lovers and our list of those which, like the yellow-wort, depend on lime as such, has become significantly shorter.

A new look at the Gower cliff flora reveals it as one which is essentially lacking in its ability to compete with more usual plants. Only here, in

128

these shallow, windswept soils, where common inland plants are suppressed by a shortage of the bare necessities for growth, can these more interesting 'strangers' stake a claim to unwanted territory and hold it against invasion. The 'golden hoof' of the sheep, with its accompanying dung, and the spreading of artificial fertilisers boost the common and spell doom to the rare. Swards once starred with tiny flowers wax lush and green and the flowers are choked to death in a glut of verdure.

Some of Gower's special plants seem to be a relic from Pre-Boreal and Boreal times just after the Ice Age, when summers were hot and winters cold. Slowly, over long years, they crossed the land bridge from Europe, filtering North in the wake of the retreating ice—probably travelling through the developing forests along the rocky ridges of old moraines. As the shady forests spread, these sun-loving plants were pushed back to the screes, dunes and marginal lands where trees could not grow—and the fierce salty winds saw to it that woodland obtained no hold on the thin soils of most of Gower's cliffland.

The "Gower Coast National Nature Reserve" in the South-west corner of the peninsula was established by the Nature Conservancy in 1958. It occupies about 115 acres and extends along $1\frac{1}{2}$ miles of mainland coast and onto the tidal island of Worm's Head. Much of the remaining cliffland has been designated as Sites of Special Scientific Interest and over the past two decades almost all West of Porteynon has come under protection. The Glamorgan Naturalists' Trust manages 220 acres of this cliffland—the Long Hole Cave Cliff Reserve at Overton donated by BP Chemicals and the Deborah's Hole Reserve by Marks and Spencers, whilst the National Trust holds most of the rest.

Best known of the rare plants because of its local abundance on near vertical rock faces above paths and the brightness of its flowers in early March, when little else has started to grow, is the yellow whitlow grass (*Draba aizoides*). It grows all along the South Gower cliffs from near Worm's Head, where the initial discovery was made in 1795, to Pwll Du Head, where it was first seen in 1904. It seems to have spread during the last few decades and is now to be found on old quarry faces and limestone walls, although native to the Mediterranean region and growing nowhere else in Britain.

Spring cinquefoil (*Potentilla tabernaemontani*) is another western cliff species, extending East to Pwll Du. This is at home in Western and Southern Europe and is very local on dry, base-rich soils in Britain, with its only other Welsh sites on the North Coast. On Gower it makes a pleasant mosaic with the blue flowers of the spring squill (*Scilla verna*) from April to June.

Also on the Pennard cliffs, but introduced, is the white rock rose (*Helianthemum appeninum*) which is otherwise confined in Britain to the coastal limestones of Brean Down in North Somerset and Berry Head in

South Devon. A more 'genuine' speciality is the hoary rock rose (*Helianthemum canum*) from both the European and African sides of the Mediterranean. This too, has its only other British sites on the North Wales Coast and a mere four sites in England. It grows with the common rock rose (*Helianthemum nummularium*) and overlaps in flowering time but is generally earlier, the flowers smaller and the leaves not only hoary but lacking the two leaf-like projections or stipules which occur at the leaf bases of the other. Visitors to Pennard in May and June will find more of the rare species than the common one.

35. Common rock rose (left) and the rarer hoary rock rose

Spiked speedwell (*Veronica spicata* ssp. *hybrida*) bearing tall blue flower clusters on the western cliffs, is like all the others so far, an early flowerer, but much rarer. It too, comes from South and West Europe and has a similarly restricted distribution in Britain to the last, plus extra sites at Strumble Head, Stanner Rocks and Avon Gorge.

The small rest harrow (*Ononis reclinata*) is elusive and escapes notice altogether in some years. It has only three other British sites if one includes the Channel Islands, the two mainland ones in South West Wales and on Berry Head, Devon. The species ranges from the Mediterranean South through Asia Minor to Arabia.

Clary (*Salvia horminoides*) is very much a plant of the chalk and limestone of South East England, just penetrating into the three Welsh coastal limestone regions of Gower, Pembrokeshire and the North. The tiny outpost on the Porteynon cliffs gets bitten off by cattle or sheep most summers, but manages to persist.

Basil thyme (*Acinos arvensis*) of the same family has a similar distribution in England and Wales. This usually escapes grazing on Gower by growing only one inch high (though capable of a great deal more in the Mediterranean) and by seeking refuge in rock crevices or springing up as a minute early colonist on soil blackened by fire and not likely to attract livestock.

130

It extends from Southern Europe into Asia Minor; clary from Southern Europe into Algeria.

Two common members of the bedstraw family on the Gower cliffs are essentially southern in Britain. The bristly madder (*Rubia peregrina*) is mostly coastal in South West England and Wales: squinancy wort (*Asperula cynanchica*) grows mostly inland, following the chalk ridges. This latter occurs on the shell sands of Glamorgan as well as the limestones and is a plant of Central and South East Europe. Madder grows on pebble beaches as well as cliffs and is centred in South and West Europe and North Africa.

The Nicholaston rarities have already been mentioned. The two helle-bores grow no further West in Britain as natives and the wild service tree is found nowhere else in Gower since its disappearance from Pwll Du Head in the 1930s. The rock whitebeam (*Sorbus rupicola*) is very local on limestone rocks in the country as a whole, but occurs in other Gower sites at Brandy Cove, Caswell Head, Horton and Ramsgrove.

Goldilocks aster (*Aster linosyris*) has only five stations in Britain, all westerly and coastal, and is extremely rare in Gower. The related golden samphire (*Inula crithmoides*), on the other hand, is a colourful feature of most of the lower cliff faces in late summer. It, too, is local in Southern Britain, confined to limestone cliffs and boulders in Glamorgan and Pembrokeshire, but growing also on granite, pebble beaches and salt marshes elsewhere. Both these members of the dandelion family are commoner in Southern Europe.

Rarest of the spurges on the open grasslands of the Gower coast are dwarf and wood spurges (*Euphorbia exigua* and *E. amygdaloides*), but rarer on a national scale are the essentially coastal Portland and sea spurges (*E. portlandica* and *E. paralias*), the former commoner on the Gower cliffs than on the dunes. Although all these cliff rarities are more rigorously confined to limey soils on Gower than they are in their usual haunts in Southern Europe, the onset of Britain's milder wetter climate some 7,000 years ago is making life difficult for them and spiked speedwell and goldilocks aster may well be on the verge of local extinction. It is notable that none of Gower's rarer plants tolerate shading by others. This they escape by growing on small ledges, unstable ground of cliff scree or sand dune or on heavily grazed turf where potentially larger plants are cropped back.

Gower's mildness has been exploited by landscape gardeners as well as growers of early potatoes. This is evidenced in the choice of exotics planted around human habitations and in the tourist haunts, particularly on the South-eastern cliffs from Oystermouth to Langland and Caswell Bays. There is a strong flavour of the Scillies and Channel Islands here —where wind-worthy but non frost-hardy plants from gale-swept lands like New Zealand come into their own.

131

The tropical touch introduced by the palms and sisal at Oystermouth is strengthened by the New Zealand cabbage trees (*Cordyline australis* and *C. indivisa*) and New Zealand flax (mostly the smaller coastal *Phormium colensoi*, with less of the larger, greyer *P. tenax*). New Zealand has also contributed the purple-flowered woody Veronica (*Hebe lewisii*) and the shrubby grey-leaved ragworts, notably *Senecio greyi* with its massed golden flowers. Other New Zealand 'daisy bushes' are the Maori holly (*Olearia ilicifolia*), *O. macrodonta* with larger, holly-like leaves and the smaller leaved *O. bastardii*, which can tolerate a lot of air pollution in town gardens.

The Falkland Islands at the opposite side of the South Pole (and formerly connected to New Zealand by a land bridge) have contributed *Fuchsia magellanica*, perhaps the most salt-worthy of all the Fuchsias. *Escallonia microphylla* comes from the adjacent continent of South America. Massed yellow-green flower clusters are produced on the evergreen Japanese spindle (*Euonymus japonicus*) in favourable summers, and pink and orange fruits in 1976, an unfamiliar achievement by a familiar hedge plant.

Mediterranean trees and shrubs are well represented with holm oak (*Quercus ilex*), strawberry tree (*Arbutus unedo*), bay tree (*Laurus nobilis*), edible fig (*Ficus carica*), rosemary (*Rosmarinus officinarum*) and the aromatic yellow button daisy *Santolina chamaecyparissus*.

36. Four of Gower's rarest plants: From left to right: Rock whitebeam, goldilocks aster, spiked speedwell and wild service tree

Various *Cotoneaster* species crop up along the coast, often on old quarry faces, but they are particularly obvious on Mumbles Hill. Here woody branches, closely set with small, evergreen leaves, spread over wide areas of ground, sometimes associated with 'lime-lovers' (betony and salad burnet), sometimes with 'acid-lovers' (ling and fine-leaved heath). The woody mat persists on well-used paths and is much fasciated in some years, with adjacent twigs fused together. Although from an artificial source in the first instance, such well naturalised plants are undoubtedly spread around by fruit-eating birds. Blackbirds, thrushes and their kin gorging themselves on the berries, are quite likely to cough up a crimson crop pellet at once to make room for something tastier. Whether ejected, thus, still surrounded by the fleshy fruit wall, or later in the droppings, after passing through the digestive system, the transported seeds are fully viable.

Introduced members of the herb layer in the East Gower cliff woodlands which are more typical of the frost-free Scillies are three-cornered leek and Spanish bluebell (*Allium triquetrum* and *Endymion hispanicus*.) Alexanders (*Smyrnium olusatrum*) and 'mind-your-own-business' (*Soleirolei Solierolei*) are other southerners and the deep purple sea stock or gilliflower (*Matthiola incana*) of Mediterranean coasts and the Canary Islands is established on Mumbles Head, as it is at Nash Point on the coast of the Vale of Glamorgan.

The comparative warmth and dryness of soil which is welcome in spring can be an embarrassment to plant life in a dry summer. Most of the survivors, like those of the Scilly bulbfields, and Mediterranean, flower in spring, only those with deep roots to tap underground moisture coming to their climax in late summer. May is a beautiful month, predominantly gold with gorse and rock rose, kidney vetch and horseshoe vetch, cowslip, primrose, and wild mignonette. The rich red-purple of dwarfed early purple orchids are followed by veritable sheets of the similar-hued bloody cranesbill and, on the eastern cliffs, by the deeper purple of wild columbine. The more subdued mauve of the rock sea lavender co-habits with sea pink and sea campion on the lower rock faces. Later flowerers like the purple-flecked eyebright (*Euphrasia nemorosa*), the wind-dwarfed, almost stalkless devil's bit scabious and equally stunted betony conserve their water resources by remaining small.

The relative freedom from frost experienced by the Gower cliffs is not only a matter of their southerly aspect and free air drainage. The sea which washes their foot is warmed by the Gulf Stream, moving North-east from the Caribbean area past Valencia Island and affecting plants and animals of the water as well as the land.

One of the unexpected 'southern' seaweeds to be found is the 12-inch-long peacock weed (*Cystoseira tamariscifolia*), which is named in English for the green-blue iridescence of the fronds and in scientific jargon for the spiky side branches which resemble tamarisk leaves.

133

Both of the southern acorn barnacle species are spreading North, *Chthamalus stellatus*, which lives in a little shelly wigwam of six plates, is a genuine native. *Elminius modestus*, which has four sides to its wigwam, is a rapidly advancing invader from Australia. The thick top shell or toothed winkle (*Monodonta lineata*) is another lover of warm water to be found on rocky shores of Gower prior to the 1962-63 freeze-up, but only very rarely since.

17 THE CLIFFLANDS AS A PLANT HABITAT: ROCK, SOIL AND WIND

CLIFF scenery and vegetation are largely determined by the dip of the rocks; the disposition of the deeply incised bays by geological faults. Carboniferous limestone beds wear smooth if their surfaces are exposed, whether as cliff faces or beach platforms, but more jaggedly if their edges are exposed, these presenting fewer problems of adherence to land plants and seaweeds—as they do to climbers.

Where the rock sequence is cracked through by a fault the sea finds the line of weakness and works back along it to form a bay. Similarly the fresh water draining from the land may be fault-guided and flow to the sea along these same cracks. Immediately after the Ice Age, when the meagre warmth thawed only the surface soil, the meltwater flowed seaward across this surface, unable to penetrate the permafrost layer below and so carving surface valleys. As the climate warmed up and the subsoil was released from the icy grip of the glaciers, the rivers percolated underground, leaving dry valleys where we see them today. The emergence of fresh-water springs from rifts in the sea bed just offshore suggests that the rivers are still flowing—unseen—in deep recesses of the rock.

They have left a fine legacy of caves scattered along the coast and used by various creatures, including man, during Gower's pre-history. Bases of stalactites and stalagmites 2 ft. and more across are testimony to aeons of dripping water and suggest that the caves were formed by river action rather than (or as well as) marine action. The calcite columns themselves were no doubt removed to grace the garden grottoes of wealthy Victorians. Before despoliation the caves must have presented a fine spectacle —the ancient craftsmen who polished the bone and ivory tools recently excavated from interglacial deposits at Bacon Hole, East of Pennard, having dwelt beneath imposing natural fan vaulting.

Today's plant inhabitants of Bacon Hole are adapted in weird ways to survive in the diffuse light which penetrates the gloomy interior. Seedlings (mostly of scurvy grass) bend sideways on emerging from the cave floor and spread their young leaves at right angles to the entrance to intercept a maximum amount of light, their hunger for this overcoming their innate response to gravity. They grow lank and spindly, like the maidenhair spleenwort of the cave walls. Liverworts (mostly *Conocephalum* and *Marchantia*) survive even to the hindmost parts of the great chamber but are tissue-thin, their delicacy ensuring that every part is at the surface and able to use the available light to make food for itself without having to pass some of its energy on to bulky internal tissues.

Green algae penetrate hardly at all into the shadows, but blue-green algae are more versatile, covering much of the walls and ceiling with a brownish jelly. Their unusual colour is due to a resorting of their internal pigments, the red, yellow and orange pigments coming to dominate the green ones, as in red seaweeds growing in deep water. These are better able to photosynthesize food materials in dim light than are the more widespread green pigments. Some of these tiny plants are of single cells, others of cells strung together to form threads. Both kinds help to bring about the formation of the calcite flows, taking calcium carbonate from the water flowing over them and depositing it in their cells. When the plants die the reconstituted limestone is left as crystals on the rock surface. The 'blue-greens' are thus incorporated right inside these travertine rocks—and account for their colour.

But back to the surface again, and those dry grassy valleys laced with gorse which are known as slades. A glance at the map will reveal eight such along the southern cliffs where 'slade' appears in the name: Limeslade, Rotherslade, Hareslade, Sevenslades, Heatherslade, Eastern Slade, Slade Bay and Mewslade. The name of Bracelet Bay may well be a corruption of Broadslade.

Gower's blocky Carboniferous limestones are the thickest in South Wales. With the limestone shales below and above they are some 3,700 ft. thick at Porteynon, most, of course, below sea level, as cliffs seldom exceed the 320 ft. reached at Pwll Du Head. Well West, towards Rhossili, the Lower Limestone Shales and underlying Old Red Sandstone are exposed at the cliff base. The detailed succession to be seen in the Lower Carboniferous sediments here is unique in South Wales. Red staining at Porteynon, where rocks were once quarried for paint-making pigments, suggests that the limestones were formerly overlain by younger red rocks like the Trias of the Eastern Vale of Glamorgan, these having long since worn away. An ancient iron mine, said to have been worked by the Romans, can still be seen at the head of Limeslade Bay.

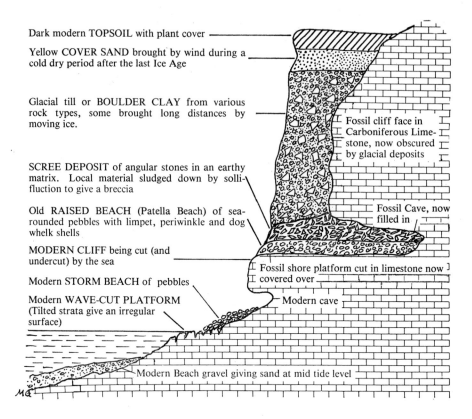

Dark modern TOPSOIL with plant cover

Yellow COVER SAND brought by wind during a cold dry period after the last Ice Age

Glacial till or BOULDER CLAY from various rock types, some brought long distances by moving ice.

Fossil cliff face in Carboniferous Limestone, now obscured by glacial deposits

SCREE DEPOSIT of angular stones in an earthy matrix. Local material sludged down by solli-fluction to give a breccia

Old RAISED BEACH (Patella Beach) of sea-rounded pebbles with limpet, periwinkle and dog whelk shells

Fossil Cave, now filled in

MODERN CLIFF being cut (and undercut) by the sea

Fossil shore platform cut in limestone now covered over

Modern STORM BEACH of pebbles

Modern cave

Modern WAVE-CUT PLATFORM (Tilted strata give an irregular surface)

Modern Beach gravel giving sand at mid tide level

37. Diagrammatic profile of the cliff face and shore East of Langland Bay, showing glacial deposits and raised beach with the limestone cropping out above and below. After John Evans (Not to scale). See also colour photographs 6 and 7 on page 2

Glacial clays and gravels dumped over Gower during the Ice Ages have been eroded off the steeper slopes and headlands, but a lot remains between the spurs. The sketch of cliff deposits on the East side of Langland Bay shows how the limestone crops out above and below them. Caves caused by undercutting of the cliff when the sea was at a higher level became filled with scree material, but the old sea beach protrudes well to seaward of this as a weathered shelf resting on the old wave-cut platform immediately below. This natural 'concrete' of sea-rounded pebbles, limpet, winkle and whelk shells now supports tufts of land plants and today's sea is cutting a new platform across the upended strata some 10 ft. below. This ancient raised beach, although visible in a number of places around the South Gower cliffs, has been eroded away entirely from the softer Lias cliffs bordering the Vale of Glamorgan.

Among the chunks of Old Red Sandstone and ironstone nodules eroded out of the soft Coal Shales, the boulder clays above the beach contain rocks which can be recognised as having come from Pembroke, Lleyn, Anglesey or as far afield as Scotland. The soil in which they occur is acid, supporting heathy vegetation in which gorse and bell heather give fine contrasting colours in late summer.

Bracken is common on the deeper clays, but avoids areas where the rock is near the surface because of drying out of the soil in summer. Quite different herb mats grow with spring-flowering gorse on the native limestones, so the cliffs present a patchwork of 'lime-loving' and 'lime-hating' plants when viewed from a distance. When clay slumps downwards into a wooded area ash and lime, the two most characteristic trees of the limestone woodlands, give way to oak and birch.

Vegetation changes are illustrated quite strikingly on a boulder clay deposit west of Limeslade in the South East. The limestone beds dip at an angle of about 45° towards the sea and loose soil has persisted on a sloping middle shelf, leaving the blocky strata exposed above and below The rock above is bright with rock rose, horseshoe vetch and kidney vetch in Spring; that of the brink below bears a windshorn fringe of blackthorn, privet and gorse above salt-tolerant crevice plants. Amidships the clay deposit is occupied by a wilderness of purple moor-grass with gorse where the soil shallows above and bracken where it deepens below. Bush grass or wood small-reed (*Calamagrostis*) is sometimes to be found on deeper soils, as at Ram's Tor and Overton Mere.

Further substrate complications are introduced by reworked glacial drift from an earlier Ice Age, which has slid over many of the southern cliffs. In the most recent glacial period ice reached only as far West as Langland Bay—as the outer edge of a great frozen lobe penetrating into Swansea Bay. Further West the glacial till is much older—from the Riss Glaciation—but sludged downwards during the freeze-thaw sollifluction regime of the later icy spell. This reworked material is known as glacial 'head'. It is of varying consistency, but can most readily be likened to a coarse concrete or consolidated scree. Where it is thickest, in the Long Hole Cave Cliff Reserve, some of the apparent 'concrete' is covered by a few inches of crusty lithified sand, which weathers down to form little sand patches. Some is looser and gravelly in texture, the matrix a reddish loam.

The contained pebbles were shuffled as they slumped downwards and tend to lie with their flattened surfaces horizontal. This, together with the fact that their angles have not been rounded off by the sea and that there are no sea shells present, distinguishes them from the raised beaches. Both head and old beach material can become cemented, the first resembling Breccia the second Conglomerate or pudding stone.

Head spilled over cliffs which were already present in the Ice Age as the edge of an uplifted wave-cut platform, straight into what is now the sea. Marine erosion has removed it from the steep headlands but it accumulated in the valleys and bays. The material may be fused firmly enough to form beetling overhangs.

Golden samphire is much the most characteristic plant of the head—on which it grows unusually high above sea level, getting tall and spindly under the overhangs, although normally quite succulent just above the splash zone where it most often occurs. Rock samphire and sea beet also grow on head, but very erodible faces may support only rock sea lavender and buck's horn plantain.

On the East side of Pwll Du Bay is a series of ledges formed in different ways. The uppermost is of cemented head. The next is an abrasion bench or wave-cut platform on which the Patella (limpet) beach was formed—some remaining still, fused fast to the platform. Three minor benches below are probably related to more modern tidal levels, whilst the lowest, irregular shelf is an unconsolidated mixture of glacial drift and old scree material. There is a good exposure of raised beach in the fault gully of Brandy Cove—the texture of concrete above and gravel below—and others West of Overton Mere some 8-12 ft. above present high water mark.

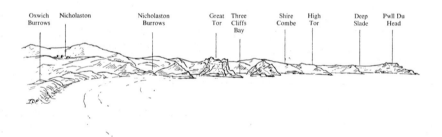

38. Oxwich Bay

Another rubbly type of habitat is provided by the frequent patches of scree, which form an inhospitable plant medium and remain largely bare. Their very bareness may prove an asset to the intrepid plants which do manage to establish themselves, however, because the stony waste acts as a fire break. Juniper bushes have a higher chance of survival here than in more inflammable sites and whole spinneys of hazel or blackthorn and isolated hollies may be preserved in this way. Blackthorn, in severely wind-cut form, is probably the most widespread of the scree shrubs, with dwarf privet running it a close second.

Plate 27 TYPICAL CLIFF FLOWERS

109. Golden samphire growing below rock samphire on the Mumbles *Author*

110. Foxglove, characteristic of more acid cliffs *Author*

111. Portland spurge, a typical scree plant *Author*

112, Spring squill *Harold Grenfell*

113. Thrift or sea pink *Author*

114. Bird's foot trefoil *Author*

115. Horseshoe vetch *Author*

139

116

117

118

119

Plate 28   BIRDS OF THE CLIFFS

116. Fulmar Petrels at Lewes Castle, where the first
Gower pairs chose to nest   *Harold Grenfell*
117. Raven on Overton Cliffs   *Harold Grenfell*
118. Kittiwake cliff (bottom right) and potato field—
Tears Point and Fall Bay to near Mewslade   *Author*
119. Rock Pipit at clifftop nest   *Arthur Morgan*

Arboreal plants may be the only ones able to colonise the screes of larger stones, as these are the only ones with sufficient food stored in the seeds to enable them to grow out to the light from the quite deep crevices between. Herbaceous seedlings starve in the interstitial darkness, with no chance of becoming self-sufficient. Ivy, with big, indigestible seeds which get ejected as crop pellets by fruit-eating birds, can be quite successful on screes. Its stems ramify among the stones and help to stabilise them, though not overtopping them for a while. Only as the star pointed leaves of the vegetative phase give way to the lighter green ovate ones of the flowering phase, do shoots rise above the surface. Screes of smaller stones, as in the neighbourhood of Ram's Tor and Deborah's Hole, can accommodate less robust plants like the locally abundant meadow rue, Portland spurge, common milkwort, basil thyme and madder along with the more widespread herb Robert, pellitory-of-the-wall and cleavers. Thrift is characteristic of spray-washed screes.

The angular nature of both northern and southern cliffs has been accentuated by past quarrying which has produced artificial screes on talus strewn slopes. The vertically ridged eastern face of Pwll Du Head has been shaped by quarrying. Bracken, bramble and a few small hawthorn bushes are established on the older ridges, which have had a certain amount of clay added as downwash from the clifftop, whereas younger ridges tend to be grassed. *Cotoneaster microphylla* has a good hold and produces abundant crops of berries for birds to distribute further afield. Quarried surfaces behind Bracelet Bay which were innocent of vegetation in the 1930s, were nicely clothed with grassland plants and the beginnings of scrub by the 1970s.

The process of revegetation can be greatly hindered by sea winds. On windswept cliffs scrub is slow to become established, if at all. With medium exposure the plant succession may be held at a bramble phase, or move on to stunted blackthorn. If the fury of the winds is further alleviated, hawthorn bushes may get away and provide shelter for pioneering saplings of a scrub woodland of sycamore, ash and hazel, but with the climax phase of oak seldom reached as yet.

Herbaceous plants are similarly curtailed by wind—and their flowering period shortened. Where the winds are stilled in local declivities, however the winter mildness allows some to flower all the year. About 20 species can be found in bloom at Mewslade in early March of a normal year and 45 by mid April, but few of these crest the gale-seared outcrops.

Plant regeneration in quarries is a recapitulation of the natural succession leading to wooded East facing cliffs and scrub-covered West facing ones. Where scrub woodland advances round the back of a bay onto the exposed side, it is tightly wind-clipped, as by a giant hedging machine, each layer compacted snugly against a slightly shorter one to windward. A typical sequence from the cliff edge inland near Sevenslades is prostrate blackthorn merging into a sloping zone of gorse and so to hawthorn, then hazel, then holly and finally to ash. Wood spurge advancing beyond the cover of the trees in such sites gets severely wind-scorched.

After the phenomenal September gales of 1974 just about everything was thoroughly browned off on its seaward side, even holly, but some of the worst hit were sycamore, privet and elder. The equally ferocious May gales of 18 months earlier did far more damage, because they blasted the tender new leaves and bursting buds of spring instead of the hardened leaves of summer's end and buds already well wrapped against the coming winter.

It was interesting to observe the state of havoc wrought by the 1974 gales among the planted exotics in Bracelet Bay. Fuchsia and escallonia had all their leaves stripped to windward; tamarisk, cotoneaster and rosemary were partially scorched, veronica and the various composites were harmed very little. Bay trees suffer badly, adopting a wind-nipped shrub form on the cliffs at Caswell and flowering well only in the taller woodland behind. Herbs with annual shoots, like hemp agrimony, nettle and bracken were prematurely cut back for the year in 1974; whereas more wintergreen ones like red valerian and yarrow were sprouting new leaves among the dead within a week, illustrating that damage was only 'skin deep'. Even the salt-tolerant rock samphire was browned locally.

The old sea cliffs of the Burry Inlet, with their sheltered northerly aspect, were originally all wooded. Ash is the dominant tree of the upper slopes where the limestone is near the surface, but oak and elm dominate below if the soils deepen.

Tor Gro, between Cheriton and Landimore, consists of near vertical slabs of exposed bedding plane in parts, few plants finding roothold sufficient to alleviate the barren-ness. When the adjacent soils are cleared of

39. Raven at Caswell Bay

trees by felling or burning, they regenerate to hawthorn scrub luxuriantly draped with wild clematis and a little wild rose, but with patches of spring-flowering gorse as well. The last is vulnerable to fire, but if not burned too frequently, young ashes of the future woodland will begin to push through. When deeper soils such as those of Cilifor just East of Llanrhidian are kept clear of trees by burning, they tend to revert to bracken.

The Tor Gro cliffs are tucked well into the lee of Whiteford Point, so that although the highest tides reach to their feet, the sea can be millpond calm. (Further up the estuary at Penclawdd there is sufficient 'fetch' for quite big waves to buffet the sea wall when the marsh is inundated). Thus it is that at Tor Gro the lowest gorse bushes wear a skirt of broken sea rush drifted up by the tides. The basal scree, with its partial covering of thyme, merges into the upper 'beach' with its silvered sea wormwood; red fescue being common to both.

The understorey of these craggy woodlands contains a good range of plants. Two of the more interesting in the Cwm Ivy Nature Reserve at the base of Whiteford Point are meadow saxifrage and a taller form of meadow rue than that of the screes, whilst cowslips figure among the spring flowers.

East of Cilifor the hills bordering the estuary are of Millstone Grit shales. These are softer and less craggy, weathering down to give soft contours, sometimes disturbed by past mining activities and now occupied by rough grazing, poor farmland or durmast oakwood. Although still old sea cliffs, they are more deeply recessed than those of the West (as is the section containing Weobley Castle, West of Llanrhidian)—a width of two fields having been won from the sea at their base.

The natural rock walls, with their irregular rectangular patterning of crevices, are the precursors of man-made walls and bear a similar vegetation. The lime demanding rusty-back fern and all the common wall spleenworts are present, particularly wall rue, but there is less of the rarer sea spleenwort.

Flowering plants growing on these vertical faces with the yellow whitlow grass include wall pellitory, wall, or rue-leaved saxifrage, wall lettuce, birds-foot trefoil with brilliant orange flowers and shining cranesbill. Towards the cliff base there is a preponderance of sea pink, sea plantain, rock sea-lavender, rock samphire and golden samphire. Sea campion is less common than sea mayweed but showy, nevertheless.

Chunky plants of ox-eye daisy form a showy fringe along some of the lower cliff brinks. The large white-flowered scurvy grass (*Cochlearia officinalis*) is a typical crevice plant; the smaller mauve-flowered Danish scurvy grass (*C. danica*) is more a feature of the close turf of shallow soil pockets.

Four stonecrops are to be found, the yellow-flowered wall pepper or biting stonecrop most often. White stonecrop, which is more of a garden plant in most of Britain, is well established on cliff faces and screes. Pink-flowered English stonecrop is the least common of the three 'classic' stonecrops and prefers the more acid rocks, as of Rhossili Down. Most spectacular and rarest of the genus on Gower is orpine or livelong which bears flat heads of rose pink flowers above broadly succulent leaves in a few spots between Fall Bay and Three Cliffs Bay. Ivy stands considerable exposure on these natural walls of limestone, its roots frequently parasit- ised by ivy broomrape.

All the soils derived directly from the limestone are not necessarily limey, because of the phenomena of 'leaching' and 'flushing', so the nat- uralist will be faced with endless puzzles of distribution, as 'lime-lovers' mingle with 'lime haters' in apparently random fashion. Limestone or calcium carbonate is not, in itself, soluble in rain water, but is readily converted to minerals which are. Hence all the lime may be leached or washed out of a shallow soil which comes to support heather and the like jumbled up with relic limestone species which continue to maintain root contact with the underlying source of lime. Shallowness of soil may thus be significant on more counts than those of root restriction and drying out.

Lime washed from the soil of the upper cliff may be deposited in the soil of the lower cliff in a process known as flushing. As mineral-charged waters seep downwards the lime may be precipitated out, immobilising the soil iron so that it cannot be absorbed by 'lime-hating' plants, which yellow and die, yielding place to lime-lovers which can cope with the situation better. In this way it is possible to get a more lime-loving flora in a formerly acid drift soil which becomes neutralised than in a native limestone soil which becomes acidified.

Soils from the limestone are, in fact, usually slightly acid—the silty red- brown loam of the subsoil having a pH around 6.8 and the humus-rich surface layer a pH around 6.3. Where there is active flushing, readings may be on the alkaline side of neutral, around 7.7 or even over 8.0. The scrub community of the Fall Bay Cliffs in the West is predominant- ly acidic with sheep's fescue, western gorse and bracken, but exhibits a contradictory assemblage of lime-loving rock-rose and salad burnet with heathers and tormentil among the subordinates.

These complications do not arise on the non-calcareous cliffs between Worm's Head and Burry Holm in the East. Here the Old Red Sandstone of Rhossili Down slopes steeply seaward with Boulder Clay slumped across the lower two-thirds of its face and fluted outwards into a narrow strip of farmland. This terminates in a stony earth cliff with a little dune sand piled at its foot. From beach to summit twelve different plant commun- ities can be recognised.

Rhossili Beach is one of the finest on Gower and it is surprising that more sand has not been whipped off its spacious surface by the wind and deposited on the land behind. The sand seems mostly to be blown away

40. Thrift and buck's horn plantain on eroding earth cliff at Rhossili Bay

northwards, little accumulating against the Rhossili Down cliff. North-wards at Hill End there is a fair deposit on the Boulder Clay of the caravan park, the unmown parts colourful in the summer with bloody cranesbill, lady's bedstraw and white clover. Northwards again vast accumulations have been wind-moulded to form Llangennith Burrows.

The fragmentary deposits against the southern clay cliff are steep and mobile, supporting little apart from the deeply anchored sand couch and marram grasses. Less well entrenched annuals such as sea rocket and prickly saltwort can seldom maintain a roothold.

Where sand clings less precariously to shelves of the underlying clay, a colourful mat of wild thyme, bloody cranesbill, rest-harrow and lady's bedstraw is spread across it, the mat dissected by narrow sheep tracks and roughened by low-growing dewberry.

Some of the stones speckling the boulder clay face are puddingstones from the Quartz Conglomerate which tops Rhossili Down. Glacial till and blown sand mingle to give a red, iron-stained soil which becomes wind sculptured to the texture of a giant chocolate flake bar. The match-box sized cavities scoured by wind and abraded by flying sand form re-positories for old snail shells—*Helix*, *Cepaea* and *Helicella*.

Buck's horn plantain is much the most typical plant of the eroding face, with thrift not far behind. Both produce wind-worthy leaf rosettes each on a stout, deeply penetrating root whose tip thrusts further in as its upper part is blown free of soil. At first the leaves become curved back

145

over little mounds which they have immobilised by their presence. Later the mounds are undermined and dissipated and the half excavated rosettes dangle at odd angles, the flower stems turning outwards and upwards again in a negative response to gravity.

Field bindweed creeps out over the surfaces and tiny plants of centaury get established. Slabs of turf slipped from above are spread with bird's-foot trefoil and yellow clover and starred with tiny field daisies. Behind an overhanging fringe of fescue and soft brome-grass the earthy cliff is topped by bracken which borders the narrow strip of farmland. Tough unpalatable crested dogstail grass invades as the sown perennial ryegrass is grazed down and and the sward is short enough for slender trefoil (*Trifolium micranthum*) to survive. The wall behind the narrow fields shelters lusher bracken on the deep soil slipped from above.

Big bushes of spring-flowering gorse make a fine show of colour here before the bracken fronds reach their full summer luxuriance—merging gradually upwards into the smaller western gorse. At the transition the foliage of the two produces a marbling of yellow-green and grey-green, so that they can be distinguished even when neither is flowering, which is seldom. The smaller species gets closely 'hedged' to windward, the larger one, if not sufficiently in the lee of the other, gets killed on the side facing the rumbustious salty gales. 'Hedging' is also effected by sheep, only the larger species having the potiential to grow away from the centre out of reach of the punitive incisors. The result is a series of dark green domes between the smaller, paler anthills, each with a shaggy topknot of wind-browned spikes.

As the soil shallows towards the summit, bracken peters out and the 'lanes' between the gorse bushes are paved with slender grasses or fine-leaved heath. The sward gets progressively more stunted until it grades almost imperceptibly into a 'waved heath' of bell heather and ling. The waved effect is caused by the bevelling off of the twigs to windward with more robust ones growing away to leeward. The resulting ridges are set more or less across the prevailing wind and separated by peaty, partially grazed sheep tracks. This is the sort of plant community found in windier parts of the Scilly Isles and Holyhead Island at Britain's western extremities. In fact, the plant cover of Rhossili Down as a whole is strongly reminiscent of that on the Old Red Sandstone of Skokholm Island in West Pembrokeshire.

Wind-dwarfed ling continues over the summit, providing no song posts for the stonechats of the lower slopes, but cover enough for skylarks and meadow pipits. On the very top, at 633 ft. bilberry shoots sprout among the heathers and the mounds are overtopped by wispy, breeze-tossed heads of sweet vernal and sheep's fescue grass.

Specialists in lichens and mosses inevitably gravitate towards Rhossili Down when on Gower, particularly to its more humid northern face.

41. Stonechats

One species, known to the weavers of old as cudbear lichen (*Ochrolechia tartarea*) was formerly collected from the rocks and used for dyeing wool at the Whitemoor weaving mill in the valley behind. Conspicuous on the summit rocks are grey-green patches of *Parmelia saxatilis* and yellow green lobes of *Parmelia caperata*, which might not be there if the air were less pure, as it sucumbs readily to sulphur dioxide pollution. On the thin peat among the heather are various kinds of *Cladonia*, some with scarlet spore-bearing tips, some with the mealy grey shoots ending in tiny 'pixy cups'.

One of the special mosses here which is particularly sensitive to pollution is *Pterogonium gracile*, which looked distinctly unhappy with bleached shoot tips when the Pembrey Power Station was opened on the Llanelli side of the Burry Inlet and started adding its effluent to that of the Pembroke power station, whose stack can be seen from almost anywhere in Gower.

Hedwigia ciliata, a westerly species of sites such as St. David's Head in Pembrokeshire, has its only Glamorgan site on Rhossili Down. *Campylopus introflexus* was first found here, but has turned up at several places in the Glamorgan coalfield since 1974. Atlantic species here, though more typical of North Wales woodlands, include the robust *Dicranum majus* and *Rhytidiadelphus loreus*.

18 MODIFICATIONS OF CLIFF VEGETATION BY BURNING AND GRAZING

CLIMATE and soil, as considered in the last two chapters, are basic ingredients of the ultimate vegetation. Animals, with the exception of man and his attendant livestock, have little effect, but the history of exploitation of the clifftops by man is a long one. It starts with the clearing of woodland for timber, then to make way for livestock and later for arable farming. One of the most potent modern threats is tourist pressure, but this is more serious on dunes than cliffs.

Graziers assist their sheep, cattle and ponies to prevent the return of woodland by setting fire to the pasture at intervals and maintaining an uneasy truce at what can be called a 'scrub grassland' phase. But fires too often get out of hand—and not all are started in the interests of pasture management. Even without interference, full woodland could not exist on the more exposed cliffs, and the low woody carpet of impenetrable thicket on the windward side of Oxwich Point probably represents the aboriginal cliff vegetation as closely as any.

The primary plant succession (which can still be traced on newly bared rock faces) built up through algae and lichens, with few mosses if the atmosphere was at all salty, to a crevice vegetation and so to herb-rich grassland, which was readily choked out by the contorted wind-thwarted branches of the scrub.

Slowly, with the plants, comes a thin soil cover gathered tediously over the years from trapped dust and dead organic fragments. But a topsoil which has taken thousands of years to form can be irretrievably destroyed by a discarded cigarette end in a matter of moments. The organic content is dissipated as smoke and the mineral matter, no longer bound together by the quick and the dead, is at the mercy of wind and rain. All too soon the harsh contours of the rock are once more uppermost.

A bad burn can completely destroy the humus-rich topsoil and with it the micro-organisms responsible for the myriad activies of the 'living soil', leaving a sterile subsoil. On the Boulder Clays this is open to invasion by cosmopolitan weeds less specific than the new arrivals on the limestone. Thistles and docks colonise the drift soils at this stage, with opportunist annuals from the arable fields behind. A surprisingly tender non-maritime invader to turn up at Newton Cliff West of Langland is the ramping fumitory, in a luxuriant cliff edge fringe 2ft. high, with stems straggling to 3ft.

Purple moor-grass is resistant to burning, sprouting green again from charred stools. Sweet vernal grass enroaches tentatively after burning on the drier soils, Yorkshire fog-grass and yellow sedge (*Carex demissa*) on moister parts. As recovery proceeds, sheep's bit and heath milkwort appear in profusion. Conspicuous in the post-burning regeneration on these acid soils are tormentil and wood-sage. The bulbs of bluebell and corms of pignut survive a winter burn and sprout unharmed in spring along with tough little common dog-violets, whose spherical yellow seeds are spurted tiddliwink fashion from contracting boat-shaped containers into the shelter of the grass bases. Fierce fires, as at Sevenslades Bay in 1973, leave sheep tracks snaking through the blackened stumps of gorse and bracken like pale green threads, their surfaces so worn as to have been leapt by flames voracious for larger spoils.

42. Manx shearwaters over Rhossili Bay

Heather burning on Rhossili Down scorches and blackens lichens plastered over boulders—undoing in a single searing moment the imperceptible growth of many decades. Charred remains of mosses are equally incapable of recovery, but succulent English stonecrop may retain just sufficient moisture to try again.

Red sheep's sorrel, yellow tormentil and blue heath speedwell (*Veronica officinalis*) appear while the new heather shoots are still quite rudimentary. The most successful survivor of this treatment on shallow soils is the pill sedge (*Carex pilulifera*), which sends up a sward of rich green shoots from undamaged underground stems while the less deeply entrenched grasses and heathers are still licking their wounds. On deeper soils it is the bracken which gains the upper hand. One of the most adequate new colonists is the foxglove, whose numerous tiny seeds invade sheltered depressions. The bold trumpets of these are buzzing with five or six different species of bees in years when the viscous heather honey is likely to be in short supply.

Furze bushes, scorched tinder dry to windward, succumb to the carelessly thrown match in a brief blaze of fiery glory, leaving a fragmented

149

blaze of golden blossoms in ensuing years, dissected by lanes of grass and bracken. Entwined, flower-starred threads of the tangled dodder (*Cuscuta epithymum*)—as abundant on the Gower cliffs at the end of last century as they are still on the cliffs South of St. Davids—had gone by 1908 — consumed by the flames. The tenuous hold which dodder seedlings have on the soil is soon severed, so the parasite cannot sprout again from below with its host.

The sheets of scarlet pimpernel which become established on blackened soil at Overton make a splendid spectacle in early summer. Some colonies show as many pink flowers as red ones, offset by an occasional bloom of gentian-blue. Similar sized associates are the mauve field-madder, tiny blue field forget-me-not (*Myosotis arvensis*) and pink, white and blue common milkwort (*Polygala vulgaris*). Yellow-green swards of dwarf spurge though local can be very striking on the scorched acres West of Porteynon.

Sometimes these attractive annuals are overshadowed by extensive stands of 2ft. high heath groundsel (*Senecio sylvaticus*), as in the Pennard-Pobbles Bay area. Spring squill bulbs, like the larger ones of bluebell, may remain unscathed below ground and push up a crop of blue flowers among the charred remains of earlier formed leaves.

The community usually progresses to a rough grassland phase dominated by Yorkshire fog-grass, which is less inflammable than most, because of rain and dew retention by the fluffy coating of hairs. Cocksfoot, sweet vernal and carnation grass (*Carex flacca*) shelter in its soft dampness, and harebells achieve elegant perfection in late summer. Bramble and sloe sometimes compete with the regenerating gorse, but fire permitting, gorse is likely to win in the end.

Not all the rarities are adversely affected by fire, columbine and spring cinquefoil sprouting unabashed through the felt of regenerating gorse sprigs East of Pwll Du Bay. A green fringe of honeysuckle and privet on the cliff brink can prove an effective fire break, but a profuse crevice flora may provide fuel for lines of flame to spread down the cliff face. In such instances recovery may start with annuals more typical of dunes than of cliffs—the little thyme-leaved sandwort, rare rock hutchinsia and fairy flax. Deeply penetrating perennials like rock spurrey, bird's foot trefoil and kidney vetch (sometimes a distinctive lemon-yellow form or with crimson flecks) can shoot again from surviving rootstocks.

The confused pattern of soil reaction in the South West allows the recovering vegetation to pass through lime-loving squinancy-wort and mouse-ear hawkweed to ling and bell heather as minerals are washed from the fire-denuded earth. A feature which these four plants have in common is their ability to thrive on light, dry soils—this preference probably overriding the affinity of the first two for lime.

Heavy grazing by rabbits, sheep and ponies, coupled with regular burning and the resultant leaching of vital minerals (or incipient podsolisation) ensures a progressive loss of soil fertility on the cliffs. Para-doxically, floral diversity and the presence of rarities is usually greatest on these poor soils, although the 'biomass' or total quantity of vegetable matter is smaller. There is no surer way of losing a speciality than to treat it with fertilisers or enclose it in a protective fence and allow it to be swamped by the lush grasses and shrubs which were formerly starved out, eaten up or burned off.

Shrubs and trees are destroyed by fire; palatable broad-leaved herbs by grazing. The end point is bracken cover where soil depth,wind strength and snapping of the young fronds by trampling cattle permit; otherwise some sort of grassland. The limestone grassland of the South Gower cliffs is botanically as rich as any in the country. Largely dominated by sheep's fescue with crested hair grass and carnation grass, it is nevertheless full of broad leaved herbs, notably salad burnet, rock-rose and thyme. The last, whose aromatic foliage proves unpalatable to most herbivores, increases with intense grazing on the Fall Bay cliffs, where its main associates may be grey soil lichens, principally *Cladonia*.

The leaves, if not the flowers, of rosette plants such as autumn hawkbit, field daisy and ribwort plantain escape most of the nibbling. Yellow bedstraw and similarly hued members of the pea family can persist at a fraction of their normal size. In the doing they become more immune not only to grazing but to the water loss occasioned by drying wind, shallow soil and destruction of water-retaining humus by fire. They are also less damaged by trampling hooves and human feet. In effect, they 'stoop to conquer', enduring at ground level environmental factors which could not be tolerated by normal sized plants.

When the Botanical Society of the British Isles held its summer field meeting on the Pennard cliffs in the bitter squalls and deluging rain of May 1973, its members also functioned at ground level, avoiding the elements less effectively. Tiny grasses visible only at close quarters include the early and silver hair grasses and abbreviated chunky specimens of crested dogstail and seaside brome (*Bromus ferronii*). Larger grasses like the downy oat (*Helictorichon pubescens*) take shelter in crevices.

Sea pearlwort (*Sagina maritima*) and two mouse-ear chickweeds (*Cerastium atrovirens* or *diffusum* and *C. semidecandrum*), seldom exceed an inch high. The similar sized water blinks, revelling in the douching of a a normally dry site, is the westerly coastal *Montia fontana* ssp. *amporitana*, distinguished only by the sculpturing of the seed coat. The inch high spring whitlow grass overtops by half its length the rue-leaved saxifrage and parsley piert. Lesser trefoil (*Trifolium dubium*) is so minute as to be recognisable from slender trefoil (*T. micranthum*) only by the shorter inflorescence stalks.

The intense blue of the minute early forget-me-not (*Myosotis ramosissima*) is dwarfed by the $1\frac{1}{2}$ inch high changing forget-me-not or scorpion grass (*M. discolor*), with its yellow flowers changing to a paler blue. Brighter again is the tiny wall speedwell (*Veronica arvensis*), the flower dashingly large to be borne on so small a plant. The 2 inch high common dog-violets look almost vulgar beside the petite eye-bright and milkwort.

Such scraps of vegetable matter are easily desiccated by summer sunshine and most have disappeared by the time the visitors arrive for the holiday season. One of the more interesting small plants recorded on Mumbles Hill before the advent of quarrying, but not since, is the cat's foot or mountain everlasting (*Antennaria dioica*) which is still present in the Western Vale of Glamorgan.

The Glamorgan Naturalists' Trust's Long Hole Cave cliff reserve was less heavily grazed in the mid 1970s than the National Trust land to its immediate West. A difference which, on climbing the fence, appeared to be merely quantitative, proved on closer investigation to be qualitative as well. But the situation could change in a matter of months with an alteration in the grazing regime.

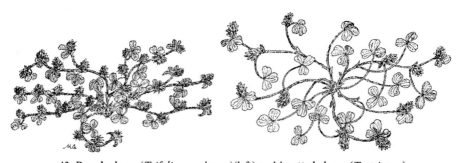

43. Rough clover (*Trifolium scabrum*)(left) and knotted clover (*T. striatum*)

Infertile, open communities, can provide Lebensraum for low-growing rarities unable to compete in the press of plants occupying more fertile sites, but there is moderation in all things. East of the fence is a limestone grassland suffering medium pressure of grazing and floristically rich. West of it is a closely razed, badly trampled turf, dotted with domes of gorse, smoothly rounded by the munching of the non-prickly shoots produced in spring, but affording brief shelter to some of the choicer species which have been eaten out completely from the turf between.

There is no shortage of species, but many are cosmopolitan 'weeds' likely to be found in overgrazed pasture almost anywhere and lacking the distinctive flavour which is the nationally recognised perquisite of the Gower clifflands. No less than 38 kinds of flowering plant can be found within a square yard, this representing perhaps three fifths of the total, so small are most.

Within the square yard may be six kinds of *Geranium*, four each of storksbill, bedstraw and plantain and as many as nine clovers. The Geraniums are dovesfoot, cut-leaved, long-stalked, shining and bloody cranesbills and herb Robert; the closely related *Erodium* species common, sticky, musk and sea storksbill; the bedstraws cleavers, crosswort and heath and lady's bedstraws. The two most unusual clovers, though quite well distributed on Gower cliffs, are the knotted clover (*Trifolium striatum*) and rough clover (*T. scabrum*). These are rather similar, with unassuming oval heads of pinkish flowers, but the sepals of the rough clover are sharply pointed and spread to give a bristly fruit head.

To survive at all, palatable plants must be small or prostrate, with their perennating buds at ground level. Unpalatable plants have more scope. Distasteful aromatic oils afford immunity to dead nettles such as wild basil (*Clinopodium vulgare*) and ground ivy. Buttercups are avoided because of their poisonous alkaloids, the temptingly juicy biting stonecrop because of its acrid sap. Thistles are physically armoured, two of the most characteristic on the cliffs being the yellow carline thistle and mauve slender thistle (*Carduus tenuiflorus*), with showy purple clumps of musk or nodding thistle (*C. nutans*) in places. Height is no obstacle in these where grazing is concerned, but salty winds are no respecters of prickles and usually relegate them to declivities in the limestone or leeward slopes. Saw-wort (*Serratula tinctoria*) ventures into the wind in abbreviated form and ragwort forgoes flowering in its windier localities.

Felted growths of Yorkshire fog are unpalatable and seldom grazed close. In windy situations they become streaked with a pattern of ridge and furrow, resembling the 'waved heath' of the Rhossili Down heather —this creating turbulence at ground level, with pockets of local shelter for more tender plants.

Rabbits, whose numbers have ebbed and flowed since the severe Myxomatosis check in 1957, congregate on the fine short turf, leaving the dew-spangled fog to animals with less aversion to getting their feet wet. Their fluctuations are reflected in the quality of the sward, which got a general boost in the early sixties when the rabbit population was at a low ebb.

Woodland herbs may survive grazing for longer than the woodland which spawned them, and relict populations of black bryony, pignut and hemp-agrimony can sometimes be found in the open, though stinking iris, which is very much a plant of cliff grassland in the Vale of Glamorgan, is normally in woodland on Gower when not on dunes.

Rabbit predation is partially offset during a wet summer, which is more appreciated by the plants than the rabbits. In such years the autumn lady's tresses orchids which pierce the short turf at Langland and elsewhere, are at their best. Orchids generally, are not greatly affected by grazing and the dwarfness of twayblade, early purple, heath spotted, southern marsh and pyramidal orchids is more likely to be a response to wind.

In years of little grazing, lusher grass pulls the subordinates up with it and the primroses of Brandy Cove and elsewhere can be as robust as on the West Wales cliffs. Bracken, though seldom eaten, can be damaged by trampling cattle and withdrawal of cattle in the Pwll Du area in the sixties is thought to be responsible for its increase there with an under-storey of dewberry.

Most livestock was removed from the Langland cliffs around 1968 because of losses of sheep, chased by dogs, and a number of plants are flowering better and earlier as result—among these the thrift of the lower ledges, although this always flowers earlier on cliffs than on the cold, wet soils of saltmarshes.

On the narrow cliff edge strip at Rotherslade, which is normally free of grazing, tree mallow thrives. This usually survives only on innaccessible faces and stacks where it benefits greatly from sea-bird droppings. Here, beside the cliff path, it grows with Duke of Argyll's tea-plant, lords-and-ladies and tall pellitory-of-the-wall very different from the tiny plants of exposed cliffs.

44. Curlew and fulmar petrel with golden samphire and a branch of dwarfed tree mallow

Ants are widespread on the cliffs—particularly the little yellow ants, *Lasius flavus*, which throw up oval mounds of finely pulverised soil a foot or two across. Their effects on the plants, although localised to the ant-hills, can be very striking, as at Porteynon, where hemispheres of closely flowering thyme rise among the deeper purple of fine-leaved heath and pollen-peppered sea plantain—an extraordinary combination of dune, heath and saltmarsh plants to find on a cliff.

Thyme, although so common on limestone, does not need lime as such, only the warm, freely draining soil which is associated with it. Moreover, it grows the better for periodic inundations by the fine soil particles which prevent it from straggling into legginess—hence its success on sand dunes. Ants do not only supply these top dressings during their summer 'heavings', but they also actively collect the hard, oily thyme seeds for food and carry them back to the anthill, where some 'get away'.

These take a while to establish, however, and a new anthill is more likely to support annuals such as hairy bitter cress, thyme-leaved sandwort and the silver and annual hair grasses. When the ants finally stop work and the soil begins to consolidate, it is likely that the thyme of the mature, occupied dome will be swamped by grasses and others from round about.

Anthills rising above the general level of a limey soil may have all the lime washed out by rain, which percolates freely through them. Drought-resistant mosses, particularly *Polytrichum juniperinum* and *P. piliferum*, grow on the bared soil, along with lime-hating plants such as sheeps sorrel, heath bedstraw and tormentil. After the ants leave, the little islands of acid-loving plants persist until the hills sink down or are trampled into the general sward, where they will become subject to flushing by lime-charged drainage waters and gradually disappear among invading lime-lovers.

Ground water rises by capillarity through the fine air spaces of the ant-worked soil, so that streams trickling alongside will soak upwards to supply neat mounds of button-leaved marsh pennywort among the shaggier vegetation alongside. Aspect, too, is important, moisture-loving mosses like *Pleurozium schreberi* occuring mainly on the northern side of anthills, with the hardier Polytricha occupying the sunnier aspects.

19 MAMMALS, REPTILES AND BIRDS OF THE CLIFFLANDS

THE broken cliffs afford shelter in plenty for mammals, with crevices to fit the needs of all—from fox to vole. Difficult terrain confines most walkers to the paths, leaving steeper and looser parts to the surer-footed. When sea winds carry the man scent away to the fields behind, the watcher on the clifftop may surprise a fox emerging from the 'dead ground' below. The watcher on the shore can observe the antics of stoats, which descend even among the intertidal boulders where access is good, as at Overton Mere, in their search for titbits. Moles and shrews seek their invertebrate food beneath the matted grass: rabbit populations wax and wane and hares lollop over the cliff slopes.

Adders are as likely to be seen on the naked rock at Mewslade as in the cliff woodland at Nicholaston. Late March sunshine can entice them from their winter hideouts, to bask in neat diamond-patterned coils on the short turf and the writhing mating dance can be witnessed in late April. Dead ones, their sinuous passage stilled, may tempt omnivorous field mice to help the ants and sexton beetles in removing all trace. Lizards scuttle over beds of thyme and rock-rose and slow worms thread the ramifications of the screes.

The western cliffs in the Thurba, Mewslade, Tears Point sector are both more remore and more precipitous than most and only these among the mainland cliffs provide nesting sites for the sea-birds. There are no auks—these congregate on the tidal island of the Worm—but there is a steadily increasing colony of kittiwakes on tiny ledges at Devil's Truck west of Mewslade which had built up to 146 nesting pairs by 1974 and 166 by 1976. With them at this site in 1976 were 28 nesting pairs of herring gulls and there were others at Thurba Head and elsewhere along the southern cliffs. That these often feed quite locally can be appreciated if the flotsam along the shoreline is compared with the coughed-up crop pellets on the cliffs above. Thus the long pincer arms and slender breathing tubes of masked crabs (*Corystes cassivelaunus*), so common on Rhossili Sands, loom large among the rabbit bones and bivalve shells of gull pellets on the cliff behind.

About 10 pairs of cormorants have reared their gawky Mephistophelian young on Thurba Head in recent years, off duty birds resting on a sea-girt stack nearby. A count of 51 adults and 11 juveniles in 1976, however, suggests that they may be increasing. Fulmar petrels have included the

45. Herring gull off the Mumbles

Gower cliffs in their general spread southwards from the parent colony on St. Kilda but sit around for several seasons before gaining sufficient confidence to lay. They were first recorded nesting in 1957 at Lewes Castle and have been gradually consolidating their position as a breeding species ever since. 51 birds were counted in 1976, when 31 sites were occupied at Lewes Castle, Thurba Head and Yellow Top, Paviland, but not all of these would be nesting. Unfortunately some of the less considerate cliff climbers practise their skills on the fulmar cliffs and may hinder the establishment of a viable colony.

There are unconfirmed reports of swifts nesting in the cliffs. It is difficult to observe their progeny, but adults can be seen entering and leaving holes in the steeper faces. Their departure in the early autumn is compensated for by the arrival offshore of the 'sea-swallows' or terns. House martins, which are well entrenched as cliff nesters on parts of the Vale of Glamorgan coast, seem to stick to buildings on Gower and are nowhere common. Perhaps the fly swarms on which they like to feed are dissipated by the wind. Nor, apparently, do starlings use cliff holes for breeding here, as they do in Pembrokeshire.

Much the most numerous of the nesting land birds are the jackdaws, which dive in and out of slightly larger crevices, or stand, watchful, on the ledges. These have completely replaced the choughs of former years— their noisy circlings a poor substitute for the aerobatics of their more graceful relatives, performed to the accompaniment of evocative, high-pitched 'mewing'. Choughs persist no nearer now than West Wales.

A census of nesting birds on the Gower cliffs carried out from 1968 by members of the Gower Ornithological Society, has recorded around 83 jackdaw nests in a non-continuous strip along some 1,100 acres of the South Gower cliffs. Although not absolute figures, the counts provide a useful baseline for comparing the status of the various breeders and show trends of change from year to year.

Most numerous after jackdaws, at about three-quarters of their strength, are linnets, with around 67 pairs in some years on this same area. Yellow hammers maintained a fairly even population over the years at about 55 pairs. Blackbirds, with 45 pairs, are fairly generally distributed, the windshorn scrub quite sufficient for their needs. Skylarks and stone-chats tied at about 40 pairs each but both suffered badly in the frigid winter of 1962-63 and, the stonechats particularly, again after the chilly February of 1969. The latter had taken 4-5 years to recover from the earlier mortality (which was more severe on the South Gower cliffs than on the North Gower ones or Cefn Bryn). Luckily not all of Gower's breeding stonechats stay on through the winter. Those which do are likely to die in hard weather, along with first winter birds arriving from elsewhere the previous autumn, so that none may breed in the summer which follows a prolonged freeze of the 1962-63 kind. But other birds travel north to Gower after wintering in the Iberian Peninsula and these can serve to replenish the stock in the succeeding year.

Cold, however, is not the only hazard suffered by stonechats. Gorse fires can prove their undoing, particularly when these occur late in spring. Notwithstanding this danger, stonechats have a long-drawn-out breeding season and can nest late into August or even September. By this time the gorse has usually begun to sprout again and the bracken fronds have unfurled to provide song posts in lieu of the more traditional twiggy ones. The birds are not easy to miss, with their constant 'chinking' from vantage points, and they were particularly vociferous on the fire-denuded clifftop at Sevenslades in 1973, although not necessarily nesting.

Dunnocks frequent the same sort of low, brambly scrub and are next on the list, with 30 pairs in the same area censused—a few more than the meadow pipit, which is a rather more obvious bird, less given to skulking. Whitethroats were much the most numerous of the warblers, but their numbers in Gower reflected the nationwide crash experienced in 1969, following drastic losses through drought in the Sahel area of the Sahara where they winter. Recovery was rapid, however and after dropping from 21 pairs to 5 pairs, they were up to 13 pairs again by 1970. But they may not be out of the wood yet, although the drought and food shortage in the wintering areas was at least temporarily alleviated by 1975.

Rock pipits and wrens, around 17 pairs of each, are both foreshore species, foraging, mouse-like, among the boulders of the upper beach as well as in the scrubby grassland. A very small patch of scrub suffices for wrens, whilst rock pipits utilise rock crevices nearer the sea and were forced to desert a stretch of intertidal rock near Pennard which became heavily polluted with oil during the 1970 breeding season.

The drop in robins, from 15 pairs to 5 in 1969, is probably another reflection of the icy February of that year making their invertebrate food hard to come by. Song thrush numbers dropped less, from 16 pairs to 12, and it may be significant in this connection that 5 of the 12 pairs were in a single stretch at Pennard where houses and the artificial food supply from these enroach close to the cliff edge. Another artefact of use to song thrushes is the tarmac path along the cliffs East of Caswell, which is handy for cracking snail shells open.

These 14 species are the most numerous of the nesting land birds, but there are at least 28 others. Of the finches, greenfinch and goldfinch are more likely to be seen than bullfinch and chaffinch, though the last is often the most numerous of all species on farmland. Chiff chaffs are commonest of the remaining warblers, then willow warblers, with fewer blackcaps and just the odd grasshopper, sedge and garden warblers. Interesting absentees as nesters are starlings and house sparrows.

Very conspicuous because of their echoing calls are the green wood-peckers which probe energetically in the anthills, and the slate-grey cuckoos, running the gauntlet of mobbing by the small birds which they exploit. Both were censused at 6-7 breeding pairs. Magpies and carrion crows averaged 6 pairs each and these are also hard to miss, as are the ravens, with a number of established nesting sites within the census area, not all of which are occupied every year.

The clifftops are so essentially 'wheatear country' that it is hard to believe that so few nest—only 1 or 2 pairs. All have left by the last week of September. They are considerably rarer than the pied wagtails which potter on the beaches—or even the 4 tit species and missel thrush which are associated so much less with the open cliff habitat. Tawny owl and little owl breed on the cliffs, Thurba and Overton Mere being among their haunts.

Kestrels are more abundant than buzzards, about 5 pairs of which nest on trees in Gower, avoiding the cliff sites favoured elsewhere. The un-spotted young kestrels rely on the adults for much of their food when flying free in August—maintaining contact with a penetrating 'kee kee kee' call. Merlins have decreased dramatically as a nesting species in Wales and visit Gower only occasionally, mostly in autumn, winter and spring.

The peregrine which formerly bred on both the Southern and North-ern cliffs has also declined, the latest record of occupation of an ancestral eyrie being for 1955, in which year the last 3 young bred in the whole of Glamorgan flew triumphantly from the cliffs. The next attempt by these rare and noble falcons to nest in Glamorgan—in the North in 1974 —was frustrated by a gun-happy pigeon fancier!

Stock doves, with their liking for rock crevices, are commoner on the cliffs than collared doves, although the latter have increased apace around farms and gardens since their initial colonisation in 1962. Rock doves have not bred on the South Gower cliffs since 1925 and have been replaced by feral pigeons on the cliff faces. Turtle doves breed no further West than the Vale of Glamorgan, with only the odd bird to be seen during the summer months on Gower.

Wood pigeons not only breed in quite small spinneys near the coast, but congregate in flocks of several hundred during winter. No doubt some get diverted into pigeon pies, which are not a new dish on Gower. The ancient lords supplemented their larders with home-bred pigeons —in evidence of which are the columbaria of Penrice and Oxwich Castles with their deserted nesting niches. But the most famous columbarium is that of Culver Hole—a curious natural slit in the cliffs, to which entrance can be gained along sloping limestone ledges. This was walled off many centuries ago, legend has it for use by smugglers, though these would scarcely advertise their presence so blatantly. The story goes that when the coastguards got suspicious and moved their headquarters to nearby Porteynon, they were altogether too close for comfort and the cave changed to the more blameless use of supplying fresh meat to the fourteenth century inmates of Porteynon Castle. At this period a shortage of winter feed necessitated the slaughter of many cattle in autumn and succulent pigeon flesh provided a welcome break from the winter monotony of salt beef.

46. Culver Hole

Kingfishers find their way down to the sea occasionally at Mewslade. Ring ouzels—unexpected birds from the inland mountain crags—are sometimes spotted stoking up their depleted fat reserves on the short grass turf as they pass through. The black redstarts seen occasionally at Caswell, Rhossili and Llangennith may be wintering. Snow buntings have been seen on the Langland-Caswell cliffs in late October and a hoopoe in early May at Cwm Ivy. This last is a haunt of pheasants and very occasionally of corncrakes, which are seen but rarely, on autumn passage. A purple heron flew wearily over Langland Bay golf course in April 1970 and dropped exhausted into a garden—perhaps the one seen a few days earlier on Lundy Island in the Bristol Channel.

Brent geese and the ocasional whooper and bewick swans fly along the coast, as do migrant waders, and common gulls join the resident species off Pwll Du head in winter. Gannets diving offshore during the breeding season may have come a full fifty miles from the nearest nesting colony on Grassholm. Rhossili beach receives a number of storm victims during autumn gales—a time of year when the newly fledged gannets are too heavy to fly (though too buoyant to submerge for fish without the impetus afforded by a high dive) and get washed, helpless, onto lee shores.

Scoter are the commonest of the sea duck, massing in flocks of several hundred on inshore waters, and the occasional velvet scoter is spotted in winter. A red throated diver has turned up in Overton Mere, as well as among the big flocks of waterfowl off Whiteford.

20 SMALLER CREATURES OF THE CLIFFS

CLIFFS as flowery as those of Gower cannot fail to be alive with butterflies in suitable weather. Almost any of the common kinds are to seen, one species waxing as another wanes. Small tortoiseshells were out of hibernation and flying at Langland as early as late February in 1976, then disappeared from mid May to await the coming of the first brood of the year in mid June. A second hiatus through most of August is terminatated by the emergence of the second brood, which flies through September and October before tucking into some cosy crevice for the winter.

The various yellow pea flowers supply nectar for many species from early spring and thyme is a great favourite in high summer, along with the small and devil's bit scabious and so on to the heathers. The dwindling honeypots of the scree ivy supply the laggards well into autumn —and continue to victual the hoverflies, bluebottles and wasps long after butterflies have ceased to be abroad. Flying close to the ground on the windier knolls the small pearl-bordered fritillaries often sip exclusively from the blue sheep's bit flowers, ignoring all else. In lusher habitats, however, they are much less discriminating than the more methodical bees, flitting haphazardly from orchid to ragged robin and buttercup, then back to orchid, in wholly butterfly-minded fashion.

These small pearl-bordereds are the commonest of the fritillaries and emerge earlier in summer than most. They are characteristic of the western cliffs from Porteynon to Rhossili, although a feature of woodland rides and marshy commons elsewhere. The dark green fritillary has thriving colonies on the west side of Oxwich head and at Nicholaston. Fritillaries generally vary in numbers from year to year rather more than most. Both 1971 and 1974 were good years for the dark green but not for the silver-washed.

Commas are rare this far west, though gradually spreading in through South and Mid Glamorgan over the past few decades. Meadow browns and small heaths rise to their numerical zenith in late June and early July, with small tortoiseshells and large skippers almost as abundant. Other skippers are the small, the grizzled and the dingy, and gatekeepers are widespread, but ringlets are more usually found inland and in North Gower. Brown argus and holly blues are often to be seen while small blues, which are common on Whiteford burrows as well as on the cliffs, thrive wherever there is kidney vetch and storksbill as food for their caterpillars. The brown argus usually lays its eggs on rock rose but can, like the small

47. Comma butterflies on bramble

blue, manage with storksbill. Graylings begin to emerge on the cliff grazings during the first week of July and bask on sun-warmed rocks, with obliquely aligned wings. Wall browns, too, delight in such heat absorbing surfaces, including those of the walls for which they are named.

Any waning of butterflies on a national scale (weather apart) is likely to be correlated with the waning of flowers brought about by close cutting of road verges and weed eradication from farm crops and is not reflected on the Gower clifftops where there are flowers in plenty for all. Such fragile creatures can, however, be incapacitated by the prevalent high winds of the open cliffs and are most likely to be found in pockets of local shelter.

On days of sunshine and stiff breeze in late May and early June 1976 only small heaths were on the wing on the exposed cliffs East of Pennard and West of Mewslade, fluttering close to the ground in the lee of vegetation tufts, and leaving the massed flowers of rock rose and kidney vetch to the hardier bees.

The woodland leading down to Pwll Du Bay on the other hand was alive with speckled woods and all three of the common whites fluttered at the edges of the clearings. On the grassy flats at the back of the bay common blues were rising constantly to converge in pairs and execute little aerial pas de deux. Similar sized 'browns' ornamented with rims of orange discs, became indisputably brown argus and not just more female blues when they temporarily left the yellow pea flowers to indulge in bouts of mating. Wall browns sunned themselves on refractive pebbles and a high flying orange tip got swept away on a puff of wind. On the leeward cliff beyond a dingy skipper rested at the foot of an upstanding early purple orchid among billowing, wind-smoothed scrub and small coppers sampled the sweets of the packed ox-eyed daisy florets. All these except the speckled woods frequented declivities of the cliffs between Mewslade and the Worm, where small blues were also in evidence and male yellow brimstones became locked to their creamy white partners in pairing flight, after long fluttering pursuits, during which he maintained a position decorously 3-4 inches below hers.

The long, hot summer of 1976 was exceptionally good for Lepidoptera and saw an increase in commas, dark green fritillaries and marbled whites, as well as commoner species like red admirals and peacocks. Most exciting, however, was the invasion of clouded yellow butterflies at Pwll Du and the frequency with which humming bird hawk moths were seen feeding on buddleia, honeysuckle and other long-spurred flowers.

Cinnabar moths are already about by late May. Where blackthorn, hawthorn or willows abound, broods of lackey moth (*Malacasoma neustria*) caterpillars, elegantly striped in Cambridge blue, cluster on the outside of their homespun gossamer nests. The cylinder of discarded eggshells from which a family has emerged may be found girdling a nearby twig, emperor fashion. If not the commonest moth caterpillars of the cliffs, dunes and woods, lackeys are certainly the ones most likely to be spotted, The emperor moth (*Saturnia pavonia*) is one of the most spectacular where there is gorse or bramble, even at beach level in coves such as Overton Mere.

Yellow shell moths (*Euphyia bilineata*) flip among the Pwll Du bracken, whilst Mother Shipton moths (*Euclidimera oni*) and burnet companions (*Ectypa glyphica*) fraternise with the more familiar burnets and cinnabars behind Rhossili beach. Cinnabar caterpillars, with their tiger striping are unmistakable on the ragwort and groundsel plants. Black banded moths (*Xanthomista antityte*) are abundant on the cliffs, feeding on sea plantain and other cliff plants, but are of a south-westerly species, rare in most of Britain.

A typical insect of the lower cliffs is the fever fly (*Dilophus febrilis*), a hairy relative of the larger and often equally common St. Mark's fly (*Bibio marci*) . It does not cause fever and is a useful pollinator, being particularly addicted to the flowers of rock samphire.

On the debit side the maggots or larval phase sometimes parasitise plant roots, but they also feed on decaying organic matter. Males of both these flies engage in communal aerial courtship dances over the more acquiescent females crouching in the grass below.

Long-headed flies (*Aphrosulus celtiber*) descend even lower on the cliffs to rocks wetted by the tide. A dung fly (*Ceratinostoma ostiorum*) has also been recorded at these low levels, together with a shield bug (the forest bug, *Pentatome rufipes*, which is more usually found on oak or alder trees, overwintering as a nymph in crannies of the bark).

Higher up in the short grass are empid flies (*Rhamphomyia variabilis*), often frequenting the flowers of yellow Composites. Other visitors to flowers are hover flies (*Syrphus corollae*) and fruit flies (*Parascaptomyza disticha*). The blue bottle or blow-fly (*Onesia biseta*) is a new record for Glamorgan.

All the common bumble bees can be found on the cliffs, the white-tailed *Bombus lucorum* being especially partial to the nectar of bird's foot trefoil in wet weather, when the shape of the flower before the 'keel' is sprung by the bee's weight may save the sugary fluid from becoming diluted. The white-tailed cuckoo bee (*Psithyrus vestalis*) which parasitises it resembles it quite closely. Buff-tailed and orange-tailed bumble bees (*Bombus terrestris* and *B. lapidarius*) occur, along with the carder bee (*B. agrorum*). It is always amusing to watch the big orange-rumped *B. lapidarius* edging sideways into the slightly asymmetric pink trumpets of lousewort. Ants abound, and common wasps in season.

Empty snail shells are sometimes put to use before being reincorporated in the soil for return to the snail population via its food plants.

Plate 29   PWLL DU BEACH AT THE MOUTH OF BISHOPSTON PILL

120 and **121.** Pwll Du Outer Storm Beach with Bishopston Pill looping Eastwards behind   *Author*
122. Dwarf Privet bush growing among beach pebbles   *Author*
123. Hemp Nettle seedlings among sea-rounded cobbles **124.** Lackey Moth Caterpillars on communal web   *Author*

165

126

Plate 30   PLANTS OF PENNARD DUNES

125 and **126.** Isle of Man Cabbage at its most southerly British station
127 and **128.** The rare creeping Wild Asparagus
129. Storksbill flowers and rapier-like fruits   *All Author*

125

127

129

128

166

130

Plate 31   THE SOUTHERN
   STRANDLINE BEETLE:
   EURYNEBRIA COMPLANATA

130. Adults Mating   *Phil King*
131. Egg in sand   *Phil King*
132. Larva on mm graph paper   *Phil King*

131

132

167

133

134

135

Plate 32 PRIMITIVE DUNE PLANTS

133. Variegated Horsetail   **134** and **135.** Adder's Tongue Fern, with orchid and creeping willow

All Author

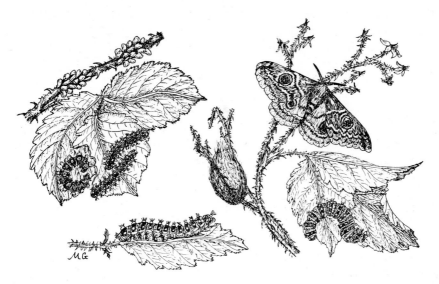

48. Emperor moth, eggs, caterpillars, cocoon and adult

A relative of the leaf-cutting bees (*Osmia aurulenta*) finds them appropriate for nesting. A shell partially filled with peat and sand is ideal for its purposes. Even after ten hours in a polythene bag, all that may be visible of the indefatigable bee is a waggling bottom as the front end busies itself with the excavation of a burrow around the coils of the *Helix* shell.

Another small creature taking refuge in the Rhossili cliff snail shells is a rather strikingly coloured little beetle (*Cteniopus sulphureus*). This is a delicate pea green, with big black eyes to guide its rapid scuttling over swards of thyme and trefoil. Similar in shape and size is *Lagria hirta*. This is a rather drab brown with hairy wing cases, black head and thorax and straight antennae of little triangles threaded neatly together.

Sheltering in living snails rather than abandoned snail shells is the carrion beetle, *Phosphuga atrata*, which does not wait, like the sexton and burying beetles, for its selected food supply to die. By biting the snail's foot it causes it to retreat into its shell and slips in with it. Further bites and a spraying with noxious fluids produced by glands at the hinder end prevent the snail from re-emerging, and there is then no let or hindrance to the beetle's consumption of its enormous meal.

The bloody-nosed beetle (*Timarcha tenebricosa*)—largest of the British leaf beetles— resembles a dor beetle until it is picked up, when the handler's fingers become stained with blood-like fluid which it spits from its jaws. Both it and the related bedstraw beetle (*Sermyla halensis*) are found mostly on lady's bedstraw. The latter is recognised by its bright blue-green body and yellow crown. Two ground beetles found on the cliff

169

grasslands are *Pterostichus madidus* and *Harpalus latus*. The brighter green tiger beetles with primrose yellow spots (*Cicindela campestris*) are often to be seen sunning themselves on cliff and dune, where the light dry soils suit the burrowing larvae. Although not long distance fliers, they whirr repeatedly into the air, only to alight again after progressing a few yards. Both larvae and adults are fiercely carnivorous.

The remains of other beetles turned up in the crop pellets of a little owl which used the old gun emplacement on Rhossili down as a perching place in 1974. Brighter beetles living alongside this wartime relic are seven spot ladybirds (*Coccinella 7-punctata*) which stuff themselves with aphids, these fattening themselves in their turn on the juices of stinging nettles. Ladybirds rose to almost plague proportions in 1975 and 1976. The nettles receive extra nutrients from the dung of sheep which shelter among the tumbled masonry and of birds which perch on eminences, giving orange lichen patches above and white guano patches below.

Beetles to be found among the heather of the upper cliffs include *Licinus depressus* and one with the somewhat contradictory name of *Longitarsus curtus*. Here too, the tiny cockroach (*Ectobius pallidus*) scoots among the woody stems with frequent bouts of flight on sunny days. This is the only one of the three British species to be found in Wales and the only one in which the females as well as the males are able to fly.

Grasshoppers are a familiar part of the summer clifflands, be these clad in grass, gorse or heather. The two common species are the field grasshopper (*Chorthippus brunneus*) and the green grasshopper (*Omocestus viridulus*). Both are very variable in colour and start up their chirping in late June, but the first stays around for a month longer than the other, into mid November. Larger, rarer and more spectacular are the great green bush crickets (*Tettigonia viridissima*) of southern and western coasts.

Bizzare members of the autumn fauna on both heather and grass are the two big daddy longlegs or harvestmen, *Phalangium opilio* and *Opilio saxatilis*. Unlike spiders, these subsist on vegetable as well as animal matter.

Hyctia, a rather uncommon jumping spider which is more often found among duneland marram, also frequents the cliffland heather. To prevent his spell as a mature adult being even briefer than it is, the male *Hyctia* has to persuade the female that he is more to her than just another meal. To do this he uses a complicated semaphore system of the wolf spider pattern, swaying alluringly from side to side with extended legs alternately raised and lowered for a full half hour before the subject of his attentions is sufficiently mesmerized to allow him close enough to mate.

Spiders whisking nimbly over the short turf are so much part of the every day scene, that they are accepted without thought, but many have fascinating life histories. There is, for instance, the crab spider *Xysticus kochi*) where the male dexterously avoids the danger of being gobbled up by his larger spouse after he has fathered her children. He embarks on his wooing by scrambling purposefully all over her, tying her down with silken threads. Then he tilts up her abdomen and slips in underneath to do the necessary. Maybe she enjoys it. Certainly she has little difficulty in breaking her bonds to move away after he has finished.

Male wolf spiders (members of the *Lycosidae*) wave hairy legs and palps in front of their espouseds in a sort of semaphore designed to convey their good intentions. After a successful wooing, mating and laying, the new mother bundles her eggs into a silken cocoon which she tucks under her 'pinny' and fastens securely to her spinnerets. The developing embryos thrive on the perpetual motion and the baby spiders clamber onto their mother's back when they emerge from the cocoon, to be carried round for another week before going on their several ways to hunt for provender on their own—leaping, wolf-like, on unsuspecting prey. Other spiders in the grassy areas are *Drassodes lapidosus*, *Trochosa terricola* and a *Tarentula*. Broad-mouthed funnels of cobweb penetrating to the grass roots are a familiar sight in the taller swards, their densely woven meshes surprisingly strong.

Common millipedes (*Cylindroiulus latestriatus*) and pill millipedes (*Glomeris marginata*) are both present, with woodlice (*Porcellio* spp.) grovelling in the surface soil. A rather odd little millipede (*Polyxenius lagurus*) can sometimes be distinguished on bare rock surfaces, although highly cryptic. Only 2-3mm. long, it is not armoured like most of its kind, but is covered with tufts of greyish bristles

A snail which finds refuge in the crannies of these same rock surfaces is the round-mouthed snail or land winkle (*Pomatias elegans*). The flat coils of the rayed or glass snails (*Retinella* or *Oxychilus*) are more likely to be found where gorse overshadows the rocks.

Even where leaching has occurred, there is sufficient lime for large numbers of snails to build their mobile homes. The white-lipped and brown lipped banded snails (*Cepaea hortensis* and *C. nemoralis*) are sometimes almost as common as on the shell sand dunes, but the little flat wrinkled snail (*Helicella caperata*) and elongated pointed snail (*Cochlicella acuta*) are less so. The grassy clifftop between Rhossili and Worm's Head has also yielded *Cochlicopa lubricella*, *Retinella nitidula*, *Clausilia bidentata* and the garlic snail (*Oxychilis alliarius*). Toothless chrysalis snails (*Collumela edentule*) frequent the damper hollows, their 'toothlessness' referring to the absence of projections within the shell mouth.

All snails appreciate moisture, which enables them to husband their slime reserves economically. In drizzly weather, when the cobwebs are jewelled with raindrops, great gatherings of common or garden snails (*Helix aspersa*) march out across the wet sandy cliffs below Rhossili Down, interrupting their browsing for long bouts of copulation, during

171

49. Common porpoises

which all else is shelved. The sluggish hordes do an amazing disappearing trick during the midday heat in dry weather, even in spots where the bloody cranesbill would appear to provide the only hiding places.

A snail survey at Foxhole Slade near Paviland has shown that the three intermingled habitats of rock face, short grass and loose scree support distinct assemblages of snails. Species finding shelter in crannies of the bare faces are little conical chrysalis snails (*Lauria cylindracea*) and flat rock snails (*Pyramidula rupestris*). Threading through the closely cropped grasses are ribbed grass snails (*Vallonia excentrica*) and wrinkled snails (*Helicella* spp.)

Quite different species inhabit the shady interstices of the scree and these are of two kinds, depending in the amount of leaf litter and other plant material incorporated among the rock fragments. Where there is much debris the snail fauna consists mainly of woodland species such as *Discus rotundatus* and the two-toothed door snail (*Clausilia bidentata*), with smooth snails (*Retinella*) quite frequent. Where plants and leaf litter are sparse *Discus* is again dominant but *Vitrea*, absent before, is abundant and *Retinella* absent. There are no open country snails at all in the scree, although the country could scarcely be more open and such species predominate only a few yards away on the bordering grassland. Here we are looking into a world much more circumscribed than ours, where a humid woodland environment is reproduced in miniature among the stones.

Green plants cannot live in the darkness of caves, where vegetable matter living or dead, is as sparse as in many screes. The resident snails must be able to subsist on animals which wander in or are washed or blown in from outside if they are to survive. 15 species of snail have been found at Foxhole and no less than 29 in Long Hole Cave at Porteynon. Typical carnivores of Long Hole Cave are the glass snail (*Oxychilus cellarius*), *Vitrea contracta* and *Discus*.

Snail shells are extremely durable and have been studied during the early seventies in relation to the fossil bone faunas of the Gower caves. Comparison of fossil snails with living ones can shed light on the climate and terrain prevailing at the time each particular deposit was laid down. Care must be taken, however, to differentiate between snails living in the rock material when it was being formed and those which crawled down to those levels later after the caves had been eroded out.

Thus at Longhole, where the small mammal remains and other signs show that the cave scree represents a cold climate of late Pleistocene age, the land snails found must have been living in a temperate climate and could not have existed earlier than post-glacial times. Three quarters of the snails found, particularly *Oxychilus* and *Vitrea*, are 'troglophiles' characteristic of caves and cellars and must have populated the rock rubbles long after the rocks themselves were formed.

Woodland snails may have been contemporary with them, but vegetable feeders could only have survived after a certain amount of plant material had sifted in for them to feed on. Species of open country may well be contaminants washed in later with soil from outside and settling among the stones of the cave floor. If the whole complex gets cemented together into a limestone breccia, it needs an expert to sort out the origins of the various components.

It seems that an interglacial fauna of animals living between the last two ice ages is coming to light in Minchin Hole Cave West of Pwll Du Head. This contains both bones and shells and is the only fossil fauna of the kind in Wales. Not only land shells are represented, but limpets, whelks and edible periwinkles, some of them associated with old beach deposits and some with the kitchen middens of early man further inland. Some of the middens were Roman, others much earlier.

The 'Red Lady of Paviland' (actually a young Cro-magnon man steeped in red ochre) was found associated with flat periwinkles and animal bones and is thought to have lived in the Upper Paleolithic. His chief claim to fame is that his is the earliest known ceremonial burial in Britain.

When he and his contemporaries occupied the caves around 16,500 BC, they looked out over a broad wooded valley where now the unruly tides of the Severn Estuary surge past daily. The wealth of fossil mammal bones in the caves is thought to indicate a population greater than the existing land could support, these ancient herbivores and carnivores having ranged widely to graze and hunt over land now submerged, and to be hunted in their turn by early man. But they did not all live simultaneously: some were animals of cold climates, some of warm climates.

Among the Pleistocene bone and ivory implements of Paviland cave were found remains of cave bear, hyena, Irish deer, wild ox, bison, woolly rhinoceros, mammoth and reindeer. Higher up, in the post-pleistocene deposits of the same cave, among pottery, coins and a polished axe, the remains were of less outlandish creatures, including brown bear, badger, fox, red deer, sheep, pig, horse and water vole.

Other Pleistocene mammals yielded by the Gower caves are lion, wild horse, soft-nosed rhinoceros, straight tusked elephant, vole, water shrew and wolf. Pleistocene animals of the Mesolithic, Neolithic and Bronze and Iron Ages and Roman Era were wolf, dog, wild cat, mountain hare rabbit, polecat, otter, marten, mole, shrew, roe deer, ox, puffin, guillemot, razorbill, gull and thrush.

Part Four

The Tidal Islands
and the Sea-shore

Sea Spider (Nymphon gracile) and masked crab

The rough rectangle of Gower, suspended from the mainland by its North-east corner, has its three extremities punctuated by tidal islands. In the South-east the lighthouse tump and its sister island off Mumbles Hill form a natural breakwater deflecting the South-westerly swells from the Swansea seafront. In the South west these same swells are cleft by the long, three-partite island of the Worm thrusting westwards from Rhossili Head. In the North-west they slide northwards around the craggy bastions of Burry Holms into the Burry Inlet. Berges Island, on the old glacial moraine projecting from the North coast, was long since swallowed up by drifting sand and merged into the spit of Whiteford Burrows, so no longer justifies the designation as an island.

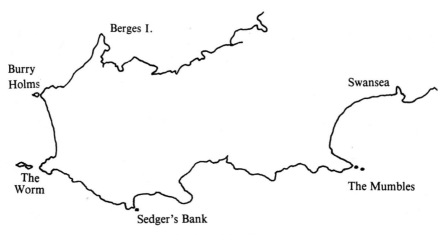

50. Map of tidal islets

21 THE MUMBLES

WHEN equinoctial spring tides rise to 31ft. or thereabouts, the Middle and Outer Mumbles are separated from the mainland by a good depth of water. As the flood recedes, wrack-covered reefs reach progressively further into the kelp beds beyond—marking the wave-scoured base of an old headland, of which they were once part. The twin, curvaceous mounds, carved by the sea and smoothed by wind and rain, can conjure up an image of matronly breasts and are thought to have derived their name from "mamelles".

An 1861 defence fort crowns the seaward extremity of the Outer Mumble—undershot by a lofty cavern and backed by soft red fescue grass. The sward leads up to the summit lighthouse, losing thickness as it gains in elevation. To windward of the tower, where sightseers from the mainland linger at low tide, it is short enough to be overtopped by thrift, bird's foot trefoil, white clover and autumnal hawkbit. To leeward it is more densely matted and only taller plants like cocksfoot, rock samphire, ribwort and thistle can compete successfully. Rock samphire was pickled and eaten in Gower at one time.

The old lighthouse, built in 1793, affords good shelter from the prevailing winds and some of the ivy shoots which penetrate the turf emerge to climb a little way up its leeward face. A few elders have grown to nearly 9 ft. behind the tower, but all appeared dead after the equinoctial autumn gales of 1974. These salt-charged blasts had shrivelled the leaves of the lowly brambles and nettles but could find no bracken or sloe on the outer isle to ravage, although these two dominate the leeward side of the middle isle. Sea beet, yellow-wort and kidney-vetch crouch immune in crevices.

The speciality of the outermost tump is the sea stock or gilliflower (*Matthiola incana*) which is well entrenched, in spite of picking of the wine-red flowers from the more accessible summit clumps. Lower plants, on both East and West, are spared to produce their long fruit pods and scatter seed, so that the velvety grey leaf rosettes can spring up to replenish the stock, even in such unpromising sites as the crumbling bases of old walls. This attractive plant is more typical of Britain's southern chalk cliffs and is known at only one other site in Glamorgan—on the Lias coast of the Vale.

Another botanical surprise among warped and cracking concrete on the outer islet is some wispy marram grass—possibly introduced with the sand from which the concrete was made. The most characteristic plant of the old ground level walltops in 1974 was the pink centaury, which germinated in profusion in the late summer among the starry yellowish *Trichostomum brachydontium* moss and shaggy, hair-tipped *Tortula muralis*. By 1975 much of this had been replaced by yellow-wort.

A count of flowering plants in 1974 gave totals of 35, 58 and 80 species on the Outer, Middle and Inner Mumbles respectively (the Inner one being the elevated tip of the adjacent headland.) This gives an approximate ratio of 5:8:11—very much what would be expected in view of the increasing exposure and isolation—the differences accentuated by the slightly smaller size of the most remote tump.

The Middle Mumble is cut off from the mainland for only 2-3 hours each side of the high tide. Sea plantain here varies from a dwarf component of short, rabbit-grazed turf to a lush plant of low crevices. Golden samphire affords a gay spectacle in August, but extends upwards from the splash zone less far than in the splashier West. In fact, it goes only half as high as the associated rock samphire, whose larger airborne fruitlets need a strong draught to carry them up the cliffs. In spite of this evident liking for sea spray, a few plants grow on leeward rocks, the related ploughman's spikenard extending down to within ten feet of them.

The belt of orange lichens is particularly well developed on some of the limestone slabs, partially obscuring the shining calcite veins. An abundance of food pellets, expectorated from the crops of gulls, gives a clue to the lichen's exuberance. The birds have a wide choice of sites from which to gather their nutrients, with a wealth of shoreline and farmland, rubbish tips and domestic effluents at their disposal, and the Middle Mumble provides a handy retreat where they can digest their spoils undisturbed for at least part of the tidal cycle.

The wealth of spring colour from thrift and squill is carried on into late summer by the harebells and small scabious. Grassland plants are mostly lime-lovers, with burnet saxifrage, perforated St. John's wort, quaking grass and the like, but there are the usual Gower anomalies. Limestone brinks are as likely to be clad with ling and bell heather as with thyme and rock rose, with the added complication of the lime-loving salad burnet pushing up among the heather!

Deeper soil on the leeward slopes is occupied by more cosmopolitan plants, though madder (*Rubia*) straggles up through the bracken, ragwort and ivy of the lower slopes, and Portland spurge edges among the gale-shorn sloe and hemp-agrimony of the leeward crest, where wind-stripped bramble shoots arch raggedly upwards.

Some of the extra species to be found on the Inner Mumble are garden escapes—red valerian, snow-in-summer and mind-your-own-business. Knotted hedge parsley, which produces twinned bur fruits among the burred heads of rough clover in seaward crevices, and yellow rattle with the knapweed and nodding thistle of the more inland sward, are genuine natives.

51. Mumbles Head

This grassland harbours busy ant populations. When the nuptial flights take place on September evenings after the flood of holidaymakers has ebbed, crowds of gulls come flocking to strut to and fro gathering up the surplus 'royalty' which is destined not to attain full queenhood. Gulls occupying the Middle Mumble at the time of the swarming— which extends along the mainland coast of Bracelet Bay and beyond— seem not to be after ants, but dozing and preening. It is evident that large numbers retire here from Swansea Bay when driven from their foraging grounds on the shore by the incoming tide.

As these tides start to flow, driving the fishermen in from the seaward reefs, gulls close in behind them, snapping up the moribund edible crabs which they collected for bait. These, after lying around all day in netting bags, with their life-giving moisture ebbing away, are unable to make good their escape when tipped out at the end of the day, and are easy prey for the opportunist gulls. (Shore crabs are more resistant to desiccation than are edible crabs, but fewer seem to be used for bait). Thoughtless crabbers, too, cause many marine creatures to die by drying when they fail to turn stones back the right way up.

More traditional fishers off the Mumbles are the common and arctic terns which linger on passage to exploit the small fry which ghost through the shadows among the kelp stalks. These elegant sea swallows course back and forth over the oarweed meadows at a height of 4-6 ft., dropping frequently among the arching fronds to grasp a shining morsel some 2 inches long. About one dive in six proves successful, the bird emerging with a silvery fish held crosswise and juggled into the head-first swallowing position even as the surplus water is flicked from the fluttering wings.

When wave action is at all severe, terns choose to fish on the leeward side of the Mumbles, flying back 'empty' towards the pier and transacting all the 'business' on the outward flight towards the point. This, of course when the wind is blowing in from the sea, because a slow watchful passage and the necessary hovering to judge diving distance can be achieved only by flying into a headwind. During apparent pauses, when the bird's

179

ground speed is nil, it is actually flying up wind at the same speed that the wind is pushing it back, and may have an air speed of 10-20 m.p.h.

Not being as well waterproofed as gulls, terns cannot rest on the sea surface, and they resort to boulders further upshore when their hunger is appeased. The occasional sandwich tern may join them in September and a black tern has been seen in August. Onshore they consort with turnstone and oyster catcher, or redshank and ringed plover from the more level beaches. The Mumbles, too, provide one of the Gower haunts of purple sandpipers—busy little foragers whose dark forms merge invisibly into the wrack-wrapped rocks.

Auks are occasionally sighted offshore, some of them oiled, and an immature razorbill strayed in from the point to watch for scraps beneath the fishermen on Mumbles Pier on 1st November 1967. Gannets fly past on their fishing trips up channel and a dark phase Arctic skua stayed around Mumbles Head for two days in April 1970.

During autumn passage the projecting row of tumps may form a peeling off point for migrants flighting across the Channel and big loose flocks of swallows may drift through during September afternoons for hours at a time on their leisurely passage South, after following the western curve of Swansea Bay. Even butterflies may use the Mumbles to help them on their cross Channel leg. 1974 was a dreary summer for butter-flies, with Vanessids less in evidence than usual, but odd individuals were winging out across the wrack-covered rocks throughout at least one September day that year. A school of dolphins was playing off the lighthouse in mid June, 1975.

22 THE WORM

The rocky causeway leading to the Worm stretches for a little more than a third of a mile and is exposed for about 5¼ hours at low water during calm weather. The tidal headland—37 acres in all and a mile long—consists of four small hills, with the highest rising to almost 150 ft. Ab-ruptly truncated cliffs at the outer end are equated with the Worm's head, the other three hillocks with the convolutions of its body. But the mythical beast may be altogether nobler and more Welsh as "Wurm" means dragon.

Of the hillocks the inner Head is much the largest (up to 200 yds. across) and is bevelled off flat, representing part of Gower's 200 ft. marine platform although lower. Middle Head and Low Neck are less lofty than the Outer and Inner Heads, and the narrow causeway immediately beyond the Inner Head is only just above high water mark.

The sea-girt peninsula represents a limb of the Worm's Head Anticline—an upfold of Carboniferous Limestone. The lower or Zaphrentis Zone of the Tournaisian geological succession is exposed only in the core of this anticline—where it is visible below high water mark on the ridge of foreshore leading out from the mainland. Next up are the Lower Caninia limestones and Caninia Oolite, which surface both on Worm's Head and further East along the coast at Mewslade. The Upper Caninia Zone limestones of the overlying Visean comprise the southern border of Worm's Head and can be be recognised at the base of the mainland cliffs as far East as Porteynon.

A cave opens out to the West on the Outer Head. This is associated with a raised beach, but the sea no longer enters. It is, in fact, 15 ft above present high water mark and difficult of access, but has been investigated and some of its contents removed to the Royal Institution in Swansea. Bones from the Pleistocene Period here include those of mammoth and rhinoceros, those from the Post-Pleistocene assemblage above include bear, badger, wolf, dog, wild cat and reindeer. Human bones and flint flakes are of uncertain age, but possibly Neolithic. An impressive booming and hissing of air and water under pressure emanates from the Blowhole on the North side of the Outer Head when the waves are pounding fiercely below.

52. Guillemots and chicks on Worm's Head

With an average of twenty gales a year—or almost as many as are experienced by exposed parts of West Wales and the Cornish Peninsula—the plants of shallow soils suffer severe drought during dry summers. And there are plenty of shallow soils, since the disastrous accidental fires of 1957, which burned for several days. These soils come in three kinds. Two are derived from the underlying limestone (though with much of the lime washed out)—a reddish soil comparable with Terra Rossa and a black Rendzina soil pocketed in hollows of the rock. The third type is a glacial drift on the southern shore of the Inner Head, derived mostly from Old Red Sandstone and more acid, with a pH of 6.3 overlying an alkaline subsoil with a pH of 8.0.

An organic sandy loam has evolved on the plateau of the Inner Head, slightly alkaline in reaction (pH 7.5). This was formerly covered by a humic topsoil, but much of this has been destroyed by fire and the wind and rain erosion which inevitably follows. There have been fires before but never one so severe as that of 1957, when plant organs formerly underground indicated a loss of a 4-10 inch layer of soil during the subsequent winter. Charred bulbs of spring squill were left perched on little pedestals which were held together by their fibrous roots and much of the denuded rock lay once more naked to the elements.

To help rectify the post-conflagration erosion, the Nature Conservancy broadcast some 80 pounds of unimproved Danish red fescue seed over about three acres in the autumn of 1958. It would have been preferable not to risk impairing the genetic purity of the native strain of fescue (*Festuca rubra* ssp. *eurubra* var. *genuina* subvar. *pruinosa*) but seed of this, perhaps not surprisingly, was unobtainable. There was no cause to worry, however.

The Danish plants established sufficiently to curb the rate of soil run-off during the winter which followed but proved finally unequal to the salty gales which lashed them. By the summer of 1959 they were yellowing and, as they died out, the native strain moved in to give a fairly full cover after a decade or so.

There was probably little genetic contamination by hybridisation because flower production was curtailed by a fungal infection on the native plants and most of the spread was vegetative. During the transitional years other volunteers helped to heal the scars—thrift and buck's-horn plantain on the shallower soils, scurvy-grass and sea beet in cracks and rank hogweed and Yorkshire fog on the deeper residues.

Two decades later the largest scars are still apparent—marked by a rank growth of hogweed, mayweed, dock, sorrel, sea campion and field bindweed.

Rabbits have access to the entire Worm but have had relatively little effect on the plants, even before the severe myxomatosis check which, providentially, was when the fire damage was being made good. Not so the sheep, which habitually graze the Inner Worm, fifty or more at a time and have brought the fescue grassland there into line with that of the mainland cliffs. Few gain access to the Middle and Outer Worm, and there the fescue persists as a thick 'mattress'; although seldom to the depth of 2ft. recorded by Professor McLean in the 1930s. The palatable sea beet and golden samphire are able to grow in the thick sward.

Such 'mattresses' are very much a feature of ungrazed stacks and islets off South West Britain, reaching a high degree of purity on Grassholm Island, 11 miles West of the Pembrokeshire mainland. It seems to represent the climatic climax vegetation of windy sea cliffs which suffer disturbance from neither man nor herbivores, but can easily be destroyed by fire or grazing. At its best, where not trampled flat by sightseers visiting the Worm at low tide, most plant competitors are choked out and seek refuge on the more open communities of the cliffs or Outer Head. Successful survivors are sea beet, sea mayweed and unusually robust spring squill, with rock spurrey, thrift and white clover where the grass is not so dense. Some of the sea campion gets affected by smut, *Ustilago violacea*, which loads the stamens with purple fungus spores in lieu of pollen. In pockets of local shelter on the Inner Head the elm-leaved bramble (*Rubus ulmifolius*) can get established, and woodland herbs such as bluebell and wild arum persist under gorse and bracken. Bloody cranesbill and a tiny red-purple eyebright (*Euphrasia curta*) are to be found on this sheltered corner.

The summit of the Outer Head and further end of the Middle Head formed a magnificent spectacle in midsummer during the late sixties, when the mallow (*Malva sylvestris*) fabricated a rose-red cap and mantle for the 'dragon'. This filled the ecological niche more often occupied by the related tree mallow and contrasted splendidly with the white of sea-bird wings and creaming surf on those delectable days when neither sea nor sky are marred with grey. The lesser plants with which it consorted were of chunky maritime form, like the luxuriant knot-grass and little soft-brome and darnel-poa grasses. Crevice flora below is brightened by golden and rock samphire and rock sea-lavender.

A botanical survey carried out on the Worm in 1910 enables us to trace some of the changes occurring during the past 65 years. Mallow in 1910 was represented by a few plants only, on the Middle Head. Its rise to dominance during the sixties was almost certainly due to destruction of the more indigenous plant cover by nesting gulls. By the middle seventies when visitor pressure had relegated the gulls to the lower cliff faces, the mallow had been largely replaced by sea campion and sea beet.

Formerly the Outer Head was almost entirely given over to thrift and sea campion, as is the outer tip of Burryholms at present, and it will be interesting to see if the thrift, too, returns. The thick mats of sea storksbill have dwindled somewhat, as have the formerly common

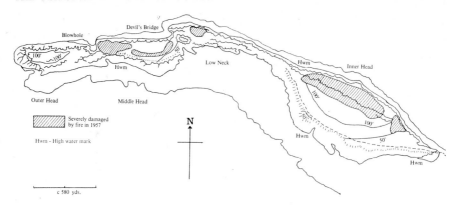

53. Map showing the extent of the 1957 fire on Worm's Head. After the Nature Conservancy Council

bluebells (which are such a feature of bird cliffs in the South Pembroke-shire Islands). Cowslips, described as common and luxuriant in 1910, are still present, as is the gorse, which was apparently as abundant then as now on the landward end of the Inner Head. Bracken is not mentioned at all in the 1910 report. Fifty-five years and several conflagrations later it has become deeply entrenched and was estimated to be covering some 1,200 square yards by the end of the sixties.

In 1910, when the Worm was described as a 'great breeding place for gulls' the inner end of the Middle Head was stated to be 'bright red to the distant observer with masses of sorrel'. Gulls started to nest on the Worm in the latter part of the nineteenth century, so it seems that the dense sorrel cover may have been a response to their presence during the first decade or so, as it was on Flatholm Island further East where gulls moved in during 1954 to produce a blaze of sorrel by the middle sixties. But on the Worm, as on Flatholm, the sorrel gave way to dock and nettle, ragwort and thistle.

These vegetation changes brought about by nesting gulls are retrogress-ive from the human standpoint, leading to rank plants which we choose to call weeds. Some of the more short-lived arable weeds, so charact-eristic of gull colonies and recorded at the beginning of the century, are still present—notably the common chickweed and knot grass, but rather less of the scarlet pimpernel, which received special mention at that time.

Distributed among these short-lived ephemerals is the aftermath of many kinds of meals. Some gulls dine from tellins and banded wedge shell fish, scattering the shiny coloured shells across the summit rocks. Some fly off to glean in the cornfields, expectorating the chaff in little golden heaps. Others gulp forth a brickmaker's mix of straw-filled pulp which, likely as not, contains viable seeds of the next plant colonisers. But the most novel pellets coughed up are from the 'sanitary squad of

184

litter pickers' and contain every sort of artefact, including screwed up paper bags moulded neatly into the tapered oval of the crop which has rejected them.

Since disturbance by holidaymakers during the post-war period of increased mobility has dissuaded the gulls from nesting on the more accessible areas where they pause for cogitation and digestion, the vegetation is slowly recovering. In due course the scars caused by both fire and gulls may heal, to be replaced—not by the indigenous fescue mattress, but by a close-trampled grassland more reminiscent of the sheep-grazed cliffs of the mainland.

Lesser black-backs, present to the extent of 30 pairs in 1925, have now dropped to 1 or 2 pairs and even these fail to nest some years. There were none in 1976. Formerly they occupied the flatter more approachable zones and were the first to succumb to visitor pressure.

Great black-backs, too, started to decline from 25 pairs in 1941 and dwindled as regular breeders to one or two pairs by the late fifties and early sixties. One pair nested successfully on the Middle Head in 1976.

Herring gulls, with their preference for cliff faces, have fared better, but are down to a fraction of their former numbers. From 1,000 pairs in 1941, they decreased to 460 pairs in 1945 as a result of egg collecting for food during the war, and the decrease continued to 1958. 1959 saw a rise from 160 pairs to 200 pairs. By 1964 they were up to 262 pairs and by 1966 to 361, which averaged a production of a little over two eggs apiece on a count in late May. 'Operation Seafarer' in 1969 recorded only 150 pairs. They are now wardened by volunteers during the breeding season but not all the disturbance is from humans, both eggs and chicks falling victim to foxes and rats on occasion. Fox predation was particularly severe in 1975. To escape all three hazards, the gulls are now domiciling themselves mostly on the steeper ledges. Over 100 nests were found in 1974, more than half on the Outer Head, the others divided between the steep northern faces of the Inner and Middle Heads, which last is white with the massed flowers of scurvy grass during April and May, a species which thrives on liberal sprinklings of guano.

Kittiwakes choose even more precipitous sites and theirs is a success story. The first 2 pairs were recorded breeding on the Worm in 1943, but the species may well have been present before as most of the nests are visible only from the sea. Fifteen years later they were up to at least 20 pairs with 100 pairs by 1965, 150 pairs by 1966 and 393 pairs by 1974 (plus another 146 pairs on the mainland nearby.) The 1976 total was 629 pairs. 166 of these were on the mainland at Devil's Truck near Mewslade. Of the 463 nests on The Worm 84 were on the Inner Head, 38 on the Middle Head and 341 on the Outer Head—320 of these last on the steep north face. These graceful birds are more pelagic than the other gulls, dipping daintily for fish in the Bristol Channel and taking no interest in the greedy gobblings of the rest on the middens of the mainland. The haunting "kitt-i-wake" call is highly nostalgic and a visit to this—Glamorgan's finest sea-bird site—in the nesting season is not easily forgotten.

The tubby forms of puffins, seemingly so much too large for the frantically whirring wings which propel them, are sometimes to be seen passing the Head or bobbing on the sea surface in summer. These birds were well established as breeders in holes of the northern cliff face as far back as 1948, but their numbers dwindled and the last authenticated breeding record for this population was in 1925. There ensued a long gap when puffins were rarely seen, but a bird was watched carrying fish to a chick in 1963 and again on 15th June 1976, while others have been seen flying into the cliffs in recent years. It seems that a new population may be setting up home again, in spite of the wide-spread diminution of puffin numbers in the South.

54. Puffins off Worm's Head

It will be splendid if the new colony succeeds, because the other two common auks still breed on the Worm and this will give us further cause for thinking of Gower as a smaller replica of South Pembrokeshire with its fine sea-bird islands at the western extremity. These others, the guillemots and razorbills, maintained their numbers on the Worm through the sixties but suffered the 1970 setback felt by other British colonies. This was shortlived, however, and guillemot numbers had risen from 70 pairs at the 1969 count to about 200 pairs in 1974. 191 birds were counted on two occasions in mid June 1976, other counts that year (all from the sea) ranging from 152 to 164. The conformation of the sheer cliffs supplies their needs more readily than those of razorbills and these, with their

186

liking for crevices rather than open ledges, are also more difficult to count. It is probable that up to 30-40 pairs were breeding about a decade ago, but by 1974 no more than 10 or a dozen pairs reared their single stubby chick to the stage where it could topple prematurely off the cliff into the sea below. Nevertheless, the 1976 counts yielded up to 85 birds at a time, so razorbills too may be increasing.

At least 6 juvenile shags were hatched successfully in crevices of the Outer Worm in 1976, when there were probably no more than 2 pairs nesting there. A few fulmar couples complete the tally of breeding sea-birds, but these find more scope on the adjacent mainland cliffs, along with cormorants. Upwards of 1,000 Manx shearwaters and 100 or so gannets can sometimes be seen fishing off the Worm in May and June. A fine but rarer sight is that of an Arctic skua harrying the resident kitti-wakes in the hope that they will give up their hard won fish to lighten the load and make good their escape. Both light and dark phases of this species appear occasionally.

Most conspicuous of the wintering sea duck are the jet black scoter, which sometimes occur in ones and twos but can build up to flocks of several hundred between September and April, when the males usually outnumber the females. They seem in no hurry to get back to their north-ern breeding grounds. Most will be going to the the Arctic to breed— Novya Zemlya, Lapland or Spitzbergen—but a few may be heading only to some Scottish loch or Irish lough. Off Gower they gorge themselves on the crowded mussel beds.

Other visitors from the North are the Arctic terns—but these do not linger through the winter. Theirs is the longest migration of any, possibly from within the Arctic circle to another brief summer within the Antarctic circle—a flight of 22,000 miles or more return! And yet they seem so fragile as they drop lightly onto passing fish under the cliffs. April and September are the months to see them as they pause in their marathon journey from Greenland or the Canadian Arctic, though some, like the common terns, with whose visits theirs may coincide, may be British born.

Whimbrel may be around in May and very occasionally a grey phal-arope turns up in winter, possibly taking refuge in a rock pool from a severe swell, but these come more often as waifs of the storm during Sept-ember gales. The odd red-throated diver has been seen here in early March.

Gower in general and the Worm in particular act as a landing and launching platform for migrants other than sea-birds. Many waders drop in to grub among the sand and rocks of the causeway with the familiar turnstones and oyster catchers. Passerines sometimes turn up in force. As many as 150 wheatears have pitched down on the Worm in September —with 100 pied wagtails and 100 rock pipits passing overhead on the same day. Some rock pipits breed here, as do meadow pipits and linnets, jackdaws and carrion crows. The odd wheatear to be seen in summer is unlikely to be doing so, and the odd summer whitethroats probably find the cover a bit sparse for setting up home.

Investigation of the red fescue mattress has yielded records of several kinds of obscure creatures living secretive lives in its cover. Larger invertebrates found on the Inner Head include a well armoured millipede (*Cylindroiulus latestriatus*), which is the only one of a group of six species to be found on the coast as well as inland. This is equally at home on arid sand dune, in moist woodland litter or on areas disturbed by man. Of the three kinds of woodlice here (*Porcellio rathkei, P. ratzeburgh* and *P. scaber*) the last is the one most likely to be found also on dunes. Pill bugs and St. Marks flies can be seen.

Round-bodied daddy-longlegs or harvestmen (*Phalangium opilio*) become very abundant in autumn. It is not difficult to spot them scurrying lightly over the grass on their octets of elegantly angled limbs because they are less nocturnal than most of their relatives. The inappropriately named female harvestman possesses a long protrusible ovipositor with which she lays her eggs in the ground—like that other daddy longlegs which reaches its population peak in autumn, the cranefly.

A spider (*Clubiona*) has been recorded, and a snail (*Vallonia*). The striped tortoise beetles (*Cassida nobilis*) have none of the metallic sheen of most of the leaf beetles. Their flattened dull green bodies with silvery blue stripe along each side merge into the grey-green of the fescue. Or they may be found hiding among the roots of some of the small members of the chickweed family.

23 BURRYHOLMS

ALTHOUGH merely tidal, the separated land mass at the mouth of the Burry Inlet bears the ancient Norse appellation of 'Holm', meaning Island. This it shares with a number of others, from Flatholm in the East to Grassholm in the West. But there is no archaeological evidence to show that the Vikings ever landed here. It seems likely that these ancient Norse terms were common parlance among medieval seafaring men and have less historical significance than they have sometimes been accorded. The reason for the plural form in this case is not clear, although a smaller southern tump is partially demarcated from the main island block by a grassy depression.

Burryholms belongs to the parish of Llangennith, thrusting out beyond the rolling sandhills to define the northern end of the splendid sweep of Rhossili Bay. Its massive beds of Carboniferous Limestone are less steeply inclined than those of the Worm, which is its opposite number at the southern end of the bay. Circling landwards from the Worm, the view from Burryholms encompasses the heights of Rhossili and Llanmadoc Downs and the Peninsula's northern cliffs to the Foxhole Tunnel and Whiteford sandspit beyond. The island's imposing seaward cliffs rise to 100 ft. in the West and were formerly crowned by a small navigational beacon, which was removed in 1966. The plateau curves smoothly downwards from this summit to 25 ft. or so at the sheltered landward end.

55. Razorbills on Worm's Head

The tidal channel which separates it for 5 hours at high water has done so at least since medieval times, the site being mentioned as an island in a charter of 1195. Nobody knows when the actual severence occurred, because the ancient promontory fort might as well have been built on a headland as an island. At present the channel is some 100 yds. wide.

The earliest known inhabitants left Mesolithic flints behind to tell of their existence. Pre-war excavation of a small Bronze Age cairn on the seaward summit yielded a bronze pin. These early clifftop dwellers lived within the 5 acre fort which occupies the western tip of the island and is separated still from the remaining $10\frac{1}{4}$ acres by a double earth rampart and broad ditch. The ecclesiastical settlement of the Middle Ages occupies the lower, landward end of the island and there are several fourteenth and fifteenth century references to hermits using the chapel of St. 'Kenyth at Holmes'. Detailed excavations of this site were carried out during 1965-7.

The taking of mussels and oysters around the shores was reported by William Worcestre about 1478 and the shell fisheries continued to operate during the seventeenth century. They operate no longer, but there is a wealth of marine life in the lee of the island. Hermit crabs scuttle among the wracks in their purloined armour of shiny pink necklace shells and spiny cockles burrow among the 'green strings' (*Enteromorpha*) in sandy-floored pools. Brittle stars lose an alarming number of arms among the wave-rolled pebbles and common starfish get stranded high on the shore after storms. Few seaweeds can survive the waves pounding on the vertical rocks of the island's seaward end. Here dog whelks and mussels cling to a wall of acorn barnacles—the scuffle marks and broken shells on nearby sands showing where some have fallen prey to oyster catchers.

Sheep grazing on the island plateau is spasmodic, and less now than formerly, when the sheep were driven in along the beach at low tide rather than risk them straying in the wilderness of dunes opposite. Some of the 'sheep lairs' where they sheltered on the southern side have been eroded back to show a soil profile of 4 inches of dark, loamy topsoil over several feet of stony reddish clay above the limestone.

Rabbits were abundant in 1973 and 1974, especially towards the seaward summit where large drifts of their rounded dung pellets had accumulated in hollows. The less conspicuous oval dung pellets of short-tailed field voles are also to be found. The turf is nibbled very short around the entrances to their tiny burrows and there is a local increase of sheep's sorrel and autumnal hawkbit—as around the larger burrows of rabbits.

A mosaic of deep green and blue-grey fescue forms the summit grassland—wind-wisped into tussocky undulations and mixed on the less turbulent end with Yorkshire fog. Lesser celandine and bulbous buttercup supply colour in spring, ragwort and carline thistle in autumn, but the main burst of flowering is in May, when the varied pinks of a multitude of thrift cushions spreads upwards from the South and West and the north-western turf is starred with the blue of spring squills.

Land winds have brought sand from the mainland dunes to cover the landward slopes and spill sideways into gullies. The accumulation in the valley separating the southern tump is clothed with almost pure marram grass. On the other sanded slopes the marram is senescent and spring squill is advancing along the intervening alleys from the North—an unusual combination. Rather more than half the total of about 60 flowering plant species are represented in the sandy areas.

Much lusher grassland with cocksfoot, curled dock and germander speedwell occurs in the broad sheltered gully between the earth ramparts delineating the promontory fort. This is the main site for salad burnet, centaury, lady's bedstraw and cleavers and contains a third of all the flora in spite of its small area.

A similar proportion occurs in seaward rock crevices where the abundant flowers of thrift and sea campion are followed by those of golden and rock samphires. Special succulents here are the pink-flowered orpine and rock spurrey. With the thrift and sea campion in the landward crevices is a wider range of species with abundant buck's horn plantain of a woollier white than usual. Others are common and Danish scurvy grass, bird's foot trefoil and thyme.

The presence of summer visitors is manifest mainly on the paths. Much used tracks are marked by sea storksbill and buck's horn plantain with common sorrel and autumnal hawkbit: less used ones by dovesfoot cranesbill, two small mouse-ear chickweeds, common and annual meadow grasses and dwarf soft brome. Lead coloured puff balls (*Bovista plumbea*) are bowled around by the wind and two fine dark green circles have been drawn by the fairy ring champignon (*Marasmius oreades*) on the nearest point of the mainland opposite.

Green tiger beetles, ants, pill bugs and wolf spiders find shelter sufficient among the short grass. White-tailed bumble bees gather floral nectar on calm spring days whilst common blue and small heath butterflies weave cautiously among the marram tufts where the danger of being blown away to sea is minimised.

Twenty pairs of herring gulls were found nesting on Burryholms at the 1959 census, but no more than half a dozen or so birds flew from the cliffs during a visit in the seventies. Smashed seashells and dis-embowelled shore crabs on the summit, however, testify to the fact that they still use the island as a dining room, particularly when unmolested at high water. Fulmars, kittiwakes and cormorants fly past and migrating terns may pitch down on the rocks among purple sandpipers and turnstones.

Skylarks, meadow pipits and jackdaws are to be seen at almost any time, wheatears and stock doves are much less regular and black redstarts are rare callers on autumn passage. But the passage to surpass all others was that of December 1967 when an estimated 65,000 fieldfares and redwings passed out over Burryholms on a single day. These

56. Worm's Head from near Rhossili

Scandinavian thrushes, with a sprinkling of song thrushes, had streamed over Swansea a day earlier, moving ahead of a severe spell of weather to less frostbound conditions on the western seaboard.

The greatest number recorded at the Lavernock migration point in East Glamorgan was then 500 a day, and congregations of redwing 2,000 strong were recorded at the beginning of the frigid winter of 1962-63, but there is nothing on record to approach this 1967 passage. An observer records that 'The sky near Burryholms was blackened by birds' and 150 per minute passed over Llangennith in that direction between 8.30 a.m. and 1.00 p.m. during that icy but stimulating morning.

Fieldfares are sociable birds, massing together in droves for these hard weather movements by day, but the flocks are more dispersed by night. Other birds were on the move at this time—among them flocks of lapwing several hundred strong, moving westwards in a more or less continuous matrix of whirring starlings. Omnivorous though they are, Burryholms had insufficient resources to serve them all, and most must have moved on down Channel to Pembrokeshire, South West England and, eventually, to Southern Ireland.

24 STORM BEACHES AT PWLL DU AND THREE CLIFFS

THE rivers of Gower are insufficiently robust to scour their mouths free of sea-borne deposits. Bishopston Pill is completely blocked for much of the year by a high bank of sea-rounded cobbles. When it breaks out as an angry flood during winter spates it does so under the eastern cliff to which this most seaward of several stony ridges has deflected it from the ford and footbridge under the western cliff.

Pennard Pill is similarly deflected by a great ridge of dune stretching from the western headland towards the conical limestone eminences of Three Cliffs opposite. Like Bishopston Pill, it crosses its valley from East to West just inland of this final meander—to round the western end of a more stable bank behind the seaward one.

The eastward deflection of the Nicholaston Pill further West is on a grander scale and the boulders of the original constricting bank reaching

Plate 33   BUTTERFLIES, BEETLES AND SPIDER OF THE COASTAL
LIMESTONES

136.	Small Pearl-bordered Fritillary	*Author*
137.	Green Hairstreak	*Author*
138.	Painted Lady	*Author*
139.	Green Tiger Beetle *(Cicindella campestris)*	*Michael Claridge*
140.	Aepopsis, a tiny beetle living on the upper seashore	*Michael Claridge*
141.	Yellow Crab Spider *(Misumena varia)* with prey, well camouflaged in a hawkbit head	*Michael Claridge*

193

142

143   144   145

Plate 34   WORM'S HEAD

142. The whole of the Outer Worm was ablaze with mallow in 1968   *Author*
143. Common mallow with knot grass on the Outer Worm in 1968   *Author*
144. North cliffs and fire-denuded slopes 11 years after the big fire   *Author*
145. Rock spurrey from spray-washed rocks   *Author*

194

north-east from Oxwich Head are exposed to view only in blowouts, where the great dunes have been cleaned out to base level by sea winds. As at Three Cliffs Bay, an extensive saltmarsh has built up behind the natural sea defences.

The Burry Pill and lesser rivers emptying northwards into the Burry Inlet are subject to a different set of longshore currents and follow tortuous courses around anastomosing sand and mud banks.

Bishopston Pill flows seaward along a line of geological weakness to where the sea has cut back along this same line to form Pwll Du Bay. The great banks of beach pebbles piled at the head of the bay are the product of not much more than a century. Most of the material which went into their making was debris from the quarry on the eastern flank of Pwll Du Head to the West—a quarry which has not been worked since 1884.

All but the most seaward rampart are composed of quite angular stones so must have built up rapidly before the pounding waves had opportunity to wear off the corners. These have for long been protected from storms by the high seaward ridge of rounded pebbles which is constantly altering its profile as minor surges pile embryo ridges at different levels along its seaward face. 'Destructional' waves comb boulders down from the crest while 'constructional' ones throw them back up again, grinding off the angles in the process. But, although changing in shape from one week to the next, there seems to be little overall loss or gain of material, so that the plant and animal succession of the main ridge complex behind the restless frontier is not subject to catastrophic undermining or burial.

The frontal ridge is lowest at the eastern end, dropping from about 20 ft. to 6 ft. above summer river level. It is here that the pill occasionally breaks through, but mostly the flow finishes in a quiet pool behind and water seeps beneath to emerge and fan out across the pebble-strewn sands of the beach below.

The seaward storm beach remains unvegetated, no scum of grey lichen smirching the polished white of the rounded limestone. Less restive pebbles of the ridge behind have become stabilised in a double terrace and are dark with crustose growths of 'ink splash' lichens and sprinkled with flowering plants.

Silverweed and red fescue spin wiry threads to help hold the stones in place and some of the host of hemp nettle, orache and curled dock seeds find suitable lodgement and spread their leaves to trap the sun's energy and transfer it to the sterile substrate for those that come after. Feathery leaf rosettes of sea mayweed throw up white-rayed flower heads and bird's foot trefoil affords dramatic patches of colour. In early summer a segment at the western end is thickly sprinkled with the pink flowers of shining cranesbill and herb Robert.

The innermost ridges have progressed further towards a stable community, with soft brome grass, wild strawberry, cleavers, mouse-ear hawkweed and ivy helping to bind the pebbles. Cushions of yellow stonecrop, pink thrift and purple thyme are pierced by spikes of viper's bugloss, wood sage and Portland spurge. Rock cress (*Arabis hirsuta*), wild carrot and the occasional green-winged orchid are to be found. Already shrubs are beginning to establish themselves—gorse and blackthorn—and the first ash seedlings, precursors of woodland-to-be, are pushing through.

Alleviation of the harshness of the habitat is swifter at river level, where rich soil is brought down from the alluvial plain to fill the barren spaces between the stones. Water persicaria produces fine displays of pink and sea sedge gives a hint of brackishness.

57. Tawny owl at Three Cliffs Bay

The pebble bank extending westwards across the mouth of the Pennard Valley at Three Cliffs Bay is much lower than that at Pwll Du and the driftlines of seaweed show that the sea sometimes tops it. But it is a gentle sea, the force of the waves broken by the parallel sandbank 'interlocking' to seaward. The surges drain readily back through the pebbles, carrying with them some of the blown sand deposit from the surface to incorporate in the rooting medium below.

The sandbank was very battered after the tidal washout which accompanied the gales of January 1974. At its basal western end the great shifting dune is now scarcely stabilised by scattered marram and sea holly and it dwindles to no more than a sea-washed sand flat with eroded mounds held by dead grass roots towards its eastern tip. But these denuded remains still relegate the river to the base of the pierced and castellated cliffs beyond.

The 'shingle' beach is double throughout, the more stable landward ridge overlain by another slightly higher one to seaward to give a groove along the crest. Where most subject to pounding by the sea at its proximal eastern end, the front and summit of the forward ridge are bare and the back clothed with the species able to advance closer to the river's edge further West.

196

Sea orache, a summer annual, descends lowest, its leaves sometimes rolled and contorted by the gall aphis *Semiaphis atriplices*. Sea beet is the most characteristic of the 40 or so species growing among the stones here. Most of these are typical of scree—rock samphire, rock sea lavender, wall pellitory and herb Robert. So many more are dune plants, however, that there must be a substantial matrix of sand sifted down among the pebbles. Sand plants growing in the absence of visible sand include sea rocket, hare's foot clover, sea holly, sea spurge and purple fleabane, with shoots of rest harrow encroaching over old camp fire sites.

A thin layer of sand is more persistent on the western tip of the hindmost ridge, allowing a wider variety of plants to grow among senescent marram shoots. These attract free-range ponies, which pay for their provender with rich dollops of dung to speed the succession on its way. There are bushes here—spring-flowering gorse, dewberry and bramble— though none more than 2 ft. high. A little yellow-horned poppy has survived into the mid seventies, along with yellow rattle and big drifts of a showy hawkweed (*Hieracium* sp.). Others are small scabious, wild basil, white gromwell, hairy violet, and cushions of thyme-leaved sandwort starred with white flowers in May.

The low scrub community is confined to the West, where shelter is afforded from the prevailing winds. To the East, opposite the river exit, the pebbles of the hinder ridge are clad with a thin skin of fescue turf made golden-olive by a felt of moss shoots (*Hypnum cupressiforme* var. *tectorum*). Thyme, bird's foot trefoil and kidney vetch are co-dominant, but all very dwarfed. Among the tiny flowers brightening the summer scene are those of knotted pearlwort, pink centaury, eyebright, lady's bedstraw and corn mint growing among trails of biting stonecrop.

A veritable sward of autumn lady's tresses orchids nestles among wispy growths of hairy brome grass in high summer. Puffballs of the lower pebbles are *Lycoperdon ericetorum*, those of better vegetated ones *Bovista nigrescens*. There is none of the classic shingle beach succession of lichens such as is seen at Gileston on the Vale of Glamorgan coast. It is, indeed, difficult to spot a lichen, in spite of the close nibbling of the sward by ponies.

25 SEDGERS BANK NATURE RESERVE

THE 86 acres of Sedgers Bank adjacent to the Glamorgan Naturalists' Trust's reserve at Porteynon was designated as a reserve in 1966. Much of it is submerged at high tide, but jagged rocks enclosing miniature lawns of sea-washed turf and smoothed deposits of sand and shingle remain exposed. These offer precarious nesting sites to a few of the birds which feed over the mosaic of rock pools and sand flats when the tide ebbs.

Bird numbers swell in winter, when curlew, redshank and greenshank are to be seen. The patterned black and white of the ringed plovers merge into the dappled background as those of the oyster catcher never do. Tiny sanderlings sprint over the sands on twinkling legs among only slightly more sedate dunlin, and purple sandpipers share the titbits of the kelp beds with turnstones. Common gulls come in the colder months to join the residents among the rich pickings of the driftlines.

Sedgers Bank is all that remains of a sand bar which once went right across the front (as the sand bar at Oxwich still does), enclosing a non-saline marsh behind. There is freshwater peat full of recognisable remains of reed stems only a foot below the surface of the beach sand behind the curve of the bank—the misidentification of reeds as sedge possibly accounting for the name.

The finding of an Iron Age smelting hearth under the beach suggests that the break through by the sea occurred during the Iron Age. Local legend has it, however, that the encroachment was much later, during the somewhat disastrous reign of King Stephen in the Middle Ages.

During that period, Porteynon prospered as a busy little port where coastal and cross channel boats plied their wares of coal, agricultural lime and building materials. Only a quarter of a century ago small craft moored alongside a jetty under the point by the old lifeboat station (now a youth hostel), but the lifeboat base itself was abandoned after 1916 when the boat was twice overturned and 3 of the crew lost. 45 lives were saved, however, in 20 years by the gallant little craft before she was superseded by more aristocratic ones plying from Mumbles and Tenby.

Not all the locals were as generously disposed to seafarers and 'wrecking' was indulged in on the South Gower cliffs as assiduously as in any of Britain's rugged West. Bobbing lights hung from cows' horns, as though from wave-tossed boats, enticed unwary mariners near to treacherous rocks and 25 ships laden with a variety of merchandise are known to have

58. Ringed plover and kidney vetch

foundered between Porteynon and Rhossili after 1865, with heavy loss of life. Now the red-painted Helwich lightship and bell buoy closer to the shore warn mariners to stay clear.

The residual reef of Sedgers Bank was protected from the sea by a fence of caulked timbers, and it was when this was breached in the early part of the century that the present phase of erosion started. Up to this time it must have formed a considerable hazard in itself to boats entering the little harbour, consisting as it does of ridges of harder rock which are taking longer than most to get planed down to the general level of the wave-cut platform stretching westwards to Rhossili. The intervening gullies are floored by boulders and crushed mussel shells, the 'foreign' stones having arrived as ballast in ships returning empty from ferrying out the local limestone.

The largest of the tidal islets is occupied by a shingle deposit rather different from the elongated spits at Pwll Du and Three Cliffs. Here sea-rounded cobbles have been dumped on the least craggy of the excrescencies, and the spaces between filled with bluish shingle supplied almost entirely by defunct mussels.

Formerly there was a well developed sand dune here, but practically all traces of sand had gone by the tempestuous summer of 1974. Nevertheless a few sand plants have outlived the sand which gave them their first foothold. Wiry rhizomes of sand sedge permeate the shingle and straggling runners of sea bindweed help to hold the surface firm. Others are rest harrow and sea spurge in the thin skin of turf and low thickets of dewberry anchored among boulders.

199

Golden samphire, although a pebble plant on Chesil Beach in Dorset and most important of the low crevice plants here, cuts out as soon as the solid rock becomes overlain by loose stones. Sea sandwort, on the other hand, is confined to the shingle, not venturing over the outcropping rocks. With it are the usual pebble species of beet, mayweed and dock. Coltsfoot and perennial sow thistle are restricted to pebbly sites; while field bindweed scrambles up through the 'summit' cairn.

Where most fine shingle has collected, a continuous turf of red fescue and white clover is pierced by odd tufts of sea couch and sea pink. To landward much of the fescue is replaced by perennial ryegrass, relic from a more stable phase, with field daisy and yarrow appearing in the sward. Lady's bedstraw, cleavers and dovesfoot have encroached over an old fireplace.

There are ants here as well as snails and woodlice, and it comes as something of a surprise to be able to see green woodpeckers feeding so far beyond the general high water mark. Rock pipits also forage on the scatter of islets and cormorants sometimes spread their wings to dry on the outermost. These sea-washed rocks are favoured gull haunts and are littered with crop pellets and scraps of rabbit, crab and mussel shell from past meals.

Some of the outcrops bear little more than a lichen flora, the yellow-orange of *Xanthoria* and deeper orange of *Caloplaca* grading down through a dark film of *Verrucaria* to a bristly sward of black *Lichina* which is submerged at high water. Saltmarsh sea-lavender mingles with rock sea-lavender and saltmarsh sea purslane (*Halimione*) grows as a crevice plant on vertical faces! Even more remarkable are the 7 inch high 'mophead' clumps of sea plantain, an anomaly seldom seen. Only the central flower spikes are normal, others grading outwards through 'bottle brushes' to 'mopheads', in which each mature seed capsule is nestled into the base of a foliage leaf about an inch long, but terminal flowers are sterile. The outermost stems splaying downwards have their succulent bracts uptilted, as all twist towards the light.

The spit reaching out toward Sedger's Bank from the mainland is a favourite basking place for adders when spring sunshine warms the rock surfaces, and there is a hybrid swarm of sea couch and common couch at its tip. Seaweeds and shells torn from their moorings infiltrate into a strandline vegetation with tree mallow and black mustard and harbour innumerable kelp flies and sandhoppers. Generally, however, the growth of seaweed is curtailed by the pounding waves, leaving acorn barnacles to reign in their stead.

In the absence of thick beds of wrack, a 1-inch-thick sward of pepper dulse (*Laurencia pinnatifida*) covers much of the mid tide zone, interrupted in parts by spreading mussel beds. Softly crisped sea lettuce (*Ulva lactuca*) and similar-textured laver (*Porphyra umbilicalis*) grow on top if it, some of the latter being taken to Swansea and Llanelli markets. The gelatinous brown mass offered for sale as laverbread looks distinctly unappetising, but can be quite palatable when rolled in oatmeal and fried with the breakfast bacon.

Insinuated into the pepper dulse sward are purple-red patches of carragheen or Irish 'moss' (*Gigartina stellata*), a delicacy prized by other Celts in Scotland and Ireland but not usually by the Welsh. *Chondrus crispus*, which goes by the same vernacular name, fills some of the midshore pools on Sedger's Bank. With it are the flat, forked, olive-brown fronds of *Dictyota dichotoma*, not a common species on Gower, and the finer red ones of *Ceramium rubrum*, its cross banding and forcipate tips just visible to the naked eye. Single green threads of *Chaetomorpha aurea* float out from the pool walls, with coarser green tufts of *Cladophora rupestris* on the rocks above.

The paucity of wrack sporelings in the pools can probably be blamed on the voracious limpets. This goes for other algae too, and some of the upper rock pools show nice 'limpet island floras', in which all the palatable plants such as *Enteromorpha* grow on the shells of the limpets themselves. Only here are they safe, because limpets, although scouring the rock surfaces free of plantlets with their audibly rasping 'tongues', do not graze over each others backs. This is not due to any highly motivated code of conduct between limpets, just that they can usually prevent another from climbing aboard. There is a fuller seaweed cover in the downshore zone of saw wrack, where limpets are fewer.

59. Wrens and wild privet

201

The Bristol Channel oyster beds have been famous since Roman times and there was once a thriving trade in these shellfish centred around Sedger's Bank. In 1674 the Oystermouth oysters of East Gower were described as the best in Britain: the Porteynon oyster fishery flourished later, in the eighteenth and nineteenth centuries. It terminated in 1870 but the lines of poles which guided the boats in remained extant until the 1960s.

Oysters (*Ostrea edulis*) were collected mostly from the Bantum Oyster Bank—in dredges towed behind the fishing boats on steel hawsers—and brought into the shallows of Sedger's Bank for storage. Still to be seen at ebb tide are the low walls of pitched stones which bounded the 'perches pools' where the catch was kept alive and fresh until needed and the under-sized ones left to fatten up. Oysters were fished from September to March, many of the fishermen working in the local quarries during the summer. When the fishery was at its height the fishermen's families ate oysters in breadcrumbs, oysters in omelettes, oysters fried with bacon and oysters stuffed into a slit in a thick steak and fried. Only the odd oyster shell now remains to tell of this past activity, these often riddled with holes made by the boring sponge, *Clione cellata*.

Mussels (*Mytilus edulis*) are now the commonest molluscs on Sedger's Bank, living crowded together downshore but more sparsely upshore, either in little colonies occupying solution pools of the limestone or singly and three quarters buried in the shingle of crevices. Dog whelks (*Nucella lapillus*) prey upon them, the mussel pigment said to have the effect of producing a dark humbug striping in their shells. (In localities such as The Mumbles, where the dog whelks feed more exclusively on acorn barnacles, their shells are white or daffodil yellow). Even more interesting is the shell shape, Bristol Channel dog whelks having longer, narrower shells than most.

Common whelks (*Buccinum undatum*) live further downshore where they are not exposed by the falling tide, and are evident only as the much larger white shells which get washed up. This is the species which produces the lightweight egg masses half way between miniature bath sponges and fossilised frogspawn, which are so often to be seen in the flotsam and jetsam. Dog whelks attach clusters of flask-shaped egg cases firmly to the intertidal rocks, these simulating oversized butterfly eggs.

The splashiness of the reef and gully system of this tidal nature reserve is shown by the height to which the edible periwinkles (*Littorina littorea*) ascend. Crowded colonies occur where water gets trapped in shallow gutter-shaped pools lying along the furrows of the knife-edged ridges; water which gets very warm and stale in summer. The only grazing available is on the orange lichens, which get a thorough soaking at high water from waves surging up the adjacent gullies.

The intermingling of rock, shingle and sand ensures a rich mollusc fauna, with sting winkles or dwarf triton shells (*Ocinebra erinacea*) and purple top shells (*Gibbula umbilicalis*) among the sea snails or univales. Bivalves are legion, from big, dull-surfaced otter shells (*Lutraria lutraria*) through rough-textured carpet shells (*Venerupis pullastra*) to tiny, gleaming nut clams (*Nucula nucleus*). Two with radiating colour bands on the shells are the triangular rayed trough shell (*Mactra corallina*) and the concentrically-ridged striped Venus (*Venus striatula*).

Familiar beadlet anemones (*Actinia equina*) abound—dark red jelly blobs when left exposed at the ebb, but 'flowering' to expose the bright blue 'beads' of the stinging cells or nematocysts when the water returns. Another anemone, which is less ready to withdraw its tentacles, is the mauvish-fawn *Cereus pedunculatus*, which lives half buried in the shell-shingle, with flakes of blue mother-of-pearl clinging to its sticky surface.

Bright green bristle worms up to 14 inches long (*Eulalia viridis*) squirm over barnacle-covered rocks when disturbed, the elegant sinuations of the body aided by the 'rowing' of multitudinous appendages. Spiral jellied egg-ribbons are produced by one of Britain's largest Nudibranchs, the grey sea slug (*Aeolidia papillosa*), which can exceed a length of 3 inches. Elusively transparent spheres swimming in quiet gullies are sea gooseberries (*Pleurobrachia pileus*). Cross-banded brown shrimps darting among the little fish of the rock pools are *Crangon vulgaris*. There is much more—guaranteed to keep fossickers happy for hours.

Beetles and bugs are essentially creatures of the land, but every now and again some aberrant species finds a refuge in the sea. *Aepopsis robinii* is a tiny carnivorous beetle of the shoreline which has not been found in Glamorgan outside Gower. This lives among rock crevices and seaweed where it is covered by every tide, but it survives by storing air with the necessary oyxgen in special air sacs within the body.

The rare intertidal bug (*Aepophilus bonnairei*, solves the breathing problem by trapping a film of air among complicated sculpturings, hairs and bristles developed on parts of its surface. An electron microscope is needed to distinguish these fine appendages, an ordinary microscope showing only the film of air. The significance of these structures, though so minute, is evident in that only where they occur is air retained.

SEDGERS Bank is representative of the more exposed shores of Gower, where wave action, fierce though it is on occasion, is not sufficiently sustained for the growth of large weeds such as tang (*Alaria esculenta*), which thrive in the turbulence off West Dyfed. Nor is thongweed (*Himanthalea elongata*) with its basal 'rubberised dummy' often found except as driftweed thrown up on the South-western cliffs.

The causeway leading to Worm's Head differs somewhat in the parts which are influenced by strong tidal currents although protected from the full force of the waves. Here it is that mussels abound, filtering a living from these same currents and themselves providing a living for the predatory dog whelks. Egg wrack, usually a plant of sheltered shores, can live at the top of the reef because the impact of the waves is lessened by the long run in over the shallows. Gullying gives a series of elongated pools which are often quite deep and contain various fish, shrimps and anemones among the attractive brown podweed *Halidrys siliquosa*. Big whelk shells washed in from deeper waters get appropriated as homes by well-grown hermit crabs.

A speciality of dry crevices on the causeway is a South westerly Isopod, *Sphaeroma serratum*, which is like the commoner, more robustly built sea slater (*Ligea oceanica*), but occurs further downshore. Also from the South and suffering severely from exposure during frigid winters is another Isopod, *Dynamene bidentata*. It lives in the empty shell wigwams of the big southern acorn barnacles, *Balanus perforatus*, and within these the male may preside over a harem of up to a dozen females. Animals best

60. Lichens and periwinkles. From left to right: *Xanthoria parietina*, rough winkle, *Lecanora atra*, small winkle and *Ramalina siliquosa*

able to escape frost are those which can migrate into deeper water before ice crusts begin to form in the shallows—like earthworms delving deeper into air-chilled soils. Species of the nearly related *Idotea* find a living among heaps of cast weed.

Much of the great sweep of intertidal rocks South of the Low Neck is covered by pepper dulse (*Laurentia*) with the deep pink of *Corallina* and red-brown of *Dumontia* in pools. Some fine potholes occur in the West, often with a red velvet covering of *Rhodochorton rotthii* on both 'pestel' and 'mortar' and a shaggy fringe of *Lichina pygmaea*, an upstanding black lichen, above. Peering down through a rock arch atop the vertical north-west cliffs at low water a rich purple carpet of carragheen (*Gigartina*) can be seen spread beneath the swaying fronds of kelp. Some 70 different molluscs were found on the Worm's Head causeway during visits by experts in May 1974 and September 1975, these ranging from the so-called sea slug or bubble shell (the pink *Actaeon tornatalis*) to the common cuttlefish (*Sepia officinalis*) and including approximately 40 bivalves and nearly 30 univalves.

The most sheltered plant and animal communities of intertidal rocks outside the Burry Inlet are probably those in the lee of Snaple Point leading into Langland Bay and to leeward of the Tutt Hill coastguard station west of Bracelet Bay, where off-shore sandbanks break the force of the waves.

Mumbles Point provides an admirable contrast of rough water and calm water species growing in close juxtaposition on opposite sides of the islets —indicating the importance of aspect in relation to wave action. South facing shores are exposed to the full swell; north facing ones to the gentler seas which bring the sand and mud to form the Swansea Bay flats.

Most of the wracks aspiring to grow on the upper and middle shores of the Mumbles' wave-lashed South are torn away, leaving the field clear for acorn barnacles (*Chthamalus stellatus*) upshore and *Balanus balanoides* downshore. Such seaweed spores and fertilised eggs which might have found a footing on the rocks are engulfed by the filter feeding mechanism of the barnacles, along with other trivia from the plankton.

B. balanoides is near the southern limit of its range on Gower, breeding in winter and releasing its larvae to feed on the spring crop of diatoms. These are inhibited, however, by the amount of silt surging up and down the Bristol Channel with the exceptionally big tides, cutting down light penetration. Hence the barnacles do not do too well. The relative new-comer from Australian seas, *Elminius modestus*, on the other hand, is doing splendidly, especially in the siltier parts. Although it only arrived on Gower shores around 1950, it is now possibly the most abundant of all the barnacles.

Downshore, below the average level of break, where wave action is buffered, is an abundance of saw wrack (*Fucus serratus*) which grows only in the deeper water, intermittently draped with reddish laver and the common 'greens', like slivers of shredded polythene.

Upshore pools are lined with crusty pink sprays of coral weed (*Corallina officinalis*) and soft maroon, spanner-tipped *Ceramium rubrum*. Some pools are so small as to hold little more than a mugful of water and in these the beadlet anemones tend to close up during the ebb when no fresh food is to be had, as do those exposed to the air.

Moving around on the surface film of these high pools are rafts of tiny animals, *Lipura maritima* with the six legs which label them as insects. Twelve or twenty individuals having the bluish bloom of a ripe sloe cluster together. Marine insects are rare; the only other one commonly likely to turn up being a bristle tail, although there is no shortage of two-winged flies able and willing to lay their eggs in the rotting seaweed.

Lipura is segmented and wingless, like a tiny ladybird larva, and has two flexible antennae which waggle vigorously as it walks. Having evolved as land animals, insects are geared to breathing atmospheric oxygen, and this can present problems in as splashy a habitat as this. But these bluish specks of floating 'dust' have solved them. When the tide threatens to overwhelm them, their body hairs trap a protective bubble of air which can last them for as much as five days if they get carried under in the backwash and held down by a temperature layer. Even then the spiracles or air tubes do not get waterlogged because their openings are so small that sea water is prevented from entering by its surface tension.

Downshore pools contain a wider range of animals, including blennies and gobies and the fry of more pelagic fish including elvers. The coral weed and *Ceramium* are larger and darker and are joined by other red algae, such as *Furcellaria fastigiata* with branched hold-fasts, the similar *Polyides rotundus* with disc holdfasts and the more diffusely branched *Gracilaria confervoides* from which agar agar gel may be manufactured.

Most red algae avoid the brighter light and drying air of the upper shore and many are never exposed by the falling tide. The murkiness of the Channel waters puts downshore ones at a disadvantage, however, and a number of 'reds' cannot survive. One of the least demanding, and hence the commonest, is dulse (*Rhodymenia palmata*). Ones usually found only as severed fronds flung by the waves into crevices include the delicate leaf-shaped *Delesseria sanguinea* and *Phycodrys rubens*, narrower fronded *Membranoptera alata* and, most frequently of all, the sturdier cockscomb weed, *Plocamium coccineum*, with its ultimate branches toothed on one side like combs.

If the whole plant comes ashore it is usually the rock which has given way, not the holdfast, so firmly does this adhere. If the frond breaks new ones will sprout from the truncated stalk. Sometimes sea snails nibbling at the base will weaken them. The debris decays and is recycled into the system, enriching both sand and inshore waters.

The wave-cut platform revealed by very low equinoctial spring tides thrusts far beyond the Mumbles lighthouse and is riven by gullies which run shorewards and deepen as they go. In some of the rifts pebbles churn around, preventing the growth of plants and animals on their sides. Others are coated with algae, sponges and anemones. The greyish-white breadcrumb sponge (*Halichondria panicea*) occurs with the encrusting orange *Myxilla incrustans*, whilst elongated purse sponges (*Grantia compressa*) sprout among protecting weed bases.

Moss animals or Bryozoons clothe some of the knobbly channelled fronds of *Gigartina*, which, along with *Chondrus*, is the Irish moss—source of jelly puddings and cottage medicines along the Celtic fringe. These sea mats are of two kinds. The greyish *Flustrella hispida* wraps itself in little cylinders around the frond bases, whilst *Membranipora membranacea* spreads its white paving of neat rectangles over the branch surfaces, as over the larger ones of wrack and kelp.

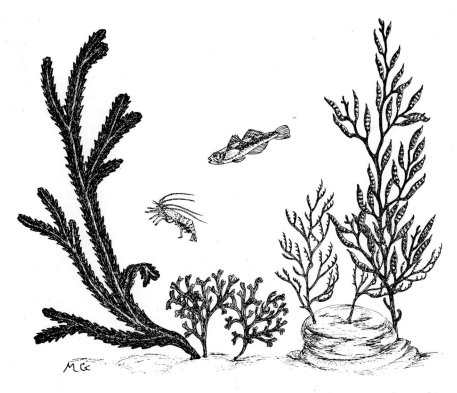

61. Seaweed, prawn and blenny. Algae from left to right: Saw wrack (*Fucus serratus*), carragheen (*Chondrus crispus*), cockscomb weed (*Plocamium coccineum*) and podweed (*Halidrys siliquosa*).

The 'Irish moss' with its burden of 'moss animals' occupies some 75% of the rock surface in summer—beneath the lower wrack and upper kelp; less palatable pepper dulse some 20% of the rest. Scattered over such as is left are crimson tufts of *Lomentaria articulata*, its shining fronds articulated into strings of sausage-shaped segments, also darker red tassels of *Polysiphonia*, dark green ones of *Cladophora* and shaggy brown ones of *Cladostephus*.

Seaweed communities, like woodland ones, are several-layered, and the ground storey here consist of a cement-like crust of pink *Lithothamnia* —red algae which incorporate into their substance quantities of lime extracted from the sea. Shattered fragments after death form something closely akin to a coral sand. Where the saw wrack gives way downshore to the kelps, tangles or oarweeds, the topmost canopy sways 6-8 ft. above the rock surface when the tide is in.

The uppermost oarweed is *Laminaria digitata*, named for the pliable fingers or digits splaying from the top of the smooth, oval-sectioned stalk. Left draped across the rocks as the tide falls, its size makes it very vulnerable to water loss. The part of the day in which the lowest tides of the fortnightly cycle occur differs in different localities. On Gower it is between midday and two o'clock, so drying out can be a real hazard, particularly if an offshore wind holds the water back.

The fingered oarweed feeds an abundance of blue-rayed limpets (*Patina pellucida*) which have the most delightful colouring of any. The translucent oval shells nestle into little depressions of their own making and bear three longitudinal lines of irridescent turquoise which fades with age, when the limpets move down from the broad shiny fronds to the rubbery branches of the holdfasts. This delicate shellfish is one of the few organisms able to hold onto this shiny host.

The next of the kelps to appear downshore, *Laminaria hyperborea*, is much more accommodating. It has rough-textured stalks, round in section instead of oval, and provides support for veritable curtains of softly undulating red algae, which in their turn give cover to innumerable animals.

Only the uppermost of this kelp is completely exposed at low spring tides. Most of it elbows out of the troughs to show some 18 inches (40-50 cm.) of arched stalk and sagging frond before being engulfed by each successive wave. Life beneath it is much richer than in the chancier conditions upshore and includes the much prized blue lobsters (*Homarus vulgaris*) and red crabs (*Cancer pagurus*), the first the rarer and usually to be located only off the end of Mumbles Point. The crabs are the edible variety, with bodies broader than long, and can live only downshore where they seek the dampness under overhanging ledges. Shore crabs (*Carcinus maenus*) are much more tolerant of desiccation and live upshore where they may lose 25% of their water content without taking undue harm.

Crab catchers follow each other round on summer weekends poking under ledges with stout wire hooks mounted on short poles. As a result both lobsters and edible crabs become quite scarce until the stocks have had a chance to replenish in spring. Nor is the threat only from those who eat large edible crabs, but from those who collect small crabs to bait their lines for sea bass (*Morone labrax*) and from those who leave few stones unturned. Hairy broad-clawed porcelain crabs (*Porcellana platycheles*) are among the many creatures which may die if disturbed stones are not replaced the right way up.

The best bass fishing at Mumbles is along the northern side of the outermost point, because the fish disport themselves more readily over sand and weed than over rock. Equinoctial springs of 16th September 1974 yielded at least one monster tipping the scales at 8 lbs., but most are a lot smaller.

There is a good range of fish available to fishermen here, one of the most commonly caught being the lesser spotted dogfish (*Scyliorhinus canicula*), a member of the shark family. Others are mackerel (*Scomber scombrus*), which are around mostly in August and September, whiting, (*Merlangius merlangius*), mainly in late autumn and winter, thick-lipped mullet (*Crenimugil labrosus*), conger eel (*Conger conger*) and the four flatfish, lemon sole (*Solea solea*), plaice (*Pleuronectes platessa*), dab (*Limanda limanda*) and flounder (*Platichthys flesus*), these last on the sandier northern side of the point.

Seventy-seven species of fish have been recorded on and around the Gower shore, these ranging in calibre from the rarely seen mako shark (*Isurus oxyrinchus*) and porbeagle shark (*Lamna nasus*) to the little sand eels beloved by terns (*Ammodytes tobianus* and *Hyperoplus lanceolatus*). One of the ones most likely to be seen by beachcombers is the common blenny or shanny (*Blennius pholis*) which can live in pools high upshore and can survive for several hours at low water in damp weedy crevices, although more plentiful downshore. It feeds on barnacles, crabs, shellfish, sea firs, sea mats and other small beasts as well as seaweeds. Montagu's blenny (*Coryphoblennius galerita*) is rarer on Gower and is confined to South-west Britain.

Gobies are the other shore fish most often found, rock gobies (*Gobius paganellus*) on rocky coasts, sand and common gobies (*G. minutus* and *G. microps*) on the muddy sands East and North of the point. As with the sticklebacks of fresh water, it is the male's job to guard the eggs after the female has laid them. Male pipefish are even more zealous about this task, carrying the eggs around in a special brood pouch like their more comma-shaped cousins the sea-horses. The great and common pipefish (*Syngnathus acus* and *S. rostellatus*) live among weed on sandy shores, the latter having been regarded as non-British until quite recently. Worm pipefish (*Nerophis lumbriciformis*) live in rockier habitats, but all have a narrow tubular snout which restricts their choice of food. Prey is of the smallest—mostly larval forms of Crustaceans—which are stalked through labyrinthine forests of weed, but also larval fish in the brief period before these grow too large to swallow. Garfish (*Belone belone*) are similar in shape, but have more of the fish and less of the worm about them, including well developed jaws and tail fin.

Other coast-hugging fish skulking in the shelter of Gower's big oarweeds include five-bearded rocklings (*Ciliata mustela*) with barbels and tentacles, sufficiently sensitive to detect the tickle of passing food, draped about their snouts. But even lethargic rocklings sometimes stir themselves and emulate gobies by becoming sprinters in order to pounce on more elusive prey. Both species consume more Crustaceans than anything else and both are capable of levering barnacles off the rocks, although less well equipped with muscular heads and strong teeth than is the barnacle-browsing blenny. Gobies develop a liking for crabs and shrimps as they wax older but rocklings remain faithful to the food of their infancy.

Long-spined sea scorpions (*Taurulus bubalis*) and butterfish (*Pholis gunnellus*) also occur along low water mark, together with pout (*Trisopterus luscus*) of the cod family. The fry of ocean-going mackerel too, mass in quiet shallows, but gales tend to break up the shoals and make them more difficult to locate.

The water is often quite opaque at Mumbles, with fine sand held in suspension, though rock pools tend to be murky everywhere in stormy weather when the beaches get churned up. (The depth of sand disturbance, though affected by the slope of the beach, is most directly related to wave height at the point of break, sand being stirred to a depth of a little less than ½ inch for every 12 inches that the wave towers above it.)

The two oarweeds, together with a sprinkling of a third, the sugar weed (*Laminaria saccharina*), fringe only the outermost Mumble on the leeward side: no doubt because the terrain becomes more gravelly and the boulders smaller towards the pier. So large a seaweed offers considerable resistance to wave action and would get thrown around if growing on too small a

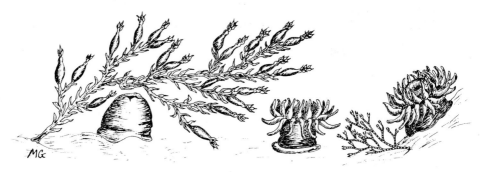

62. Peacock weed (*Cystoseira tamariscifolia*), beadlet anemones and *Ceramium rubrum*.

210

146

147

148

149

150

151

Plate 35   SEASHORE LIFE

146. Red Dulse growing on brown Kelp off the Mumbles — *Author*

147. Mumbles seashells: cowrie, whelk, periwinkle, grey top, netted carpet, cockle, scallop, limpet, sand mason worm tube etc. — *Author*

148. Mermaid's glove sponge, Fall Bay — *Author*

149. Tope, a small shark caught off Gower shores — *Author*

150. Goose barnacles on timber drifted in under Lewes Castle cliffs — *Author*

151. Llangennith beach animals: heart urchins, masked crabs, shore crab, necklace shell and egg ribbons, prickly cockle, banded wedge shell and dogfish egg case — *Author*

211

Plate 36 VARIED COASTLINE AT THREE CLIFFS BAY

152. Nearly vertical carboniferous limestone strata at Three Cliffs Bay   *Author*
153. Pebble beach to landward of sand bar at Three Cliffs Bay   *Author*
154. North Wood on the East-facing side of the sand-filled mouth of Pennard Pill   *Author*
155. Pennard Pill meanders seaward through the saltmarsh at Three Cliffs Bay   *Author*

stone. The saw wrack, which is that much smaller, extends further round into Swansea Bay, but is confined to the bigger boulders. Upshore the problem of finding a secure toehold is less acute because the weeds need to be smaller in order to avoid excessive drying out. Keel worms (*Pomatoceros triqueter*) survive within their limey tubes on quite small pebbles, without getting crushed by rolling stones.

The carpet of carragheen and pepper dulse beneath the larger browns is but a parody of its former self on this quieter shore, and half engulfed by a film of sand cemented to the rocks. Generally, however, there are more species here.

A puckered orange-red sponge in the deeper parts of the outer strait is *Hymeniacidon perleve*, but the irregularly lobed spongy masses with it are not always sponges. Some are soft corals or 'dead men's fingers' (*Alcyonium digitatum*) others are sea mats (*Alcyonidium*). Hydroids or 'sea firs' come in many patterns, including the frondose ones which are dyed green and sold for interior decoration as 'evergreen ferns'. Few who buy them realise that they are actually animals. Hydroids such as these supply much of the food of the leggy sea spiders or Pycnogonids.

After a brief contemplation of a sea spider's body girth, it will come as no surprise to learn that a branch of the gut passes into each and every leg and often into other appendages as well. As with the many-armed, small-bodied brittle star, evolution has had to work out alternative accommodation for the vital parts (see sketch on page 175).

The gonads are similarly branched and eggs mature only in the legs of the female—from whence they are released to be picked up by the male and stuck firmly on to special ovigerous legs adapted to this end. As they develop the infant sea spiders let go their hold on Papa and attach themselves instead to some more profitable source of food. *Nymphon gracile*, which is the common upshore species on the Mumbles except in December and January, has little appendages to hold and break up the prey before sucking it in through the proboscis. *Endeis spinosa*, which is also common here in the summer, has no such aids. Two to four eyes on the upper surface give sea spiders a wide range of vision and, although such lowly organisms, they are able to detect ultra-violet light beyond the limits of human perception. *Nymphon gracile* escapes the possibility of freezing on upshore rocks in winter by moving out to sea and adults have been caught in nets off the French coast at that season, so they may well be free-swimming members of the plankton during this annual escapade. Altogether a dozen different kinds of this little known group have been found on the Gower coast.

Common starfish (*Asterias rubens*) may be stranded in hordes, and little sandhoppers (*Pariambus typica* var. *inermi*) can sometimes be found clinging to them. These are new to Britain and were first found on Gower as recently as 1970. The slender fringed tubes of sand fragments belonging to the mason worms (*Lanice conchilega*) protrude from little pockets of sand much patterned by the webbed feet of gulls and unwebbed ones of oyster catchers.

The straits between the islets run more or less from South to North and the outer one is flooded for about twice as long as the inner. They are floored by smallish boulders and gravel sufficiently mobile for irregular clumps of acorn barnacles to have been chipped away, and are mostly weed-free. Shelter is adequate in odd corners, however, for the egg wrack (*Ascophyllum nodosum*) with an interrupted carragheen mat beneath it.

Chondrus crispus, the carragheen species with a fine navy blue sheen, fills the permanent pools with miniature forests, among the branches of which sport tiny fish and stripy shrimps. As the incoming tide drowns the kelp beds, the terns move in here to fish. Long-clawed porcelain crabs (*Porcellana longicornis*), not much bigger than peas, scamper among the stones on the pool brinks and hordes of hermit crabs (*Eupagurus bernhardus*) blunder to and fro in their borrowed homes. These are avid scavengers, converging on dead crabs of other species. Half a dozen or more will tug and heave at a single prize, bowling each other over in the process, but retrieving their position with little time wasted. On large prey such as this, one pincer is used to hold the food steady while the other tweaks out convenient-sized morsels to stow into the maw. Small crabs wear the white or orange shells of rough periwinkles (*Littorina saxatilis*), bigger ones those of edible periwinkles or dog whelks.

Velvet fiddler crabs (*Portunas puber*) get thrown into gullies by heavy seas. These are swimming crabs and the hindmost pair of blue-striped legs is broadly flattened and bristly-edged to act as paddles. They occur only on the South and West coasts of Britain.

Largest of the acorn barnacles here (up to $1\frac{1}{4}$ inches) is *Balanus perforatus*, also a species of the South and West and extending only as far as St. David's Head in Dyfed. The bulged and blotchy top shells (*Gibbula magus*), rare in Gower, is another which escapes cold by staying in the South and West. This disappeared altogether in the hard spell of early 1963 and is making a slow comeback in the East Gower Bays. Both the flat or purple top shell (*G. umbilicalis*) and the thick topshell (*Monodonta lineata*) of similar distribution nationally, suffered severely during this freeze-up. These live higher up the shore, and so are more subject to frost. The grey top (*G. cinerea*) of the mid and downshore zones, suffered scarcely at all. Most attractive of Gower's top shells but not very often found is the red, 1 inch (25 mm) high painted top (*Calliostoma zizyphinum*).

The blennies (*Blennius pholis*) of the Mumbles pools have their own special parasite, a marine leech, *Oceanobdella blennii*, found otherwise only in North Wales. The young sole taken by inshore fishermen support another species of leech, *Hemibdella soleae*, which is much commoner attached to bigger soles taken by sea-borne fishermen from the off-shore

63. Velvet fiddler crab and bladder wrack (*Fucus vesiculosus*)

gravel banks. Two other parasites new to science occur in Gower's five-bearded rocklings, these being *Lepidopedon cambrensis* and *Lechithaster musteli*.

Among the passage migrants feeding along the shores are turnstone and sandpiper and these act as host to another parasite, *Parapronocephalum symmetricum*. This lives part of its life cycle in periwinkles and was known only in Russian periwinkles until found in those at Mumbles and Caswell, so it is fairly safe to assume that the birds act as carriers. Yet another parasite, *Parvatrema homoeotecnum*, which is completely new to science, has been found to be shared between the local periwinkles and the oyster catchers.

The rocks over which these creatures feed are soluble to chemicals as well as soft enough to be tunnelled in, so become extensively holed by boring animals in places. Largish holes may be made by bivalve molluscs, *Hiatella arctica*, smaller ones by another bivalve, *Gastrochaena dubiosa* or by bristle worms, *Polydora ciliata*, which trap debris as it floats past and build projecting tubes. Another borer is the small anemone, *Fagesia carnea*. Larger burrows give shelter to other animals, including the hairy and non-hairy crabs, *Pilumnus hirtellus* and *Pirimela denticulata*, the white sea cucumber, *Cucumaria saxicola* and the worm-like Sipunculid, *Golfingia elongatum*.

Where sand and rock meet, the honeycomb worm, *Sabellaria alveolata*, collects the one to build reefs upon the other—crusty edifices of passages which crunch underfoot. Free-living bristle worms and scale worms hide under rocks and can be found wandering round on damp surfaces even when the tide is out.

215

Shingle pockets of the Mumbles Straits consist of pulverised shells, but the diligent beachcomber will be able to procure a few prizes intact. Two of the most charming are the little ridged pink cowries, *Trivia arctica* and *T. monacha*, as attractive in death as when actively browsing downshore on sedentary seasquirts. Others are the deeper pink banded Actaeon shells (*Actaeon tornatilis*), netted dog whelks (*Nassarius reticulatus*) and various red-ringed scallops (*Chlamys* species).

Wholly sandy shores appear much emptier of life than rocky ones but this is an illusion. How else could they provide food for so many shore birds? Plants are, indeed, scarce, as the sand surface is too mobile for attachment, but animals do not need light and can escape friction by burrowing. The presence of such as the lugworm (*Arenicola marina*) is evident to bait-seeking fishermen by the worm cast above the tail end of the U shaped burrow and the little pit where the sand is being sucked in at the head end.

Most animals have to be looked for more carefully—or dug for. Star-shaped depressions in the sand do not necessarily mean a starfish is below; the hidden animal may be a heart urchin, or sea egg (*Echinocardium cordatum*), oval and with much softer bristles than the larger, spherical, edible urchin (*Echinus esculentus*) which is seldom seen, though the little greenish sand urchins (*Psammechinus miliaris*) are occasionally found in wave-swept pools. A bristle worm (*Flabelligera affinis*) sometimes lives among the spines of this last, a little bivalve (*Montacuta ferruginosa*) among the spines of the heart urchin.

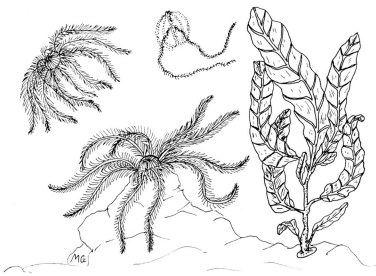

64. Sea gooseberry, two feather stars and the red seaweed, *Delesseria sanguinea*

216

It is really necessary to paddle to see live creatures above the sand, and many of these, like the fry of flatfish, become quite invisible when not in motion. Not only are there dab and sole but sand sole (*Pegusa lascaris*), turbot (*Scophthalmus maximus*) and plaice (*Pleuronectes platessa*).

Each beach has its own particular character. Oxwich is the only one outside the Burry Inlet where eelgrass grows—a sparse scattering of the slender-leaved *Zostera angustifolia*, but sufficient for its underground stems to give the stability needed by a host of sand-dwelling animals. Here, too, is a veritable forest of the shaggy shell-sand tubes of sand mason worms (*Lanice conchilega*)—showing best after the surface sand has been scoured away by rough seas. The terminal frill of each tube is cunningly constructed of sand grains strung together edge to edge and filtering food particles from the water. Tentacles emerging from the 'pepperpot' at its base wipe these delicacies off and transfer them to the 8-10 inches of worm ensconced in the tube below.

Hermit crabs along the edge of the tide at Oxwich include the southern *Diogenes pugilator*, which has the left pincer bigger than the right. The 'special' crabs on Llangennith Beach are the masked crabs (*Corystes cassivelaunus*). These back into the wet sand when alarmed, bringing their long antennae together to form a breathing tube maintaining contact with the surface. Their empty shells are abundant among the whitened heart urchin tests and cuttle bones.

Egg ribbons of large necklace shells (*Natica catena*), also abundant, look like 4 inch collars fashioned from wet hessian—a texture resulting from sand grains embedded in jelly. Wanderings of adult necklace shells just beneath the surface are marked by ridges in the sand. These are purposeful wanderings, to seek small sand-burrowing bivalves and bore through the shell near the hinge with the proboscis so that the contents can be consumed. The holed shells of the victims lie scattered over the beach.

Local hermit crabs appropriate discarded pink necklace shells, the exterior of which remain shinier than most by being more than half covered in life by the soft foot of the moving animal. Little parasitic pea crabs (*Pinnotheres pisum*) can be found in the shells of living rayed troughs (*Mactra corallina*) and thick trough shells (*Spisula solida*) of the same family at Llangennith and turn up again in the mussels of the old glacial moraine at Whiteford Point.

Razor shells are always conspicuous, the blocky pod razor (*Ensis siliqua*) and more elegant *E. arcuatus*, 8 and 6 inches long respectively, and the small, more delicately curved *E. ensis*. These burrow with alacrity when disturbed, sending up little jets of water as they go. Flooding by rains such as those of January 1974, which caused a rise in lake level at Oxwich, prevents them from burying themselves completely, presumably because of a reluctance to penetrate the much raised freshwater table a few inches beneath the surface.

217

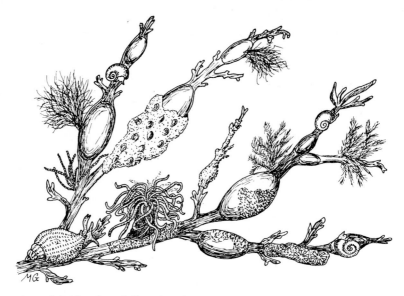

65. Flat periwinkles, dog whelk and opalet anemone on egg wrack encrusted with sponge, sea squirt and moss animals and shaggy with sea fir and the red seaweeds, *Polysiphonia* and *Callithamnion*

Jack knife clams (*Pharus legumen*) living downshore on the western beaches, are distinguished from the true razors in having the hinge of the shell amidships instead of at one end. This species is seldom recorded further North and the severe losses in the 1963 freeze-up have been replenished only from populations which escaped severe frost by being furthest downshore. Another southerner recorded here in 1967 for the first time in Britain is *Eurydice affinis*—an Isopod resembling a woodlouse. Although new, it is not rare, as many as 550 being turned up in a square metre of sand dug to a depth of 6 inches in Oxwich Bay.

No spade is necessary to sample the riches of the driftlines snaking across the sands. Here, among the plant-like fronds of the animal hornwrack (*Flustra foliacea*), are brittle stars (*Ophiura* species) and feather stars (*Antedon bifida*). Goose barnacles (*Lepas anatifera*) grow in profusion on great baulks of timber and tree trunks thrown up at Mewslade and elsewhere. Other barnacles are *L. hillii*, which occasionally turns up on wood, *L. pectinata* on floating cuttlebones and algae and *L. fascicularis* on solidified blobs of crude oil! Barnacle-bearing timber is often burrowed extensively by 'shipworm' (actually a two-shelled mollusc, *Teredo norvegica* the biggest and commonest of several species.) The breadth and extent of the tunnels can only be appreciated if the substrate splits, because the larvae enter from the plankton through quite tiny holes and wax fat inside,

218

burrowing onwards with a spiral action of the two frontal shells. A honeycomb of smaller holes can be produced by wood-boring gribbles.

Rare arrivals on equinoctial gales are by-the-wind sailors (*Velella velella*) and Portuguese men-of-war (*Physalia physalis*)—also various jellyfish from closer to home. Much commoner are mermaid's glove sponges (*Haliclona oculata*), mermaid's purses (the egg cases of lesser spotted dogfish with twirled attachment cords at each corner) and darker fishermen's purses (egg cases of skate or ray without the twirling extremities). The three rays most commonly brought up in trawl nets offshore are the spotted ray (*Raja montagui*), the painted ray (*R. microocellata*) and the thornback ray (*R. clavata*). A sting ray (*Dasyatis pastinaca*) was caught near Mumbles in 1972 and electric rays (*Torpedo nobiliana*), able to produce about 220 volts with a current of 8 amps, are occasionally fished out of Carmarthen Bay off North Gower.

More extravagant jetsam likely to get thrown up from Porteynon westward includes the metre-long angler fish or frogfish (*Lophius piscatorius*), the frontal lure which enticed prey into the formidable jaws deflated in death.

Even larger are the Cetaceans—whales, porpoises and dolphins—whose built-in sonar systems have failed to prevent them from running aground. The horizontal tail lobes, seen also in seals, label them at once as mammals and quite distinct from the sometimes similar-sized shark or tope (*Galeorhinus galeus*) which boat-borne fishermen pursue over the offshore sandbanks. There is great excitement on occasion for long-shore fishermen when some of the great finned hunters pursue their prey fish into the confined waters of Blue Pool near Broughton in the North West, and the whole surface erupts with the commotion.

The most remarkable record is that of the white-sided dolphin (*Lagenorhynchus acutus*) which turned up on Rhossili Beach in October 1967. Attempts were made to return it to the sea, but it had finally to be shot. This is a northern species, found chiefly around Norway, Orkney

66. White-sided dolphin (*Lagenorhynchus acutus*), Rhossili, 1967

219

and Shetland, and this one the first to be seen in Wales. Other species which have come ashore at Rhossili over the years include lesser rorqual (*Balaenoptera acutorostrata*) and common dolphin (*Delphinus delphis*).

Porteynon has attracted lesser rorqual and Risso's dolphin (*Grampus griseus*), Mumbles common dolphin and Sowerby's whale (*Mesoplodon bidens*). Twenty one false killers (*Pseudorca crassidens*) were stranded at Llanmadoc in 1934, a bottle-nosed whale (*Hyperoodon ampullatus*) at Broughton Bay in 1965. Most numerous arrivals, however, are common porpoises (*Phocoena phocoena*) with 19 strandings in Glamorgan between 1911 and 1973, and bottle-nosed dolphins (*Tursiops truncatus*) with 10.

The Atlantic leatherback, largest of all the turtles, which turned up off the Gower coast in September 1966, had probably drifted there in the Gulf Stream. It was described in the popular press as the size of a small car with a head as big as a football. As creatures of the Tropics and sub-tropics, these cannot live long in British waters and the few sightings in the West have all been South of Anglesey.

Part Five

The Shifting Sands

Birds foot trefoil and small heath butterflies

27 THE DUNE SYSTEMS AND THEIR DISTINCTIVE FLORA

GOWER'S rolling sand dunes are as attractive as her limestone cliffs—to both holidaymakers and naturalists—while being more accessible and more erodible; so they pose serious problems for conservationists. All are on the western two-thirds of the peninsula, cradled in bays of the southern cliffs or cutting across the north-west corner behind the rocky ramparts of Burryholms. In places the prevailing south-westerlies have carried sand to the clifftops, enabling dunes to build up well above sea level. The old village of Pennard was lost beneath dunes such as these, a remnant of the twelfth century parish church near the crumbling ruins of Pennard Castle being all that remains from the former community. These Pennard cliff dunes are the most easterly on Gower and have now been fashioned into a golf course.

Mares and foals crop the links, but not so closely as to destroy the contrasting swards of red bartsia, yellow rattle and white eyebright or the bright patches of bird's foot trefoil and lady's bedstraw. Seedling oaks are common near Pennard Castle in some years, but seldom get beyond the three to four leaf stage before being nibbled off.

Seaside golf courses can be beneficial to sward conservation except in certain crucial spots, where long rubberised carpets have been laid between fairways to halt the blowing of the bared sand. Only six months after the fencing off and returfing of a worn path on the west facing cliffs above Pobbles Bay in the Spring of 1973, the substitute path had been gouged out to a depth of 15 inches below turf level. A similar trench had been worn along the front of a bench seat nearby. Ponies were largely responsible for the first but cannot be blamed for the second. Uneven rainwashing of lime from the sand gives a mosaic of acid-loving sheep's bit scabious and bell heather with lime-loving small scabious, rayed knapweed and rest harrow.

These dunes drop to sea level in Penmaen Valley, quite precipitously by Pennard Castle, more gently to seaward behind 'Three Cliffs'. Nicholaston Burrows a little to the West lead into the extensive dune system at Oxwich and contain a central blowout where the marram grass has been trampled to death by picknickers and walkers. Although toughly invasive and able to withstand natural vicissitudes better than most, marram succumbs readily to physical pressure, leaving bare paths which funnel the wind and form the foci of extensive sand ravines and hollows.

Dunes near the Porteynon carpark are very worn but a few sections fenced off from the public showed an increase of vegetation to an 80% ground cover—oases of green in a desert of yellow. Interesting, though not very typical plants here are horse radish, ramping fumitory, with crimson-tipped white flowers, pink-blossomed narrow everlasting pea, yellow fennel and mauve vervain or Verbena.

There is a negligible build up of sand behind the great expanse of Rhossili Beach, where long lines of breakers curl constantly shore-wards in one of the most exquisite seascapes of the Peninsula. Only beyond the northern end of Rhossili Down do dunes start to accumulate, marred at first by a caravan site, but broadening into Llangennith Burrows. These still retain much of their glory, although the bee orchids and other beauties of the flatter, more stable areas have been squashed out of existence by cars and people. Where both cars and people are deterred in the wetter slacks fluffy white bogbean flowers follow the golden cups of marsh marigold and lead on to a riot of early and southern marsh orchids. Pink trumpets of sea bindweed are spread generously over the looser sand with sea spurge and sea holly, and there is unusually much turret cress (*Arabis hirsuta*,) some with galled, reddish flower clusters.

Llangennith and Broughton Burrows are contiguous, filling the depression between Rhossili Bay and Broughton Bay and riding up over the high cliffs of Blue Pool Corner. Lichens are more prolific here than elsewhere, the sheets of whitish, lobed *Parmelia* especially so, along with darker green dog's tooth lichen, *Peltigera*, spikily branched *Cornicularia* and a *Cladonia* with brown fruiting bodies.

The lichen cover, along with dry twists of *Tortula ruraliformis* moss, gives a greyness to the ground and this stage of the stabilising sand succession is referred to as 'grey dune'. This is the place to look for puff-balls, the little stalked *Tulostoma brumale* and pear-shaped *Lycoperdon ericetorum*: also for black earth tongues (*Geoglossum fallax*) and orange

67. Dune puffballs: *Bovista nigrescens* and *Tulostoma brumale*

fairy clubs (*Clavaria corniculata*). Dark jelly pustules of the blue-green alga, *Nostoc*, appear in these sparsely vegetated zones in winter.

The long sweep of sandhills continues on up the coast to the tip of Whiteford Point, fed by air-borne particles from several hundred acres of beach to windward. Complicated topography gives a variety of habitats and in high summer there is no need to range far to find a hundred different plant species. An equally rich animal life makes this a site of national importance. These are the last of the dunes on the coastal sequence: from here on, up the Burry Inlet, the sands are tide-washed and partially bound together with drifted mud.

Dunes are such a feature of the Gower scene, that it is hard to believe that as little as six hundred years ago they had scarcely begun to form. The stormy period of the thirteenth to sixteenth centuries, was the big dune building era, when offshore sandbanks were transported inland. Their advance was associated with the loss of forest—each process assisting the other. Where the trees had already succumbed to the axe or fire, there was little left to stay the passage of the sand: where they were dwindling, the advancing sand mass hastened their death.

But some woody species can co-exist with accreting sand, creeping willow positively revelling in it. These lowly bushes get established in dune slacks, trap sand and build up into mounds, with their roots reaching down to the water table. Hillocks may be 6ft. high and vertical sided, and are termed 'hedgehogs'. Smaller woody species giving extensive cover on the eastern dunes, rather less on the western ones, are burnet rose and dewberry. These get straggly and die out as larger bushes of grey sallow, spindle and the like take over in the sheltered hollows. On Oxwich the sand succession has run full term to birch spinneys with quite sizable oaks pushing through. Such progression to closed woodland is not common on British dunes. More usually grazing of the dune grassland allows only such as heather, gorse and bramble to become at all abundant—as on the clifftop dunes at Pennard, where most of the limey ingredients have been washed away.

The warmth and dryness of soil enjoyed by Gower's cliff plants are accentuated for her dune plants, the porous sands readily drying out and absorbing the sun's heat. Plants common to both habitats include bloody cranesbill, wild thyme, centaury, yellow-wort and carline thistle. Yellow stonecrop and Portland spurge grow on sand as well as on rock but the introduced white stonecrop grows only on rock, and sea spurge only on sand.

Gower is famous for her orchids and these are most prolific on the dunes. In mid summer many of the slacks become carpeted with the deep purple and crimson flower spikes of southern marsh orchids (*Dactylorhiza praetermissa*) and the two kinds of early marsh orchid (*D. incarnata* ssp. *incarnata* and *D.i.* ssp. *coccinea*). Drifts of red-tinted marsh helleborine (*Epipactis palustris*) cover many square yards and the albino variety (*E.p.* var. *ochroleuca*) with attractive cream-coloured flowers can be found occasionally, though Whiteford and Kenfig further East are its only known Welsh sites. Broad helleborine is less gregarious and prefers shade, growing largest under trees or among creeping willows. Pyramidal orchids are widespread in drier areas: green winged orchids more sparsely scattered in stonier sites. Lady's tresses orchids push up later in the year from old dune pastures, particularly after a wet summer. Twayblade and early purple orchid are likely to occur anywhere, but the more widespread spotted orchids are rarely found on dunes.

Gower's star species is the little greenish-flowered fen orchid. The 'ordinary' version of this, *Liparis loeselii*, grows in only a small part of East Anglia: the dune version (*L. l.* var. *ovata*) in only a few sites in Glamorgan and Carmarthen. Like the white helleborine, this is a speciality of Whiteford and Kenfig Burrows, from where it has recently spread to Braunton Burrows on the other side of the Bristol Channel.

Another particular rarity which likes the same type of open slack as the fen orchid, and which has only just reached Whiteford, is the maritime variety of the larger wintergreen (*Pyrola rotundifolia* var. *maritima*). This was formerly known only in Lancashire and Flintshire, but was discovered at Kenfig in 1927.

Since then it has spread rapidly and by the early 1970s it was well established at Oxwich, flowering profusely in August, in association with another late flowering rarity, the Welsh gentian.

This dull purple gentian (*Gentianella uliginosa*) forms considerable swards in these slacks—and also in the short turf of pathways on drier

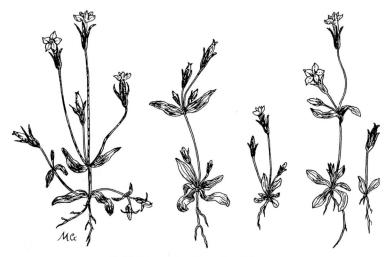

68. Welsh gentian from Oxwich dunes

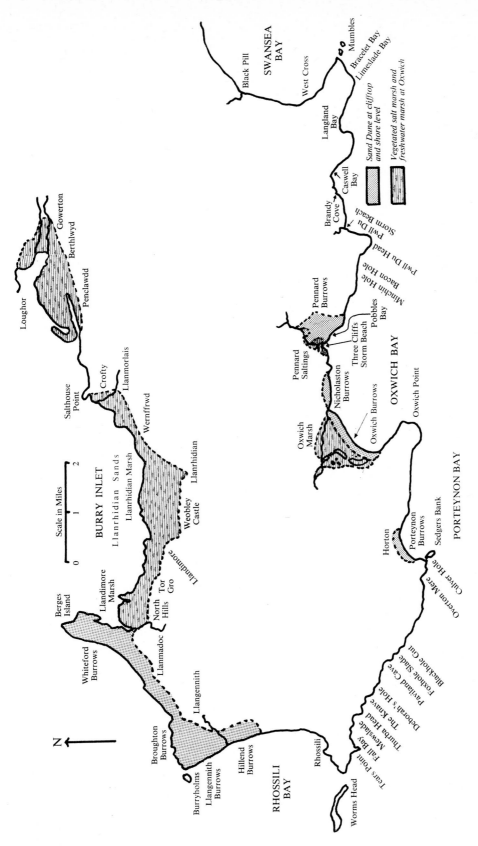

69. Map showing location of dunes and salt marshes

SWANSEA BAY

Black Pill
West Cross
Mumbles
Bracelet Bay
Limeslade Bay
Langland Bay
Caswell Bay
Brandy Cove
Pwll Du Head
Storm Beach
Minchin Hole
Bacon Hole
Pennard Burrows
Pennard Saltings
Three Cliffs Storm Beach
Pobbles Bay
Nicholaston Burrows
Oxwich Marsh
Oxwich Burrows
OXWICH BAY
Oxwich Point

Sand Dune at clifftop and shore level
Vegetated salt marsh and freshwater marsh at Oxwich

Gowerton
Berthlwyd
Penclawdd
Loughor
Salthouse Point
Crofty
Llanmorlais
Wernffrwd

BURRY INLET

Llanrhidian Sands
Llanrhidian Marsh
Llanrhidian
Weobley Castle
Llandimore

Scale in Miles
0 1 2

Llandimore Marsh
Berges Island
North Tor
Gro
Hills
Llanmadoc
Whiteford Burrows
Llangennith
Broughton Burrows
Burryholms
Llangennith Burrows
Hillend Burrows
Rhossili

RHOSSILI BAY

Worms Head
Tears Point
Fall Bay
Mewslade Bay
Thurba Head
The Knave
Deborah's Hole
Pavilland Cave
Foxhole Slade
Blackhole Gut
Overton Mere
Culver Hole
Horton
Porteynon Burrows
Sedgers Bank

PORTEYNON BAY

N

ground, where it is not in competition with the rank grass, bracken and dewberry alongside. In these drier sites it is usually with the commoner felwort (*G. amarella*), which is a taller plant of bushier growth. This biennial common felwort lacks the distinctive long flower stalks, which sometimes spring directly from ground level, and also the uneven sepals of the annual Welsh gentian. In Britain the rarer species is known only here and at Tenby further West. Unlike many of the Gower rarities, this outlier is not exploiting the milder climate to extend its range northwards, but is a native of Northern Europe, from Scandinavia to Poland.

Another straying in from further North is the Isle of Man cabbage (*Rhynchosinapis monensis*), whose yellow flowers romp across the dunes of the Pobbles-Three Cliffs area. This constitutes the most southerly population of an all British species, whose only other sites are on the West coast from South Lancashire to Kintyre, and, of course, the Isle of Man. Similar plants on the shore at Porthcawl are wallflower cabbage (*R. cheiranthos*): those across the water on the Isle of Lundy are the endemic Lundy cabbage (*R. wrightii*). All three have tenacious root systems which enable them to continue flowering when dangling upside down after a sand blow or a rock slide.

Much rarer on the Pobbles-Three Cliffs dunes and almost as rare on a national scale, is the creeping wild Asparagus (*Asparagus officinalis* ssp. *prostratus*). A native of Europe's West coast, this species is diminishing in Britain, the South Wales specimens bridging the gap between the few known populations in South West England and South East Ireland. The creamy white bell flowers are unisexual by abortion of either the male or female organs, with the functional sexes occurring on different plants, but both kinds are present on the South Gower dunes, Their hold is tenuous, however, often on badly eroding sand brinks, and the outlook for their persistence not too rosy. They nevertheless flowered quite profusely in 1976. The future of the rare rock Hutchinsia (*Hornungia petraea*) is brighter, this tiny cress being more abundant than is often supposed. Plants seldom exceed an inch or two in height and they flower early, in February and March, when few people are lying around on the sands to observe them and when walkers proceed briskly, egged on by chilly winds too fast to see all the treasures about their feet. This feathery-leaved annual frequently flowers alongside the spring whitlow grass (*Erophila verna*)—extending from Pennard to Broughton—and not far from the site of caper spurge (*Euphorbia lathyrus*) at Nicholaston.

Sea stock (*Matthiola sinuata*) turned up first at Llangennith Burrows in 1974—the flowers indicating that it had been established there for at least a year. This large biennial with mauve flowers and waved, velvety grey leaves, was rediscovered on the dunes of West and Mid Glamorgan in the 1960s, after having been thought extinct for many years (an event paralleled during the same period at the mouth of the Dovey in West

Plate 37   INSECTS OF WHITEFORD BURROWS

156. Caterpillar of Broom Moth *(Ceramica pisi)* on mint   *Author*
157. Minotaur Beetle *(Typhoeus typhaeus)*   *Michael Claridge*
158. Fly *(Physocephala rufipes)* which parasitises and mimics bees   *Author*
159. Drone Fly *(Eristalis)* on evening primrose   *Author*
160. Hover Fly *(Syrphus)* on evening primrose   *Author*

161

162

163

Plate 38   BURRY MARSHES: BETWEEN THE TIDES

161. The Evening Tide seeps shorewards at Llanrhidian **162.** Ponies set galloping by summer fly plagues
163. View eastwards across Pony-cropped Saltings Turf   *All Author*

230

Wales.) Its mode of arrival in West Gower during the subsequent decade is not known, but human agency cannot be ruled out.

One of the rarities which Whiteford shares with the screes of south Western cliffs is the lesser meadow rue (*Thalictrum minus*). This grows in fairly stable sand communities here with pyramidal orchids and dune pansies. It is another of Gower's more northerly species, which is particularly abundant around Scottish and Hebridean coasts, with only a few outliers further South.

With it at Whiteford is the white horehound (*Marrubium vulgare*) with only three native sites in South Wales, two in North Wales and seven on the South coast of England, although established elsewhere by introduction. At Whiteford it occurs also under marginal trees of the pine plantations.

Lyme grass (*Elymus arenarius*) is spreading along the seaward dunes on North West Gower, having extended from the tip of Whiteford Point along its western flank in recent years and replaced quite a quantity of marram at Broughton Bay, although some of it was washed away during storms at the beginning of 1974. Lyme grass is a species of the North and East in Britain, with few post 1930 records in the South and South West.

The distribution map of the locally common sharp rush (*Juncus acutus*) is almost a mirror image of that of lyme grass. Headquarters of this species are along the North side of the Bristol Channel with an outlier at Braunton in North Devon, around St. George's Channel in South East Ireland and along the northern flank of Cardigan Bay. Only five other British sites are known, two in the English Channel and three on the East coast South of the Wash.

Another with its principal population in South Wales, including Llangennith, Whiteford and Oxwich, is the rat's tail fescue grass (*Vulpia membranacea*), which has a very discontinuous distribution around the coasts of England and South East Ireland. Bristle bent (*Agrostis setacea*) is a local grass of South West England, extending only as far North as the southern part of Glamorgan, where it occurs in both Gower and the Vale.

Rarest of Gower's grasses nationally, however, is the early sand-grass (*Mibora minima*) discovered at Whiteford as recently as 1966. This little grass of South and West Europe is known otherwise in Britain only on the Channel Islands and in Southern Anglesey, with a naturalised population in Hampshire.

Among the ferns, the primitive little adder's tongue (*Ophioglossum vulgatum*) is likely to be one of the most exciting finds. This predominantly South-easterly species is not uncommon in dune slacks, particularly at Whiteford, but the related and predominantly North-westerly moonwort (*Botrychium lunaria*) is much rarer and probably to be found on Gower now only at Whiteford. It is interesting to see the common polypody fern as a dune plant where, no doubt, the drought resistance which enables it to live on tree trunks and walls in other parts stands it in good stead.

Most notable of the horsetails is the modestly creeping variegated horsetail (*Equisetum variegatum*). Though abundant in open dune slacks in both South and North West Gower, this is uncommon on British coasts with widely separated populations centred mainly in the uplands of the Pennines, Central Scotland and Central Ireland. It earns its name from the rings of white tipped black scale leaves which give the stems a banded appearance.

Rarities are to be found in groups other than the vascular plants and Gower's dunes are guaranteed to provide species of note for specialists in many fields.

28 PENNARD VALLEY AND THE SEA-WASHED SANDS

THE lower valleys of Gower's two south easterly rivers are similarly flat-floored and steep-sided, but their flora and fauna could scarcely be more different. At Bishopston the storm bank of Pwll Du Bay has sealed the valley mouth, excluding the sea and allowing a freshwater marsh to build up on the accumulated alluvium behind. At Parkmill an arm of the sea winds between only partially restrictive storm beaches to fill the entire valley from flank to flank for ¼ mile or so upstream at the fortnightly spring tides. When these ebb, the tortuous convolutions of Pennard Pill are revealed—the water speeding seaward with unexpected vigour in so meandering a channel.

Skin divers measuring current strength in July 1972 were sometimes submerged to their armpits, but the river shallows towards the sea and is spanned by stepping stones at the end of the inner storm bank.

It has not always been so. An eighteenth century artist painted a scene with ships moored immediately below Pennard Castle, where the river now holds a mere foot of water when the tide has left the sand flats. He is known to have had a tendency to accentuate his verticals but was otherwise pretty accurate and there is no reason to doubt that the river was navigable this far in the 1700s. The sanding up has occurred in the last two hundred years and is likely to proceed apace now that the cord grass (*Spartina anglica*) has gained a substantial footing behind the seaward bar.

The vanguard of the *Spartina* has already permeated upstream as far as the foot of Castle Hill, where it overlaps with a healthy population of water voles (and probably also of brown rats) tunnelling in the earthy banks. *Enteromorpha*, commonest of the green seaweeds, extends much further up river into the Parkmill woodland, among branched bur-reed and other wholly freshwater species. Spotted sand gobies dart through dappled shadows and black-headed gulls probe among the multitudinous breathing holes of the shallows for the creatures which rely on these for their oxygen supply.

Most of the birds, however, feed on the broad expanse of salt-marsh downstream, where the sand is muddier and is strewn with the remains of baltic tellin shells (*Macoma balthica*) and rather fewer peppery furrow and cockle shells (*Scrobicularia plana* and *Cardium edule*). Ringed plovers and pied wagtails join the larger waders and gulls on these silt washed sandflats. Linnets and greenfinches feed on the seeds of the saltmarsh scurvy grass and flocks of starlings forage among the sea plantain rosettes. Cormorants may take up their scare-crow wing-drying stance on the more remote sandbanks.

The valley floor is gently undulating, bringing loose dune and sandy pasture above the general level of a marsh which grades from fresh through brackish to fully saline. Between the western reedswamp at the valley head and the eroding sand opposite are fine clumps of dame's violet, common valerian, yellow monkey flower and yellow iris, the last muddied by the tide to a horizontal line 7 ft above river level at high water of neap tides. Where the reeds merge into reed canary-grass the first coastal brookweed occurs with orache, and false-fox sedge gives way downstream to long-bracted sedge.

Abundant sea arrow-grass penetrates upstream to meet the rarer marsh arrow-grass penetrating down, and sea-milkwort and parsley water-dropwort appear in the sward as this changes with increasing salinity from one of perennial ryegrass through bent-grass to red fescue with drifts of sea pink.

Sea aster is insinuated as a riverside fringe along the edge of all three kinds of grassland, the flower heads opening in August and September a little later than those of the sea lavender downstream, when most of the other saltmarsh flowers have faded. As elsewhere on Gower, the aster is neither the true rayed form nor the variety *discoides*. Not only do most of the plants possess both yellow disc flower heads and purple rayed ones, but the individual heads often show a mixture of floret types around the periphery, suggesting that there is not the varietal distinction that the Floras claim.

233

Sea sedge, mud rush and sea plantain push upstream to a little North of the castle—the first at the river edge, often below the aster fringe, the others more subject to drying out. Sea rush, like cord grass, reaches just about level with the castle. The main marsh from here down is peppered brown in late summer with the fruiting heads of the plantain, alleviated by the mauve of sea lavender in the western loop. Scurvy grass remains at the riverside, where it is moistened by fresh water.

The uppermost saltpans to contain glasswort are on the inland side of the pebble storm beach where sea spurrey, sea-milkwort, sea-lavender, sea arrow-grass and sea purslane (*Halimione*) mingle with the dominant sea plantain. Sea blite grows only an inch or two high in this pony-grazed sward but reaches to twelve inches where the river loops westwards around the storm bank. Many of the barer salt pans are floored with a woolly, yellowish mat of the green alga, *Rhizoclonium implexum*, which goes less far upstream than the dark, velvety green carpets of *Vaucheria*. Cord grass has taken over completely from the native saltmarsh plants in the crook of the curving dune to seaward.

Plants at the junction of dune and saltmarsh differ little from those where dunes abut onto open coastal beaches, except that there is rather more sea sandwort (*Honkenya*) associated with the sea beet, prickly saltwort and orache. A fringe of hemlock water-dropwort a yard or so wide above these, at around the level of high spring tides, is an interesting departure from normal and illustrates the importance of the river water in diluting

70. Rare flowers of the western dunes. From left to right: round leaved wintergreen, lady's tresses orchid, fen orchid and lesser centaury

the saltiness of the invading tide. Sand couch and common couch lead back to typical rough dune grassland where bee orchids, pyramidal orchids and bloody cranesbill can be found in high summer.

Pennard Pill is of hard water, charged with lime from the Llethrid Cave system and the underground river flowing through Ilston Cwm. The streams entering the sea via Diles Lake on Rhossili Bay and the Burry Inlet off Broughton Bay come from the more acidic rocks of the Old Red Sandstone and are of soft water. A six-inch-layer of peaty alluvium has been deposited over the beach sand where the Broughton stream breaks through a textbook example of parallel dune ridges which follow the curve of the bay. This supports acid-loving plants such as procumbent marshwort (*Apium inundatum*), bog stitchwort (*Stellaria alsine*) and marsh foxtail (*Alopecurus geniculatus*). Top dressings of blown shell sand ensure the presence of lime-lovers too—as the flote grass and sweet reed-grass grade seawards to mud rush and sea rush.

Reduction of wave action as well as reduction of salinity can have far reaching effects when comparing the strandlines of river mouth and open shoreline. Quite close to Broughton stream, where equinoctial tides reach right to the Berges Island bird watching hide, waves are undercutting the old foredune ridge and exposing rounded pebbles in gullies.

At Oxwich, just along the coast from Pennard Pill, damage was considerable when the high spring tides of January and February 1974 were backed up by gales. Not only the foredune vegetation of couch and prickly saltwort was affected, but plants of the main dune ridge as well. After the second onslaught of the elements on 10th February 1974 hundreds of clumps of marram grass had been ripped from their spreading roothold by wind and trundled back and forth across the beach by waves which fashioned them into elongated rolls and scattered them over the saltmarsh behind. The sand in which they had lived was also displaced, the remainder ending in a vertical sand cliff up to 10 ft. high. As the gales eased, those responsible for the welfare of the National Nature Reserve got busy with freshly cut pine branches repairing breaches which funnelled the winds into blowouts.

The eastern end of the dune rampart at the mouth of Nicholaston Pill had been attacked from three sides and new sand faces dropped almost vertically for as much as 20 ft. in parts. Two 6 ft. sycamores had toppled from the brink. Such losses of stabilising trees and shrubs are recurrent. Photographs of this end of the dune taken in 1965 show a patch of 6 ft. high scrub on a summit which had been scoured free of woody vegetation by the beginning of the seventies.

An extensive meshwork of creeping sand sedge stems had been laid bare alongside the newly carved course of the river in February 1974 and the sand brink at the water's edge was constantly subsiding as the current, augmented by floods in the marshes behind, ripped along the

235

base, undermining an edge from which a powdering of sand was being swept into the river by the wind. A super-high driftline of marine debris and polythene had settled in the foot of Nicholaston Wood, marking the junction between the riverside alders and the oakwood above—a boundary of woodland types no doubt positioned by similar high tides in past years.

Equally dramatic changes had taken place at Whiteford, where there is a constant loss of small pine trees from the collapsing sand cliff at the South-western end of Whiteford Sands. During calm spells material is deposited along the central part of this concave stretch of beach to form an irregular foredune ridge, but on 13th January, 1974 much of the pale green sand couch which had begun to stabilise this had been uprooted and relegated to the driftline, along with some of the strawy yellow marram from the dunes behind. By the following summer, healthy flowering stands of sea rocket had started the building up process over again but, being annuals, these plants do nothing to hold the beach against winter storms.

Further North towards the point a great deal of sand had been scoured away by wind and water to reveal the underlying layers. Whiteford Burrows have built up on an old moraine laid down alongside the glacier which occupied the Loughor Valley and Burry Inlet and emerging here at the junction of the Irish Sea ice and that coming down from the North. In 1974 silty clay mottled with rusty ferric iron and greyish ferrous iron was laid bare at the base of the receding sand cliff. On top of the clay bed where it emerged from the remains of the dune was an old storm beach of boulders which had previously been buried. At the foot of the new exposure was the current storm beach, forming a rugged line between clay above and sandflats below. The stones are of mixed origin, from ice-tran-ported material—as are those stretching far out around the old cast iron lighthouse to provide a suitable footing for inumerable mussels. It is probable that changes along this shoreline are a reflection of movements in the protective sandbanks offshore.

Around the corner on the Llanrhidian Sands a series of peat banks ap-pears and disappears on the upper beach as sand is washed away or drifted over. These are full of old reed stems and point to a byegone era when freshwater swamp occupied a zone now invaded by the sea. They are contemporary with the peat beds of Swansea Bay and Margam Sands to the East—relict of a time when sea level was lower in relation to land level than it is at present.

Sand removal during January 1974 storms had exposed a formerly submerged 'forest' of unexploded shells on the beach East of Berges Island to be collected up by the army—as they have been collected inter-mittently over the past thirty years when the tide lays another lot bare. Apart from what is washed away, quantities of sand from here are blown on up the estuary, in a knee-high haze of pale particles, to settle among the

236

spreading banks of *Spartina*. The invasive circular patches of this grass on the projecting sandspit had expanded and coalesced into a continuous sward by the mid seventies.

Tree trunks stranded at the top of the beach, as at Oxwich and Whiteford, provide shelter for animals of the upper shore, including the rare strandline beetle, *Eurynebria complanata*. This sizable animal, some 2 cm. long,

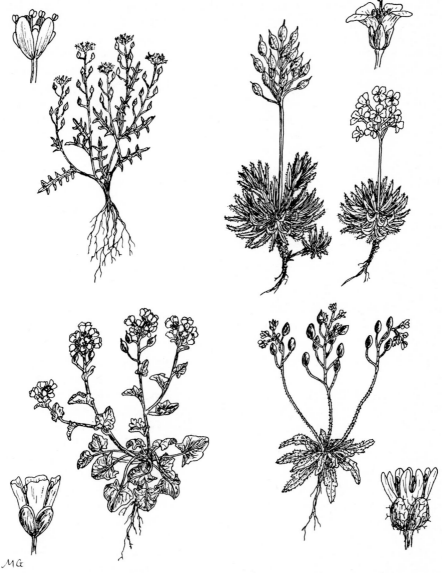

MG

71. Four tiny coastal cresses. Top left: rock hutchinsia; top right: yellow whitlow grass; bottom left: Danish scurvy grass; bottom right: Spring whitlow grass

rather resembles a cockroach, but is not related. It is a shiny buff colour longtitudinally striated and with conspicuous black eyes. Sociably inclined, the beetles can be found 30-40 together, skulking under driftwood, old sofas and other sea-washed artefacts by day. At night they emerge and are ferociously carnivorous, feeding largely on sandhoppers. *Eurynebria* is a southern species, restricted to South West Britain and County Wexford.

Another animal speciality, to be found on Whiteford only this time, is a little money spider called *Lasiargus Gowerensis* after its Gower home. This lives slightly lower on the shore among the invading *Spartina* grass.

There is always something of interest to be found in this no-mans-land where sea meets land. In early 1974 it was a grey Atlantic seal, which unfortunately died here. On March 11th, 1975, there was a passage of well over a hundred seals across Rhossili Bay, moving towards Burryholms only 50-75 yards from the shore. More often the attractions are ornithological, for the food potential of invertebrate life just beneath the sand surface is enormous.

29 OXWICH BURROWS: NATIONAL NATURE RESERVE

'THE Burrows', whilst not comprising the whole of the land deposited to seaward of the old cliffline at Oxwich, are, nevertheless, impressively large and varied in character. From the high point on Crawley Top the view westwards encompasses acres of sandhills rolling landwards for a quarter of a mile and reaching to fifty feet above sea level. They stretch for one and a half miles along the shore, from the mouth of Nicholaston Pill to the car park under Oxwich Head, and back eastwards as Nicholaston Burrows. Wet and dry hollows alternate with broken ridges which are eaten into by wind gaps. From above they present a complicated mosaic of colour—a winter jigsaw of purple-twigged birch spinneys, dark willow slacks, straw-pale grassland and wind-combed marram dunes.

But the Burrows proper are more than just the sandhills. Tucked behind them are forty acres of saltmarsh, nourished by sea water entering along the shifting channel of Nicholaston Pill, whilst stretching seawards for a quarter of a mile at ebb tide is a magnificent beach of golden sand. The

National Nature Reserve embraces more again, to include the wooded limestone cliffs of Nicholaston and the fascinating complex of East Anglian type fen peat and lakes described in sections 4 and 13. The area is nationally recognised not only for its scientific worth, but for its scenic and amenity value, figuring in various national touring guides of special desiderata for countryside viewing.

The dunes have built up on stabilised pebble deposits which are sometimes laid bare in the bottom of blow-outs. They are orientated East and West, almost normal to the shore in the South but becoming increasingly oblique in the North. The damage periodically inflicted on them by stormy seas has already been stressed and it is probable that they once extended further seaward across the underlying storm beaches. There is seldom any true foredune in process of building up, the seaward margin alternating between a newly cut erosion face and a steep sandslide which only the hardiest of plants are able to colonise and stabilise. (The natural 'angle of rest' of loose sand is about 45°; at anything steeper the surface is liable to slump, as, indeed, much of it did during the dry summers of 1975 and 1976.)

Sand is always on the move, invading the slacks of the dunes themselves and spilling over into the saltmarsh and freshwater marsh behind, so that there is no clearly defined boundary on the inner side. The topography suffered interference during the 1939-45 war when a number of East to West channels were bulldozed out and linked to the beach to give throughways for amphibious craft. These offered unrestricted access to sea winds and developed into blow-outs which have persisted over the thirty years since, in spite of attempts to block them with wicker fences and cut branches.

Longer term changes are more closely allied with natural phenomena. During the 16th and 17th centuries the Burrows were an important grazing area for local farmers and were 'preserved for all sedge and grass therein'. The deterioration of grazing quality in the 18th century is likely to have been brought about by a combination of sand blow and rabbit activity. Since then the seaward side has probably become less stable (due in no small part to the numerous day trippers) and the inland side more stable because of invasion by bracken, which so often takes over on marginal land.

Notwithstanding this, the western shell sands are more fertile than the average siliceous sands of Eastern Britain, being quite strongly alkaline as a result of the high lime content and able to support a rich flora as a result. Sand freshly arrived on the forward dunes has a pH of 9.0 or more, dropping only to a little below 8.5 when colonised by marram grass and bracken. Soil reactions to depths of 3 inches under the grey lichen mats and damp alder spinneys are still well above neutral (pH 8.5 and 8.0 respectively). Rainfall, which increases acidity by washing out the minerals, is approximately 40 inches per year (1,000 mm.), offset by the evaporation

GULLS LIKELY TO BE SEEN ON GOWER.   (Drawn by Rob A. Hume and first produced in *Gower Journal*, XXIV, p. 7)

Greater black-back, adult
Lesser black-back, adult
Common gull, first year and adult
Mediterranean gull, first year and adult
Little gull, adult and first year

Glaucous gull, first year
Herring gull, juvenile and adult
Ring-billed gull adult (seen off Mumbles)
Kittiwake, adult
Black-headed gull, first year and adult

(All adults in summer plumage)

240

occasioned by an average annual 35% of possible sunshine, so the climate is both drier and warmer than in most of West Glamorgan.

There is a wealth of wildlife, with foxes, stoats and weasels hunting through the dune woodlands, and a host of others right down to the conger eels up to 9 ft. long which forage offshore. A bed of the plant-like animal, hornwrack (*Flustra foliacea*) off Oxwich Point is the subject of a current study. The growth of other moss animals (*Bryozoans*) and sea firs (*Hydroids*) attached to it are also being investigated, along with predatory sea spiders (*Pycnogonids*), particularly *Achelia echinata* and the porcelain crab (*Porcellana longicornis*) which shelter among it.

The lowermost intertidal communities are sensitive to level, insofar as this is bound up with waterlogging and salinity and there is a clear zonation of different communities on progressing inland. Inch long plaice fry make lightning darts through the shallows at low water of springs—merging indecipherably with their sandy background on coming to rest. With them are oblong, sand-burrowing razor shells of three kinds and jack knife clams.

A little above this zone the fine-leaved eel-grass has colonised the shifting sands—the only plant species to have done so apart from invisible minutiae. Heart urchins live at this level, out of sight beneath the surface for most of the time, and among their spines their commensal bivalve partner, *Montacuta ferruginosa*. Off-white ribbon worms (*Cephalothrix rufifrons*) are also characteristic, drawing themselves lengthwise to mere threads or bunching into quite substantial jelly blobs. The protruding shelly tubes of mason worms (*Lanice*) roughen acres of sand surface here, along with the coiled casts of lugworms (*Arenicola*), but the neatly packed sand grain tubes of the trumpet worm (*Pectinaria koreni*) are models of smooth symmetry.

The best place to seek the elegant pink or cream tellin shells (*Tellina tenuis*) is a little above low water mark of ordinary tides; those of *Tellina fabula* are usually further down. Bivalves are much commoner than uni-valves on the sands, their empty shells attracting many beachcombers. Spoils range from big otter shells (*Lutraria lutraria*) to tiny but similar-textured milky lucinas (*Lucinoma borealis*) and little shining nut clams (*Nucula nucleus*). There are striped Venus (*Venus gallina*), banded trough (*Mactra corrallina*), saddle oyster (*Anomia ephippium*), spiny cockle (*Cardium aculeatum*) and several kinds of scallop (*Chlamys*).

The shrimps encountered when paddling through the shallows are likely to be *Crangon vulgaris*, the prawns *Leander serratus*. Among the hopping and crawling 'sandhoppers' or Amphipods of the middle beach are *Haustorius* and *Bathyporeia*. The intertidal Isopod, *Eurydice*—marine version of the familiar woodlouse—has been the subject of a special study. Two species from different climatic regions live together at Oxwich, their needs apparently indistinguishable. A square metre of sand dug to a depth of 15 centimetres yielded on average 520 individuals of *E. pulchra* (which are to be found right around the British coast) and 550 of *E. affinis* (a Mediterranean species which is restricted in Britain to the shores of the Bristol Channel).

The waters are clearer this far down Channel than on most of the Glamorgan coast and little transparent sea gooseberries (*Pleurobrachia pileus*) can sometimes be seen propelling themselves through the water by means of eight iridescent rows of tiny beating combs and catching their prey with 'lassoo cells'. Mauve-banded common jellyfish (*Aurelia aurita*) and the rarer south-westerly, brown-rayed *Chrysaora isosceles* may also undulate past, motivated by the rhythmic pulsating of their transparent 'umbrellas'.

73. Bog pimpernel from acid dune slacks

Sea creatures penetrate inland along Nicholaston Pill into the domain of black-headed gull and kingfisher, overlapping with those of land and fresh water. Otter spraint was found by the sluice here in July 1975. Tideline flies, *Fucellia maritima*, tempt pipits, wagtails and starlings onto the lines of drifted seaweed and the fry of flounders and mullet from the sea mingle with sticklebacks and rudd from the marshes and lakes. The red-finned rudd can be baited with bread for a closer view, the little ones racing in, bumping their noses on the bread and retiring in consternation, while their elders move in with slow decorum and scoff the lot.

Sand clams (*Mya arenaria*) and Baltic tellins (*Macoma balthica*) live in the reaches of the pill alongside the sea wall, with peppery furrow shells (*Scrobicularia plana*) higher up. There are ragworms here too (*Nereis diversicolor*), the lean, mud-burrowing Amphipod (*Corophium volutator*), the Isopod (*Sphaeroma rugicauda*) which rolls itself into a ball when upset, and the little prawn (*Paleomonetes varians*) which prefers brackish water to that of the open sea.

Some 25 years ago, in the 40s and 50s, there was a lot more open water in the saltmarsh alongside the pill and these animals were widespread on the mudflats, tempting waders in to feed. In those days the frequency of redshank, dunlin and others made the erection of photographic hides a more worthwhile proposition, but some, including green sandpiper, still winter here.

Now most of the saltmarsh is silted up and vegetated over, so that only the highest of tides can cover it. There is still some glasswort left in the low-lying parts (*Salicornia dolichostachya* and *S. ramosissima*), forming miniature, cactus-like stands of succulent candelabra stems bearing the minutest of leaves and flowers. Sea purslane (*Halimione*) of the same 'saltbush' family lines the residual creeks and another of this fraternity, the Babington's orache (*Atriplex glabriuscula*) grows on drier sandbanks. Leaves of one of the commoner oraches (*A. patula*) are affected in some years by roll gall, the rolling of their edges induced by the Aphid, *Semiaphis atriplices*.

Sea aster and sea lavender provide late downshore colour when upshore zones are brightened by the soft pink of marsh mallow and lemon yellow of evening primrose (*Oenothera erythrosepala*). The South American dock (*Rumex cuneifolius*) has got established at Oxwich, but it needs a discerning eye to spot it.

Salinity gradients are confused at the inner end of the saltmarsh, where banks of invading vegetation prevent free run-off, so that some of the stagnant water trapped upshore may be more saline than that downshore. Instead of the expected grading from *Spartina* through sea sedge to common reed on moving upstream, these three alternate and overlap. A narrow belt of sea rush and parsley water-dropwort at one point separates salt-loving sea sedge on its upper side from freshwater reed on its lower side. *Spartina*, fortunately, is not common in the upper marsh and the general sequence from Nicholaston Pill in the North to the dunes in the South is from reeds through waterlogged sea sedge to the main, drier, marsh of sea rush and so to mixed freshwater and dune plants.

There are interesting gradients within the sea rush zone with parsley water-dropwort (*Oenanthe lachenalii*) growing only downshore and tubular water-dropwort (*O. fistulosa*) only upshore. The gap between contains brackish species such as wild celery, long-bracted sedge and saltmarsh rush (*Juncus gerardi*). Some of these, like brookweed (*Samolus*) and arrow-grass occur in all communities, seedlings of the former germinating in thousands during late August. At this time of year the upper marsh is colourful with hemp-agrimony, perennial sow-thistle, fleabane, tansy, centaury and silver-weed, grading upward into water mint, gipsywort and a few late flowers of ragged robin.

Many winged insects spend their infancy in this community, among them a Hymenopteran, *Rogas punctipes*, which is very local in Britain. Two of the craneflies found here are first records for Glamorgan: *Dicranomyis sera* being quite common, *Erioptera stictica* locally common at the edge of the saltmarsh towards the dunes. The fly, *Dexiopsis minutalis* is also an 'Oxwich only' record. Such rarities may well turn up elsewhere, but the likelihood of their doing so in the diverse habitat at Oxwich, tempts the experts to seek here first.

The caddis fly (*Limnophilus affinis*) is not adverse to living in these slightly brackish waters and a typical dragonfly of the saltmarsh (as well as the dune slacks) is the libellula, *Sympetrum striolatum*. Bugs include *Notostira erratica, Stygnocoris pedestria* and the lucerne plant bug, *Adelphocoris lineolatus*, which is a pest of lucerne in America, Poland and Russia, but associated with a wider range of legumes, including clover and rest harrow on Oxwich.

A few duck and wader species still visit the saltmarsh and three pairs of shelduck nest most years. Water rail, too, breed in the saltmarsh as well as in the freshwater fens behind. Herons, including visiting purple herons, drop in to feed sometimes and an impressive number of species halt awhile as they pass through. Larger mammals such as foxes take temporary refuge among the tall grasses and rushes and short-tailed field voles occur in the mixed saltmarsh, along with the rather less typical bank voles.

There are more bank voles in the wet alder copses, where wood mice and common shrews are frequent, but in a recent survey of open dune and bracken land, only the wood mouse was found, rarely on the dunes but abundantly among the bracken. The status of the rabbits fluctuates and they are thought to have been exterminated by Myxomatosis in 1954-55, but were re-established again by 1963. Molehills of clean yellow sand get thrown up over the dark moss of the grey dunes, where the marram is wispy and has almost disappeared, but where surface organic matter is still very superficial.

Green woodpeckers and stonechats are particularly evident among the resident birds and ringed plovers, once quite widespread along the coast, still nest occasionally on the edge of the slacks. Siskins regularly frequent the alder and birch spinneys and other migrants which can be relied on to appear are bar-tailed godwit, knot and sanderling. Waders, wagtails and martins are most numerous among the birds of passage and a vagrant hoopoe turned up on Nicholaston Burrows at the end of October 1967. In 1963, when the fresh water ponds froze over, many water birds moved down to the beach to feed and were joined there by lapwings, a number of which died.

Much has already been said of the plant rarities and vegetation succession on the Oxwich dunes. 1974 was a particularly good year for the Welsh gentian and wintergreen, both of which flower in the slacks in August, well after the main burst of flowering on the sandhills round about, where the porous soil is likely to have dried out by then. Perhaps it was the long wet summer which stimulated them to extra exuberance. Certainly some of the dune annuals such as fairy flax continued to germinate and flower

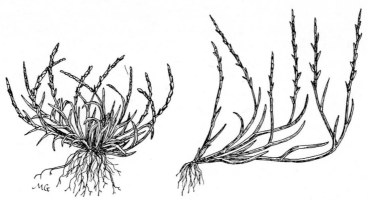

74. Curved and common sea hard grasses (*Parapholis incurva* and *P. strigosa*)

all summer instead of shrivelling by late May, as when confronted by the June heatwave of 1975 and 1976. Unusual species near the Nature Conservancy's Centre in the car park include yellow tree lupin, pink everlasting pea, Virginia creeper, soapwort and ramping fumitory.

Parts of Oxwich Burrows are as rich in flowering plant species as anywhere in the county, yet parts are practically barren. The father and mother of all blowouts near the car park shows few plants even marginally apart from sea holly and sea spurge, with sand couch encroaching up gullies from the beach. All of these have tough, well waterproofed leaves and are fitted to withstand drought in other ways. The deep roots of sea holly tap hidden reserves of water, the milky latex of sea spurge helps to retain moisture chemically and the spreading underground system of sand couch can utilise surface water from light showers or dewfall. The marram tufts planted out in 1971 looked rather pathetic at first, but those supplied with fertiliser rallied well. Given reasonable freedom from visitor pressure, these may survive and spread to form a healing callus. Underground stems ramifying sideways and shoots growing ever upwards as they are sanded over, provide a herring bone skeleton for the rising dune, which comes to resemble a collapsible version of reinforced concrete. Some unexpected plants of these yellow dunes are rock samphire, wind-dispersed red valerian and tough little fronds of polypody fern. Heath dog violets are locally abundant, their leaves darker and more slender than those of the common dog violet. Dewberry and blackberry become established in the tall grass/bracken phase of the plant succession and fruit earlier than normal on the sun-warmed sands. Spindle and privet bushes herald the full scrub phase, occupying a niche which is partially filled by wayfaring tree on more easterly dunes. Grey sallow and hairy birch are the chief spinney formers, but there are occasional self-sown ashes, yews and pines as well as oaks, helping the community on to the final woodland climax.

245

Hollows scoured out below the level of the water table become slacks in which the sand ceases to blow because its grains are stuck together with ground water. Marsh plants soon invade these, benefitting from the stability and from shelter afforded by the surrounding dunes. A surface layer of humus is laid down, sometimes above the level of the limey ground water, so that it is moistened only by rain and may become quite acid. Such peaty slacks can show an interesting mixture of salt tolerant and freshwater species with sea rush from the saltmarsh growing among hard rush from the moors and blunt rush (*Juncus subnodulosus*), which is a rare plant in Glamorgan and confined to limey habitats. Welsh gentian occurs in such communities with brookweed, suggesting that it may be tolerant of a certain brackishness. Purple loosestrife, yellow iris, creeping Jenny and various orchids are among the more colourful components of the slack flora.

The abundant lime from the pulverised fragments of razor, mussel and other seashells in the dune sands dissolves out into the ground water and is recycled into the shells of land snails via their food plants. Snails as a result are common, but a snail has a damp foot so needs a damp substrate if it is to conserve its body slime. Most species must live among moisture-retaining vegetation or in the slacks, but four or five are able to survive the rigours of the barer dunes by venturing out of cover mostly at night or on wet days.

The hardy ones include the versatile garden snail and the two grove snails, the brown-lipped *Cepaea nemoralis* much commoner than the white-lipped *C. hortensis*. The two last come in many colour patterns which are genetically stable, remaining constant from one generation to the next, and it is likely that those surviving thrush predation longest to breed their kind are those which best match their background. Thrushes need an 'anvil' on which to break the snail shells and, in the absence of natural objects sufficiently hard, a coca cola bottle or beer can may be utilised and become surrounded by shell fragments.

The little cone-shaped pointed snail, *Cochlicella acuta*, seems quite at home on the yellow dunes and is abundant, too, on Llangennith Burrows. Striped snails, *Helicella virgata*, prefer the arid habitats to more comfortable looking ones further back, where their relatives the wrinkled snails, *H. caperata*, come into their own. These latter get their name from the ribs on the shell, which distinguish them from the other, where the stripes are merely growth rings. One is tempted to wonder why they so often walk up dead grass stems—and what they eat. Perhaps there is a fungal growth that they can lick from the senescent straws.

Shells of snails get abraded by flying sand while still on the move, so that they appear dull and dead, but are heavy with flesh when picked up. Such specimens are often still shiny and colourful on the underside which has been protected from blowing particles, and on the lastest growth

164 165 166

67

Plate 39.   BURRY MARSHES: ABOVE THE TIDES

164. Great Bulrush or Reedmace   *Author*
165. False Fox Sedge   *Author*
166. Great Pond Sedge   *Author*
167. Mare and Foal come upshore for freshwater to drink   *Author*

247

168

169

Plate 40
CWM IVY MARSH 1

170

168. Common Spotted Orchid
169. White Marsh Woundwort
170. Creek lined with Sea Sedge
     penetrates freshwater marsh
     All Author

248

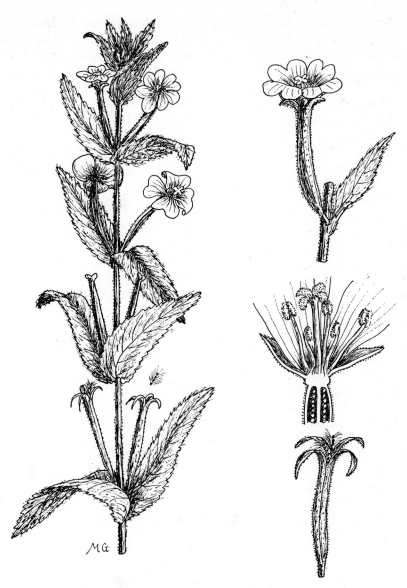

75. Greater willow herb

increment at the shell mouth, which has been exposed for a shorter time. There are, however, many sub-fossil snail shells too, particularly where long-buried ones have been re-excavated in blowouts—and these may be still intact after seventy years and more. One of the whorl snails, *Vertigo angustior*, has been found only as dead shells in Oxwich sand pockets, never alive.

249

The pill bug is another animal of the open dunes which utilises lime to strengthen its heavily armoured outer skin. This is able to tolerate the dry conditions much better than woodlice do. Harvestmen or daddy longlegs are named for the time of year when they are most abundant in August and September. Carnivorous by nature, they can prove cannibalistic and may be seen with an octet of bedraggled legs belonging to an erstwhile fellow protruding from their jaws.

Grasshoppers abound on warm summer days, mostly the short-horned field grasshopper, *Chorthippus brunneus*. The slender black and orange sand wasp, *Ammophila sabulosa* is sometimes spotted astride a caterpillar bigger than itself, dragging this to a burrow where it will be stowed away as food for a single wasp larva. The burrow is closed after the egg has been laid in the paralysed but still living victim. The black and yellow striped field digger wasp, *Mellinus arvensis*, stocks its nesting burrow with immobilised flies. Black and red cuckoo bees, *Sphecodes*, and spider hunting solitary wasps, *Pompilus*, are also to be seen in season. The mining bee, *Colletes marginata*, lives among brambles with *Prosopis communis* and *P. lyalinata*, building a paper cell which she stocks with honey for the larva at the end of a burrow 8-10 inches long. Inch-high sand volcanoes belong to tiny black ants which race busily in and out of the central funnel.

Yellow and black hover flies, *Syrphus ribesii* and others, feed on nectar and pollen throughout the summer and on into November. Drone flies, *Eristalis tenax* and, more rarely, *E. pertinax*, are also around for most of the year, wearing the warning colouration of the honey bee. Other contributors to the hum of insect wings on drowsy summer days are green bottles, *Lucilia* and *Orthellia* species. A rarer fly, *Minettia rivosa*, discovered here in 1960, is a first record for Glamorgan.

Of the butterflies small coppers and orange tips are typical in spring, grayling, hedge brown, meadow brown, peacock, small skipper and common blue in high summer. Cinnabar moths and six-spot burnet moths are abundant in season, as on all the dunes, and others have been collected by means of light traps. The shore wainscot (*Leucania litoralis*) lives on marram, the sand dart (*Agrotis ripae*) on sea holly and the barred yellow (*Cidaria fulvata*) is associated with burnet rose instead of the more usual hedgerow briars. Very similar to this moth, with barred yellow forewings and pale hindwings is the chevron moth (*Lygris testata*). Another with barred wings is the shaded broad bar (*Ortholitha chenopodiata*), one with more white on it the common carpet (*Epirrhoe alternata*).

The crimson and gold (*Rhodaria purpuralis*) is as attractive as its name suggests flitting from flower to flower in the sunshine, but it also flies after dark. Grass moths of the genus *Crambus* are particularly characteristic, no less than nine species having been identified at Oxwich in 1971 and 1973. They are quite cryptic when resting by day, narrowly parallel-sided with brown and white wings folded tightly round the body and often aligned

76. Five moths from Oxwich dunes. From left to right: shaded broad bar, barred yellow, common carpet, sand dart and shore wainscot

head downwards among the grass stems. One, *Crambus geniculeus*, is restricted to sand dune country.

Finest of all the moths are the puss moths (*Cerura vinula*) whose plump exotic-looking caterpillars are sometimes quite common on sallows in the dune slacks. They are bright green with white-bordered black saddle and yellow-bordered red and black 'face mask'. The display of this last, coupled with the lashing of two crimson tail threads must prove quite terrifying when the larva rear up in front of a would be predator. And, as if this was not enough, the visual deterrent is likely to be followed by a jet of formic acid from a gland in the thorax.

At the other end of the scale for blatant show and also living on the willows but in tiny paper cases like those of the common rush moth, are the larvae of *Coleophora palliatella*. More conspicuous on the creeping willows of the slacks are the scarlet willow leaf beetles (*Chrysomela populi*), like oversized, unspotted ladybirds. These are widespread and common in all the dune systems. Their larvae are similar in colour but elongated and segmented, with an armoury of black spines. When threatened they are able to exude milky drops of a distasteful fluid containing salicil aldehyde from these spines as a deterrent.

30 WHITEFORD BURROWS: NATIONAL NATURE RESERVE

THE fact that two separate areas of Gower dunes have been designated as national rather than local nature reserves says much for the biological diversity to be found on this captivating peninsula. Whiteford Burrows are regarded as the wildest part of Gower and, in spite of their proximity to the great connurbation of Swansea, one of the least disturbed sand dune areas in Wales. It is a two mile walk from the nearest road at Cwm Ivy to the tip of Whiteford Point—just half way across the estuary mouth to the old coast of Carmarthen (now Dyfed) two miles further on.

Likening Gower to a great lower jaw, the Nature Conservancy Council refers to the long sandspit leading to the point as a canine tooth, but it might better be thought of as the forward incisors. To the West is the mobile 'lip'—the shifting sand of the ocean beach—to the East is the equally mobile 'tongue' of shifting sandbanks in the Burry Inlet.

The morainic ridge of Whiteford Scar, the rocky foundation on which the spit is built, was deposited by glaciers 10-50,000 years ago, when sea level was at least 150 ft. (46m.) below its present level. As the melting ice poured in from the land, the augmented sea level rose, filling the former valley and eating into its flanks to form the North Gower cliffs. Waves lapping to the foot of Cwm Ivy, North Hill Tor and the limestone faces further East began to deposit particles of sand and mud which pushed the open tide further from the land and gave the dunes and marshes as we know them today.

The scientific importance of the land which has come into being during the last few thousand years was officially recognised in 1953 when the area was designated as a Site of Special Scientific Interest, so there was inevitable concern that it might fall into the wrong hands when it came up for sale by auction in 1965. Pressure on any such potential holiday area in this age of affluence is enormous and soaring prices are likely to take it well beyond the reach of any but the commercial developer who can hope to get his money back. Thanks, however, to efforts by the Glamorgan Naturalists' Trust and the Society for the Protection of Nature Reserves, along with some generous loans, the National Trust was able to buy and hold it safe for all time against indiscriminate development. This was the first property in Britain to be acquired as a result of "Enterprise Neptune", the National Trust's campaign to safeguard our coastal heritage from the inroads of unwise exploitation. (Yet another 'first' for this first 'Area of Outstanding National Beauty'.)

Three square miles at Whiteford are now leased to the Nature Conservancy Council and managed as a wildlife sanctuary adjacent to part of the eastern marsh leased to the West Glamorgan Wildfowlers' Association and managed as a shoot. The partnership is not as odd as it may seem, the wildfowlers being as interested as the naturalists in maintaining a vigorous breeding stock of birds and conserving a natural feeding habitat likely to attract them.

Gordon Goodman (first scientific secretary of the Glamorgan Naturalists' Trust), who knew Gower's natural history as well as anyone during the fifties and sixties, expressed the feeling of all local naturalists when he wrote, "The far-sighted cooperation in this enterprise of all these bodies

Plate 41   SAND DUNE BUTTERFLY AND MOTHS

171. Six-spot Burnet caterpillar and cocoons *(Zygaena filipendulae)* on dock — *Author*
172. Six-spot Burnet moth newly emerged from cocoon on ribwort plantain — *Author*
173. Cinnabar caterpillar *(Tyria jacobaea)* on ragwort — *Author*
174. Cinnabar moth among wood sage — *Author*
175. Gold spot moth *(Plusia festucae)* — *Author*
176. Common blues *(Polycommatus icarus)* pairing on ribwort plantain — *Author*
177. Cream Spot Tiger moth *(Arctia villica),* a species of South East England, photographed at Whiteford — *Author*

178

179

180

181

182

183

Plate 42   SMALL SAND DUNE ANIMALS

178. Larva of Red Leaf Beetle *(Chrysomela populi)* exuding blobs of distasteful liquid to deter predators
Michael Claridge

179. Great Green Bush cricket *(Tettigonia viridissima)*   *Michael Claridge*

180. Sand wasp *(Ammophila)* bears the same generic name as the marram among which it lives   *Michael Claridge*

181. Galls of the Gall wasp, *(Diplolepis spinosissima)*, on burnet rose   *Michael Claridge*

182. Hedge snails *(Cepaea)* showing new shell growth. Garden snail *(Helix aspersa)* on right   *Author*

183. Snail shells on thyme at Llangennith. Elongated *Cochlicella,* small *Helicella* with central hole and large *Cepaea*   *Author*

254

with such overlapping interests in the countryside is undoubtedly a milestone in practical conservation in Britain and even the most coldly scientific conservationist will forgive the feeling of exuberance one has in writing about this splendid area which is now ours in perpetuity."

The interest begins well below high water mark, beyond the spreading mussel beds where attached oarweeds were seen for the very first time during the low tides of February 1974. It is only that part of the moraine in the lower intertidal zone which remains free from drifted sand and hence able to support seaweeds. This part falls within the lowermost saw wrack zone, the four wracks which normally dominate the zones above being sparse or absent. Mussels grow throughout, well anchored by the guylines of their byssus threads. Churning of the morainic stones by waves where these are not effectively held by the navy blue multitude results in high mortality among the acorn barnacles (mostly *Balanus balanoides*), many getting scoured from their hold to leave pale circles like fossil corals embedded in the rocks.

Dog whelks have a bonanza here, with a surfeit of both mussels and barnacles for food. So, too, have the little pea crabs (*Pinnotherus pisum*) which live within the mussel shells, cleaning their hosts' gills in return for a sheltered niche in which to dine. In order to effect entry a crab will stroke the lips of the chosen shell with a hairy leg, this persuading them to relax and open. In between picking delicacies from her host's filter-feeding mechanism, the female crab lays her eggs within. Larval crabs escape soon after hatching and swim off to find cooperative mussels for themselves.

Many other creatures find shelter in the mussel banks. Some are sedentary like the snakelocks anemone, fan worms, boring piddock shells and red, orange and grey sponges, others mobile—brittle stars, star-fish, sea gooseberries and shore crabs. Pools of the middle shore hold much carragheen (*Chondrus*) but the upper rocks are partially sand-covered and characterised by the protruding tubes of sand worms.

Scuffle marks of unwebbed bird toes on otherwise untrodden sands around the upper rocks accompany little piles of mussel and carpet shells. They tell a story of contentedly feeding oyster catchers and turnstones which attack the hinges, so that the empty shells are open but often undamaged. Redshank, curlew, eider, shelduck and brent geese are also to be seen on this exposed shore, but it is to the lonelier saltings behind the spit that most of the birds repair to feed.

The vagaries of the ocean shoreline have already been discussed, one visit revealing a storm-lashed sand cliff, the next a ringed plover's nest tucked away under a fresh flowering clump of sea rocket. Within and across the spit to the marshes beyond is a spreading confusion of hillocks and hollows built in sand to heights of fifty feet and more by the interplay of winds from all quarters. These miniature hill ranges set a pattern in

255

77. Marsh pennywort. Habitat forms from dense, medium and heavily grazed plant cover.
Flower and fruit showing affinity with the carrot family

micro-climates with some plants favouring the windy or sunny slopes and others the sheltered or shady ones.

Those in the depressions may lie beneath flood water during winter with the sand remaining pleasantly moist during summer and the number of

256

species is large. Visiting botanists seem to have taken on something of the depressions themselves, wandering, apparently aimlessly, to and fro with shoulders stooped and heads bent. They are, on the contrary, having an extremely rewarding hunt, whether they are conoisseurs looking for the two rare liverworts, *Moerckia flotowiana* and *Petalophylum ralfsii*, or just out to admire the sheets of pink, purple and cream-coloured orchids in June.

The crimson early marsh orchids which precede the ivory drifts of marsh helleborine are particularly striking. By the time the carpets of bird's foot trefoil are at their best the fruit capsules of the creeping willow have burst assunder to reveal their froth of silky-plumed seeds, so the great arena-like slacks become patterned in gold and silver, with the paler gold of kidney vetch rimming the margins.

These riches can be appreciated without adopting the sad botanical stoop, but one needs to be closer to the ground to find the real pearls. One such is the newly discovered early sand grass, another the parasitic yellow bird's nest. Others are the two primitive and un-fernlike ferns, adder's tongue and moonwort, sometimes with the added bonus of a lapwing's nest tucked into the grass alongside with mottled eggs tapering to the centre to fill the available space with neat perfection. Other gems in the rough mossy grass of the slacks are the rare fen orchid and elegant lesser centaury, which is likely to be found only at Whiteford.

The drier dunes yield a different selection, from the colour contrast of pyramidal orchid and yellow bedstraw to the more muted tones of the meadow rue and white horehound. The annual sea pansies come and go —having a thin year if their seed heads have been nibbled off in the previous summer.

There is little natural woodland at Whiteford, but three successional phases are recognisable. While the marram thrives on partially open dunes associates include the pinky blue (occasionally white) spikes of viper's bugloss, wine-red hound's tongue, white gromwell and handsome heads of evening primrose—successful invaders from North America. The dune meadow which follows, as the creeping fescues succeed the tufted and annual grasses, shows a succession of many shades of yellow as the year advances. Here are hop trefoil and lesser yellow clover, crosswort and yellow-wort, mouse-ear hawkweed and hawkbit, along with salad burnet, thyme and eyebright. The dune heath which develops as the minerals seep away with the flushing of rain water is less lush—a thin carpet of thyme, mosses and lichens, pierced by a scatter of taller herbs.

Sea buckthorn threatened at one time to become a menace, as it has on the Mid-Glamorgan dunes, but the invasion was nipped in the bud by the Nature Conservancy. Plants turned up in the post-war decade, probably brought by birds from Towyn Burrows across the estuary around Pembrey, where they were introduced in the 1930s. Their increase at

Whiteford during the mid sixties sounded the alarm (though the bird watchers envisaged a pleasant increase in the cover for song birds and supply of berries for winter thrushes). A programme of grubbing out and cutting resulted in their virtual extinction but odd seedlings were still appearing in 1975.

The other big management operation is the gradual removal of some 20,000 conifers, mostly Scots and Corsican pine, planted over 100 acres or so by the previous owner from 1931 on. Some fine mature trees shelter the Nature Conservancy research hut in the Cwm Ivy corner of the Burrows and the canopy here has opened out to give a healthy ground flora where the broad-leaved helleborine orchid can grow. Elsewhere the policy is to remove the pines piecemeal before they mature and set seed, thus allowing the natural dune vegetation to regenerate in the clearings.

This is paying dividends from the faunal angle as well as the floral, with butterflies and other winged creatures (including birds) favouring the local shelter of the newly opened clearings and exploiting the newly arrived flush of nectar-bearing flowers and the ensuing crops of fruits and seeds. Whiteford supports all the common butterflies likely to be found in Gower and a number of uncommon ones as well.

Here it is that the large pearl-bordered and dark green fritillaries indulge in their fast, elusive flights, denying the watcher a long close look. Marbled whites are unmistakable and common in July and August, here in the shelter of the pines and also in dune scrub and over salt and freshwater marsh. This is much the best site for this very local southern butterfly which is more characteristically found on the chalk grasslands

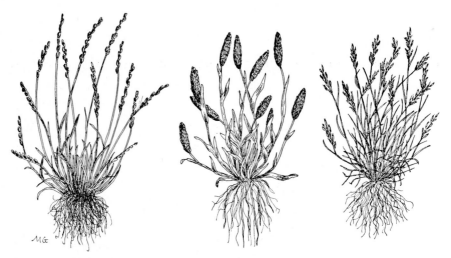

78. Three annual dune grasses. From left to right: early sand grass (*Mibora minima*), sand cat's tail and early hair grass

of Southern England. Common blues abound and, in good years such as 1975, small blues as well, often associated with kidney vetch on the dunes here, as they are on the Eastern cliffs around Limeslade Bay.

Large, small and dingy skippers, small coppers and small heaths are among the daintier species and the medium-sized gatekeeper is frequent in midsummer, particularly over the bramble thickets. Speckled woods prefer the shade near the field laboratory but graylings, like meadow browns and wall browns, are very much a part of the arid sandy slopes. Painted ladies are less regular than the other Nymphalidae (red admiral, peacock and small tortoiseshell).

Quantities of moths have been identified, as many as forty species from the owlet moth family or Noctuidae alone (a family having 300 species in Britain out of a world population of more than 6,000!). As their family name implies, these usually fly by night, hiding up by day in dark crannies, so that they reveal themselves only to those who sally forth after dark with light traps.

Most easily recognised of the moths are the red and black cinnabars (*Callimorpha jacobaeae*) with their tiger-striped caterpillars denuding the leaves of the abundant ragwort and rarer groundsels. Other black and yellow caterpillars, their stripes longitudinal this time, are those of the broom moth (*Ceramica pisi*) but there is another colour form of this in green and yellow. Six spot burnet moths (*Zygaena filipendulae*) are extremely abundant. Their speckled green caterpillars like to climb tall marram, rush, dock or plantain stems when they are ready to pupate, but can sometimes find no such elevated pitches and have to spin their yellow silk cocoons at ground level, where they are likely to get trodden on. Five spot burnets (*Z. trifolii*) also occur on the dunes, but the two species are almost mutually exclusive, though occasionally feeding on the same flower head where their territories join. The five spot favours pea flowers such as bird's foot trefoil in the marshier areas.

Silver Ys (*Plusia gamma*) fuss around the late August flowers, feeding without alighting on occasion, so that the distinctive Y marking on the wing is invisible. Brown greys (*Scoparia dubitalis*) and yellow shells (*Euphyia bilineata*) are to be seen, as are close relatives of the riband wave and spinach moths (*Sterrha dimidiata* and *Lygris testata*). The snout moth (*Hypena proboscidalis*), which is named for the long palps or sense organs which protrude in front like a snout, is likely to be disturbed from nettle beds. These fly at night in midsummer and again in autumn, the caterpillars feeding among the nettles from August until driven into hibernation by the onset of winter.

The small purple-barred (*Phytometra viridaria*) with plum-coloured bar across each forewing, lives (with its eggs, larvae and pupae) on the pink, white or blue patches of milkwort. Bordered whites (*Bupalus piniaria*) are day-flying moths of the pine plantations; their slender green caterpillars the 'pine loopers' which feed on the needles right through from June to October. Light emeralds (*Campaea margaritata*) are quite beautiful when first emerged, but the delicate pale green of the patterned wings soon fades to whitish yellow. Another beauty, in delicate yellow this time is the swallow tailed moth (*Ourapteryx sambucaria*). Both the green and the yellow are found among broad leaved trees, principally sallows.

Species new for South Wales which were discovered at Whiteford in 1972 were *Aristotelia bifractella* on the flowers of fleabane (the species on whose seed head the larvae feed) and *Eevtria purdeyi* in the pine plantations. This last is described as being distributed from Kent to the Isle of Wight only, and quite locally even there, so it must have come in with the planting of the pines. Better known kinds are the splendid eye-spotted emperor moth (*Saturnia pavonia*), whose fat stripey caterpillars feed on dewberry and bramble, and the oak eggar (*Lasiocampa quercus*) which is by no means confined to oak, haunting the grey and creeping sallow, bramble, hawthorn and broom as well. Many others have been listed and there is always a chance of something new being found by the experts.

The bulk of the Whiteford invertebrates are less far ranging and are perhaps best thought of collectively in the zones where they occur. Animals of the driftline at the top of the beach are carnivores and scavengers rather than plant feeders and no less than nine beetles have been identfied in this rather restricted habitat.

The rare *Eurynebria complanata* beetles move upshore into the foredunes if driftwood and other cover gets carried away by storms. Their immediate environment is chancy at best, presenting problems of food supply, shelter and drying out. Added to which the animals are at home in Morocco, Algeria and Tunisia and this outlying British population is at the northern limit of its geographical range. The beetles mate from September to November, laying eggs singly in tiny, uncovered holes in the sand above the strandline—as much as 180ft above in some instances. Larvae emerge from October onwards and are around until March, the first adult beetles, rather pale-coloured ones, emerging from the pupae at the end of May.

Eurynebria's chief food item, the sandhopper, *Talitrus saltator*, is rarely attacked by the other big nocturnal beetle which co-habits with it (*Broscus cephalotes*). This is what zoologists call a 'top predator' feeding on other beetles. The third big carnivore in this trio is the yellow and bronze tiger beetle, *Cicindela maritima*, which hunts by day and flies so readily as to be easily mistaken for a big fly when it takes off. The burrow in which the larva lies in wait for its prey may be as much as a foot deep. The predatory juvenile sits just inside the entrance, biding its time until it can pounce on an unwary passer-by and then retreat to the bottom of its underground hideout for an undisturbed meal.

260

79. Eider drakes and ducks

A carrion feeding beetle of both beach and dune is the black-patterned yellow *Phateria cadaverina*. Another which scavenges over bare sand for a living is the small scarab, *Aegialia arenaria*. Feeding on marram, but often wandering downshore over the beach sand is a globular brown weevil, *Philopedon plagiatus*.

Even rarer than *Eurynebria* in this forward zone is the white pill bug *Armadillidium album*, which is known from only four other localities in Britain. Like *Eurynebria*, it moves inland if cover becomes sparse in the driftline. Spiders likewise move upshore in the autumn when the flotsam and jetsam become sanded over or washed away, but they are quite abundant there in July. Gower's new species, *Lasiargus gowerensis*, was found in drifted *Spartina* grass.

That some are more choosy than others as to where they live is demonstrated by four members of the genus *Erigone*, little black money spiders. *E. arctica* forages only along the lines of tidal debris and into the foredunes, *E. longipalpis* among both foredune sand couch and main dune marram, *E. dentipalpis* and *E. atra* throughout all the available habitats from drift-line to dry dune meadow and wet slacks.

Spiders typical of the narrow foredune ridge include *Lophocarenum nemorale* and *L. stramineum* and another very characteristic animal here is the mirid bug, *Trigonotylus psammecolor*, which feeds on the sand couch.

Mixed dune vegetation of marram tufts and herbs further from the sea is the place to seek adults of the two spiders, *Agroeca proxima* and *A. inopina*, and the juveniles too, in September. In July however the latter are more likely to be found in dune meadow, and these are not the only ones to migrate to a different habitat as they grow. Most reach maturity by autumn and there are far more spiders around in September than in midsummer.

The more sparsely vegetated dune heath supports fewer spiders but one, *Argenna subnigra*, seems to prefer the low cover of moss and lichen here.

261

The harvestman (*Phalangium opilio*), with striking saddle mark on its back, is common on the main dunes in Spring and Summer as well as autumn. Two spiders which are quite localised here are the rare ant mimic, *Synageles venator*, which is restricted to the South-west coast, of Britain and *Stylotector romanus*, which seems not to occur on the East coast dunes either.

Marram tussocks of the main open dune system provide cover for a great many creatures, one of the commonest of the beetles being the ground beetle or Carabid, *Risophilus monostigma*. A chafer or scarab beetle with cock chafer-like flight to be seen crawling or flying over the bare sand is the reddish-yellow *Anomala dubia*. Another is the false ground beetle or Tenebrionid, *Phylan gibbus*.

Patches of the abundant dune moss, *Tortula ruraliformis*, shelter rove beetles, *Amara*. Members of the pea family are popular hosts in the dune grassland. The weevil, *Apion loti* feeds on bird's foot trefoil (*Lotus*), another weevil, *Sitona griseus*, on various of the legumes and the plant bug, *Dicyphus annulatus*, on rest harrow.

Glow worms, *Lampyris noctiluca*, can be seen twinkling among the marram tussocks on summer nights. The luminescent ones are unwinged females: the males have no lamps but are able to fly around and locate potential spouses by theirs. Adults feed very little but the segmented yellow-patterned larvae fare well on the soft bodies of snails. A big, attractive shield bug, often on flowers of the carrot family, is *Dolycoris baccarum*. Other bugs of the yellow dunes are *Dicranocephalus agilis* and *Coranus subapterus*. Only one of the two common sand cockroaches is likely to be found at Whiteford, this being *Ectobius pallidus*.

Certain plant-eating beetles and bugs are quite at home here, on the mosses and lichens of the dune heath, among them the glossy-coated ground beetle, *Amara tibialis*, and *Metabletus foveatus*. Some of the commonest, like the ground beetles *Calathus erratus* and *C. fuscipes*, are abroad mainly at night and difficult to locate by day.

Ponies straying up from the saltings leave warm patches of manure behind and these are welcomed by the big black dung beetles, *Geotrupes stercorarius*, which tunnel out burrows ¾" across underneath. Their own remains are sometimes found in the dung or crop pellets of kestrel and curlew. Less striking dung beetles, species of *Aphodius*, are also dependent on the marsh ponies for their immediate environment.

Lochmaea capraea as well as the commoner poplar leaf beetle, *Chrysomela populi*, feed on the creeping willow and it is here that the male scorpion flies, *Panorpa communis*, can sometimes be spotted, with ruddy, tip-tilted but harmless tails poised aloft. The rare southern spider, *Theridion saxatile*, which is new to Wales, constructs a quite specialised type of web around the steep sides of the willow 'hedgehogs'.

Plate 43 SPECIAL FEATURES AT WHITEFORD BURROWS

184. Dunes cut back by gales in January 1974 to expose basal clay layer. West side of Whiteford Point   *Author*
185. Moonwort, a rare and primitive fern to be found at Whiteford   *Author*
186. Yellow bird's nest is probably Whiteford's rarest plant   *Author*
187. Fen orchid, rarest of Gower's orchids, in a Whiteford dune slack   *Author*

Plate 44   NORTHERN DUNES AND SALTMARSHES

188. Scarlet pimpernel   *Author*
189. Sea bindweed   *Author*
190. Bloody cranesbill   *Author*
191. Pyramidal orchid   *Author*
192. Cockleshell heap and cart at top of Llanrhidian saltmarsh   *Author*
193. Sea lavender on Cheriton saltmarsh   *Author*

264

Slacks proper, with their more favourable humidity, form the richest habitat. The bright-hued ground beetles, *Feronia caerutescens* and *Chlaenius nigricornis*, live here but are not often seen by day. More diurnal is the coppery or brassy *Elaphrus uliginosus*, which resembles a small tiger beetle. Spiders vary in their moisture requirements and one of the wolf spiders, *Arctosa leopardus*, is unable to survive away from the slacks, and is replaced on dry dunes by *A. perita*.

Grassy slacks support the speckled bush cricket, *Leptophyes punctatissima*, which, though large and green, is still quite well camouflaged among the moist grass. Small inconspicuous ground hoppers with them here are *Tetrix ceperoi* and *T. undulata*. The stout tussocks of sharp rush (*Juncus acutus*) in the slacks tend to concentrate the fauna and shelter no less than four species of woodlice.

Dune pools introduce a whole new world of animal life with the big *Dystiscus* diving beetles and *Corixid* water boatmen. The keeled Orthetrum dragonfly (*Orthetrum coerulescens*) is a yellow brown colour except in adult males, which change to powder blue as they grow. Only one has ever been seen on Gower—a male at Whiteford in early September 1972. The green lestes damselfly (*Lestes sponsa*) also haunts the Whiteford pools, the metallic emerald body becoming powdered with blue at each extremity in the males as they mature.

The pine plantations support an impoverished invertebrate fauna with *Nebria brevicollis* the most often seen. (This has no English name but is everybody's idea of the common black beetle).

Foxes stalking through the reserve when all is quiet and the tracks in the sand may tell a tale of the mouse which got away or the vole which was caught on the third pounce. Two badger setts were occupied into the early 1970s but possibly not any longer. Rabbits were common in the North in 1974, when hares were also about, and the common or viviparous lizard (*Lacerta vivipara*) is everywhere. The rare sand lizard (*L. agilis*) is also recorded, but seldom seen.

Pheasant tracks, identifiable by the marks of the trailing hind toe, sometimes appear on the beaches among the neater webbed and unwebbed

80. Sand lizard (*Lacerta agilis*)

265

ones of gull and wader. Skylark, stonechat, reed bunting and yellow hammer from the land meet curlew, redshank, mallard and shelduck from the water in this marginal no-man's land of wet and dry sand.

Oyster catchers dropping cockles on the dunes—as a subsidiary method of breaking them open—unwittingly help the song thrushes, which use a number of the open but often unbroken shells as anvils for dealing with their snails. Both crows and gulls drop food items on the sands with similar intent, and are more successful with crabs and sea urchins than the tougher cockles and mussels.

Part Six

The Burry Marshes

Goldeneye and geese

31 LONELY SALTINGS OF THE NORTH

THE spacious empty saltings flanking the North of the peninsula stretch eastwards from Whiteford Point for nine miles and more, fending off the sea from the ancient coastal hamlets. Much dissected by water channels at Cheriton and Landimore, they bulge seawards at Llanrhidian, narrowing at Wernffrwd and Crofty to reach northwards again past the famous cockle beds to Penclawdd, and so to the muds of Gowerton. Beyond their western half stretch the Llanrhidian Sands, where sinuous golden ripple marks are shuffled twice daily by wind and water and where poles erected to deter landings by enemy aircraft still stand after thirty five years of tidal ebb and flow.

Geologically the Burry Inlet lies beyond the northerly edge of the blocky Carboniferous Limestones, so the seemingly limitless, often desolate expanse of sand and mud is deposited where the softer Millstone Grit Shales and productive Coal Measures have been worn down to a lower level. Sediments vary in texture from a heavy clayey mud at the landward edge to a gravelly sand in mid channel. Accretion has been going on at the mouth of the estuary at least since Burry Pill moved its course around 1830, the rate now greatly accelerated by the establishment of *Spartina* grass.

At low tide the sea is sucked back four miles from the old sea cliff at Weobley Castle and more than three from the forward thrusting edge of the reclaimed paddocks at its foot. There appears to be dry land all the way to Burryport on the misty skyline, but this is an illusion. In the grey of dawn or dusk at the time of equinoctial springs, the sombre flood will be lapping under the hedge bottoms and through onto the crops within. These catastrophic-seeming inundations occur, however, in March and September, so it is possible to snatch a crop of cereals, mangolds or Brassicas in between, the two last having wild seaside relatives and being quite tolerant of salt.

As sea water surges up the creeks and steals quietly in across the level turf, little groups of mares will find themselves standing belly-deep, patiently fasting as they wait for the tide to ebb—too often unmindful of the diminutive stature of their foals, which get swept away. Only marshland ponies which know their way around the treacherous channels and bays of no escape are allowed the run of the saltings, but there are still losses. The freedom of those wide acres would come strange to any pasture-bred pony. When hundreds of the semi-wild creatures are set in motion by biting flies in an August heatwave, the ensuing stampede is an impressive sight. Manes and tails flying and hooves thudding on the springy turf, little groups converge from near and far and thunder across the flats, scattering clouds of gulls, lapwing and redshank to the four winds.

This is common grazing land, the sea-washed turf sustaining large numbers of sheep as well as ponies. From time immemorial commoners have moved their flocks from marshland to moorland and back, according to tide and season. Until about 1904 the fleeces were spun into yarn and woven into quilts and bedspreads at Llanrhidian. Looms were powered by a water wheel, the energy giving stream led by leat from the river near the church stile.

Seven commoners graze their animals on the marshes of the Whiteford Nature Reserve at present and there are usually stray ponies which ford Burry Pill and take refuge among the alders or sandhills when driven upshore by the tide. A current ecological study is aimed at assessing the effects of their grazing on the vegetation, these effects being intensified by rabbits which live on the wooded tors and lollop over the sheep-smoothed saltings to feed.

Cwm Ivy Marsh in the South-western angle of the newly deposited land was annexed from the tidal flats in 1638 by the building of a sea wall. (It is odd that we normally refer to such acquisitive operations as a 're' claiming of land from the sea). The salt leached away and the resulting freshwater marsh was parcelled and fenced. The part nearest to Llanmadoc supports a splendid display of yellow iris in season, but the bulk is good grassland and heavily grazed. The rare saltmarsh flat sedge (*Blysmus rufus*) has been found here, but not recently.

In the February floods of 1974 some of this land was temporarily borrowed back by the sea, hedgetops a good field's width from the current shoreline protruding in bleak black lines from the hungry waters which lapped the doorstep of the cottage below the wooded Cwm Ivy Tor nature reserve. To prevent a repeat the sea wall was heightened.

81. Llanrhidian Marsh

Clods of earth thrown up from the inner ditch contained fragments of brackish-water plants such as celery-leaved buttercup, wild celery and brookweed which lived atop the bank through the drought of the subsequent 1975 summer as minute flowering replicas of the lusher plants below. Thistles rapidly colonised the earthwork from the pastures within but the clouds of thistledown wafted away over the saltmarsh in late summer reach one of the few habitats they cannot conquer. No doubt foraging seed eaters such as linnets and goldfinches see to it that the crop is not wasted.

Sea water backs up through the sluices at high tide and the main drainage dykes of the Cwm Ivy Marsh are bordered by rich green sea sedge, whilst the first few tufts of *Spartina* had entrenched themselves by 1975 well along the ditch *inside* the sea defences. Where the embankment ends at Whiteford Burrows, the midsummer yellow of irises gives way a couple of months later to the soft pink of marsh mallow peppered with the more strident yellow fleabane.

To seaward Landimore Marsh is crossed by four main vegetation belts. Sea rush is furthest inshore, forming a more or less continuous brown zone of varying width above the broad expanse of closely grazed saltmarsh turf. To seaward of the turf a belt of sea purslane (*Halimione*) leads down to the advancing mass of cord grass and below this again are the true marine plants. Landimore Beach is now the only site in the estuary for the narrow-leaved eel grass, which was formerly widespread. Fifteen or so kinds of seaweed may be found, mostly sea lettuce (*Ulva lactuca*), the rather bloated 'green strings' (*Enteromorpha intestinalis*) and Welsh laver (*Porphyra umbilicalis*).

The main sea-washed turf is of saltmarsh grass (*Puccinellia maritima*), the red fescue which occupies a slightly higher zone on most saltmarshes being quite restricted. In early summer a pink haze of thrift flowers spreads across the sward, the heads paler and closer to the ground than on the cliffs, but the pink funnels of the sea milkwort are half hidden among the neatly aligned foliage. Later the brown spikes of sea plantain give an illusion of drought.

Only west of the meandering Burry Pill, where wave action is mitigated and more mud is deposited, does the sea lavender come into its own, but the magnificent acres of purple flowers in August depend on more than the small size of the mud particles. Once this was *Puccinellia* marsh with abundant sea aster, as it still is East of the river (the aster partly ray-headed and partly disc-headed, as elsewhere on Gower). Heavy grazing led to denudation of the turf and erosion with the disappearance of much of the palatable aster and diminution of the grass. The harsher-leaved, less tasty sea lavender which was previously rare took over—at a level slightly lower than the thrift and bordered by a silvery line of sea wormwood in the medieval sea wall.

In fact the conformation of the marsh is changing all the time and there is clear evidence of both erosion and accretion. Some of the changes occurred in historic time, but they are still taking place, mainly as a result of two factors. Erosion depends largely in the great increase of sheep numbers from a few hundred in 1945 to 2,500 in the early sixties, these highly concentrated in a few areas. A dramatic manifestation of this can be seen below Weobley Castle where the army observation tower built in the second world war on the saltmarsh turf at the end of the still extant road over the marsh is now far beyond the receding edge of both turf and road and surrounded by bare sand. Hard grass (*Parapholis strigosa*) is common in the eroding turf. A small patch of the Middle Marsh fenced off from grazing showed a marked increase in succulent palatable species, with sea arrow-grass almost as abundant as the lush red fescue and sea milkwort and scurvy grass in profusion but thrift and sea wormwood missing. Such growths blanket the soil and hold it against the scouring of the sea.

Accretion in the present century is mainly the result of the alarming increase of *Spartina* which was introduced to the West of Burry Pill in 1931. A broad belt at the lower edge of the Western and Middle Marshes is now dominated by this coarse grass to about mean high water mark, usually pure but sometimes associated with residual growths of the annual glasswort, annual seablite and sea purslane. As the level is built up by silt trapped among the shoots, it is likely that these three members of the saltbush family will be squeezed out. At present the *Spartina* is invading landwards up the creeks to the upper saltings turf, where seeds and vegetative fragments drifted into bare-floored pools do particularly well. It has penetrated right up the estuary to Gowerton and the vast *Spartina* meadow below the sea wall at Penclawdd did not exist in the forties and has made an almost complete takeover in the twenty years since 1955. Silt filtered from the becalmed waters by the forest of shoots is burying the former expanse of golden sand beneath a layer of mud.

Fortunately farm livestock will eat *Spartina* before the leaves get too tough in midsummer, but unfortunately they do not usually penetrate around Salthouse Point to this stretch, being deterred by high water at high tide and a long intervening stretch of bare sand at low tide. How long will it be, one wonders, before the invasive grass swamps the whole estuary, including the commercial cockle beds, much of which it has already replaced since accumulating sand built up to a level higher than the cockles can tolerate. The marsh pea (*Lathyrus palustris*) is one prized possession lost from further upshore at Llanrhidian, its only recorded Glamorgan site. How much else will eventually be engulfed?

Flora and fauna between the sinuously parallel driftlines of dead crabs, outgrown crab shells and seaweed is a hotch potch of seaside and inland species, of terrestrial and aquatic. Near the upper end of the estuary the

82. Submerged plants of upper saltmarsh pools: beaked tassel pondweed (*Ruppia maritima*) and horned pondweed (*Zanichellia palustris*)

junction of sea and land has the novel addition of extensive dumps of cockleshells, some of which have been used to floor waterside car parks. A fine stand of yellow horned poppy flaunts fragile golden petals and narrow pods, each longer than a handspan on cockle banks between the two

273

uppermost driftlines, among buck's-horn plantain and sticky groundsel. Another interesting stranger is the least toadflax (*Chaenorhinum minus*) which is normally a plant of railway ballast and probably arrived via the now derelict line running westwards along the top of the saltings from Gowerton.

This is a rich community, with the cockleshells supporting components from all adjacent soil types—aster and Babington's orache from the marsh, sand sedge and sea couch from the beach, sea beet and sea mayweed from the pebbles, sea campion and red bartsia from the land, plus such casuals as black horehound, black nightshade and common mallow. The sixty different kinds of flowering plants counted here in August 1975 had attracted squadrons of dancing butterflies. Cockle deposits below the tidal driftlines are dominated by annual seablite with most of the usual salt-marsh species, the larger-flowered sea spurrey with winged seeds occupying slightly raised ridges of shells while the smaller, darker pink species favours siltier depressions.

Interest of a different sort is found where fresh and salt water mingle at the top of the saltmarsh—a region of sea sedge (*Scirpus*), grey clubrush (*Schoenoplectus*), great reedmace (*Typha*), branched bur-reed (*Sparganium*) and yellow iris. Roadside ditches near Crofty are occupied by crusty stonewort (*Chara*) and bordered by bobble-fruited strawberry clover. More than half a hundred species jostle each other in the marsh behind— mostly freshwater plants but with invaders such as sea-milkwort and sea arrow-grass from the saltings. The associated animals, too, are mostly non-maritime, with whirligig beetles and pond skaters, dragonflies and damselflies. A smelly ditch leading from the kennels is bordered by lush banks of orache—a species which also does particularly well when nourished by sea-bird excreta.

Two unusual water plants in pools of the upper saltmarsh further West are often mutually exclusive, each filling its pool to capacity. These are beaked tassel-weed (*Ruppia maritima*) and horned pondweed (*Zannichellia palustris*). Both bear flowers and fruits on slender August shoots, the first the coarser of the two, resembling hair plucked from a pony tail. *Ruppia* penetrates well down the saltmarsh, but only where fresh water is seeping through a string of pans to dilute the salt. Its accumulated remains cover the pool floor with loose, silty black peat, which is easily stirred into a suspension. Pools floored by greasy clay at the same level (some from former turf cutting for lawns) are occupied by true saltmarsh species. Again the animals of the *Ruppia* pools are typical of non-saline conditions —water boatman, water cricket, pond skater and the like, in spite of the salt-demanding *Spartina* encroaching downwards from above.

Some pools are bright with water crowfoot flowers the summer long, both *Ranunculus peltatus* and *R. baudotii* doing well. Rotund scarlet water mites follow invisible paths through a tangled labyrinth of jellied toadspawn strands during May. In due time a multitude of tadpoles hatches to hang with quavering tails like notes of music among a seething mass of tiny yellow Copepods, smallest of the Crustaceans. In autumn the mud of the pool floors is alive with red bloodworms or midge larvae and the water wriggling with suspended gnat larvae, the white tufts at either end of their red bodies meeting intermittently as they gyrate.

An easy approach to the marine fauna can be made along the old army causeway leading out from Salthouse Point near Crofty—the causeway itself supporting a rocky shore element in the form of edible and rough periwinkles. The muddiness of the surrounding sand with its shifting channels ensures a good supply of organic matter to sustain the myriad small creaures which, in their turn, sustain a host of shorebirds.

Favourites with smaller birds such as dunlin are the little black spire-shelled snails (*Hydrobia*) and large pink Baltic tellins (*Macoma*). Knot probe slightly deeper than dunlin, although their bills are not much longer, so the two species can feed in the same place without depriving each other. Like all waders except oyster catchers, they swallow their prey complete with shell, fragments of which can be found in the gizzard with the grinding stones. Peppery furrow shells (*Scrobicularia*) and cockles (*Cardium*) are among the larger shellfish taken here by the larger waders, but the commercial cockle beds are further West than Salthouse Point. The sand gaper (*Mya arenaria*) can attain a length of five inches and is more than a mouthful for most when fully grown.

83. Stranded false killer whales (*Pseudorca crassidens*) Llanmadoc, 1934

Members of the British Conchological Society, the shell experts, discovered two new species of sea slug on the Llanrhidian saltmarsh in September 1975 which were 'firsts' for Gower. Both are small and unprepossessing (as indicated, perhaps, by their second names—*Alderia modesta* and *Limapontia depressa*), but it is always satisfying to turn up something new. *Alderia* is most often a creature of estuaries on Britain's eastern coasts, feeding particularly on eel grass; *Limapontia* favours green algae.

Amphipods or 'sand hoppers' (*Corophium volutator*) and common shrimps (*Crangon vulgaris*) help to nourish birds feeding along Salthouse Pill and lugworms (*Arenicola*) occur further out to the North. Three bristle worms contribute to the avian diet, the free-swimming *Nereis diversicolor*, the sedentary, tube-dwelling *Nephthys hombergi* and the burrowing *Magelona papillicornis*, which picks up tiny food animals and scraps of detritus from the sand surface with two questing tentacles more than half as long as itself. The embanked slag along the south side of the Loughor Channel beyond allows rock animals to appear again with acorn barnacles, mussels and Aesop prawns (*Pandalus montagui*).

Down the estuary below Tor Gro the sea reaches to the foot of the limestone cliffs bringing the sea wormwood of the tide-washed cobbles into close juxtaposition with the rock plants of sub-aerial scree. Every stone upturned beneath the mugwort reveals a host of small animals. Spherical navy blue pill bugs and slender ginger centipedes from the land mingle with Isopod 'hoppers' from the shore. Glossy, gold-tinged beetles and shiny black spiders co-habit with oil beetles whose segmented bodies are inadequately covered by short wing cases worn like a tailed waistcoat. These exude a blood-like fluid to deter predators while they burrow rapidly into the turf to escape.

Westwards again on the Whiteford marshes the small animal life has been studied quite intensively over the years. Behind the sea wall at Cwm Ivy (outside the Nature Reserve) it rather resembles that of the dune slacks. A Carabid beetle common to both habitats is *Feronia nigrita* and there are various weevils and Chrysomelids or leaf beetles to be found. Perhaps the most interesting in July and August is the tortoise beetle (*Cassida murraea*). This resembles a big green ladybird with scattered black marks on the wing cases and the head completely hidden by the thorax, as with a tortoise in constant retreat. Although a rare species nationally, it is common at Cwm Ivy among yellow fleabane, the only plant that it will eat. Few beetles inhabit salt marsh proper but rove beetles of the genus *Bledius* will dig small burrows in the mud along the banks of creeks.

Unexpected inhabitants of sandy saltmarsh are yellow ants (*Lasius flavus*) and, at Whiteford, black ants (*L. niger*) as well. The domed anthills which rise from Whiteford's pony-grazed saltings are inundated for as much as an hour during high spring tides, becoming completely saturated with sea water, yet the ants seem to take no harm.

The mounds form refuges for sea pearlwort, buck's-horn plantain and lesser centaury above the general level of grassy sward with its sea lavender and saltmarsh rush. (Similarly sited anthills on the sandy, pony-grazed saltmarsh at Pennard are also characterised by sea pearlwort with thrift and red fescue in a bent-fescue community with sea plantain, sea milkwort and saltmarsh rush.) Buck's-horn plantain occupies anthills of the muddier, sheep-grazed marsh of similar species at Llanrhidian. Vegetation differences are less marked in the almost ungrazed estuarine

276

Plate 45   CWM IVY MARSH II

194. Branched Bur-reed   **195.** Common Fleabane   *Both Author*
196. Iris Sward at foot of old wooded sea cliff on 'reclaimed' land   *Author*

277

197

198

199

200

201

Plate 46 WADERS

197. Purple Sandpiper a bird of the rocks   *Keri Williams*
198. Dunlin   *Harold Grenfell*
199. Little Stint   *Keri Williams*
200. Greenshanks with Eel   *Keri Williams*
201. Knot   *Harold Grenfell*

278

Plate 47   COCKLE COUNTRY

202. An unusual, white flowered Thrift or Sea Pink *Author*
203. Cockle Woman and Donkey, typical of Penclawdd and Ferryside, Carms., in 1929 *National Museum of Wales*
204. Cockle Boiling Shed in 1965 *National Museum of Wales*
205. Yellow Horned Poppy growing on dumped Cockle Shells at Penclawdd *Author*

279

206

207

Plate 48　AT THE TOP OF THE BURRY MARSHES

206. Long fruits of Yellow Horned Poppy on Cockle Shell Dumps, Penclawdd　　　　*Author*
207. Pink Marsh Mallow　　　　*Harold Grenfell*

280

marsh at Llwchwr, but Babington's orache is practically confined to ant-hills here and the sea aster, so common round about, seems to be excluded.

Anthill species, (including Danish scurvy grass, toad rush and the typical dune moss, *Tortula ruraliformis*) are all adapted to life on disturbed and accreting soils and benefit, too, from the enhanced drainage and washing of salt by rain from their elevated tumps.

Warm summer days see hosts of butterflies hovering over the upper marsh and settled on the flowers, like fairies at their prayers. Wall browns and graylings can be seen sunning themselves every few yards along the sea defences. One of the typical brown grass moths which resemble short lengths of twig when settled, head downwards, is *Agriphila selasella*. Another, with broader, paler hindwings is the Crambid, *Crambus perlella*. The larvae spin silken galleries for themselves down among the grasses on which they feed. Moths of saltier zones include *Pexicopia malvella*, whose caterpillars feed on the marsh mallow, and *Phalonidia vectisana* on the sea arrow-grass.

Severed cord grass shoots and other vegetable debris drifted over the saltmarsh provide admirable cover for spiders, including the newly dis-covered *Lasiargus Gowerensis*. A single hour's searching here by an expert yielded 57 individuals of 27 different species on a July day and 68 individuals of 30 species in September. An abundant and quite local species, *Stylotector romanus* of saltmarsh drift is not found in the drift of sandy beaches. *Erigone arctica*, a shiny black money spider, builds up rapidly to vast numbers in saltmarsh driftlines and the uncommon *Cornicularia kochi* is also to be found.

These and many another form good pickings for the starlings, pipits and other small birds feeding over the saltings, but marine animals proper are more abundant in the muddy floors of pools, pans and creeks, which get covered with a meshwork of wader footprints. They provide a conveni-ent trysting ground for birds driven up from the mudflats by a rising tide or down from inland feeding grounds by a winter freeze.

84. Redshank

281

32 WILD WINGS OF THE MARSHES

THE 'Birds of Estuaries Enquiry' launched by the British Trust for Ornithology in the sixties established once and for all the significance of the Burry Inlet as one of the "top twenty" national havens for wading birds, whilst its importance for duck has long been known to wildfowlers.

Most of the birds seem to frequent the Gower side of the inlet, big numbers taking refuge on the Dyfed side only when driven off the flats at high tide. The bald statement that the estuary holds between 45,000 and 50,000 waders and some 6,000 duck in mid-winter takes no account of the aesthetic enhancement of the marshes by all those wild wings. The pied, crimson-flecked splendour of a big gathering of oyster catchers or the breathtaking black, white and chestnut beauty of a group of shelduck is something to stir the heart of the least imaginative.

There is no need to recognise whether the multitude is of dunlin or knot to appreciate its astoundingly accurate aerial manoeuvres, with never a bird out of place to spoil the sinuous rhythm of a mass movement. When the impulse to flight seizes them they rise as one, nearer flocks rustling like silk, further ones peeling skywards like a finely drawn puff of smoke. The synchronised airborne throng twists and turns, the sunlight flashing alternately on silvery bellies and dark backs. Whole cohorts will merge invisibly into their backgrounds to reappear miraculously as they expose the opposing facet.

No material value can be placed on the mournful cry of the redshank, the eerie piping of the curlew, as over some lonely mountain moor, or the evocative complaints of the peewits, but Gower—and Wales—would be the poorer without them. The muted whistling of 2,000 or up to 4,000 wigeon and more plebian chatter of 500 pintail can be stored in the memory to impart a pleasure which long outlives the originators of the sounds.

When repelled by the December desolation of moor and meadow, there is plenty of interest to be found on this northern tidal fringe. The bird hide on Berges Island at the tip of Whiteford Point is a Mecca for the ornithologists of South Wales and beyond, but interest begins well before the point is reached. At Cwm Ivy rarities such as the corn bunting have been seen and occasionally a group of crossbills tweaking winged seeds from ripe cones in the pine plantations between here and the hide. As impressive as the awesome passing of some 28,000 starlings is the sight of the occasional merlin pursuing some luckless meadow pipit in spectacular aerial chase. Merlins are quite capable of tackling small waders, whose feathers may be found at their plucking posts. A still rarer raptor was the Montagu's harrier seen at Llanmadoc in 1968.

Those who approach the winter estuary across Llanrhidian Sands may be rewarded by the blue glint of a kingfisher patrolling the upshore creeks and flocks of fieldfare and redwing probing the hedged pastures above the sea rush zone. A small flock of twite strayed into Crofty from the North in the autumn of 1969. Golden plover start moving into these fields from their northern breeding grounds in August—building up to flocks of 800 or 900 by mid winter. Grey plover come a little earlier to the lower feeding grounds most years and can reach a flock size of nearly 300 individuals by February but are usually well below the 200 mark. Wisps of snipe erupting in steep zig zag flight from the sedge beds and muddy pools occur in more modest numbers and are most likely to be encountered in February. They rise singly, one after the other, emitting short rasping calls. Jack snipe are fairly common in winter but are difficult to find.

For those taking the easy route out from Salthouse Point there are likely to be good views of pintail, which flock to Gower in winter, coming probably from breeding grounds around the Baltic. These arrive in September, building up to anything between 600 and 1,100 or so by January, but are gone by April. Although feeding ostensibly by night whole rafts may be seen upended by day, sampling the rich pickings of the estuary. Golden-eye are much rarer callers to Gower, being often represented by immature birds on their juvenile wanderings.

Where the road borders the *Spartina* meadow at Penclawdd there is a fair chance of seeing a hen harrier quartering low over the marsh in characteristic floppy flight. The long wings are retracted tardily as the raptor drops repeatedly among the grasses, but it is soon airborne again the light catching the conspicuous white feathers on the rump. Anything proteinaceous is acceptable, from insects and frogs to warm-blooded prey. Already by 1848 this noble diurnal hunter was becoming rare.

Herons feed on the marshes at Berthlwydd inland of the road as well as on the saltings. A bird mistakenly employing the stabbing method of aquatic feeding on land came to grief in 1972 at Llanrhidian. When the emaciated but otherwise intact body was found in June the beak was embedded right to the hilt in the saltmarsh turf, so firmly that it could be removed only with a trowel.

Scoter are principally ducks of the open sea, a large flock wintering regularly in Carmarthen Bay. A small group from this flock were usually present, summer and winter in the sandy sea sedge pool at the the inner end of the Berges Island spit, until this sanded up in 1975. Red-breasted mergansers, elegant fish catching 'sawbills', are more estuarine, but seldom exceed 20 on winter counts. Flightless youngsters have been turning up since the late sixties, so a few pairs must be nesting. Mergansers, like fulmars, are gradually extending their breeding range south.

Eider duck have attained notoriety as the chosen emblem of the Glamorgan Naturalists' Trust, by virtue of their presence in the Burry Inlet the year round, although breeding no further South in Western Britain than Walney Island in Lancashire. Incongruous, perhaps, when this wholly maritime symbol is met with on a Nature Reserve plaque in a mountain woodland, but the Royal Society for the Protection of Birds also went for a rarity when it adopted the avocet as its symbol. Britain as a whole veered the other way in selecting the homely robin as her national bird a few years back. Eider numbers remain fairly steady at around 35-45 birds both summer and winter, 1974 counts ranging from 65 in February to 10 in June.

Mallard skulk in freshwater pools at the top of the saltmarsh and the count of 150 in May is unusually high for summer, but there is an influx from elsewhere during winter, giving numbers approaching 200 in some months. When the human hubbub dies at nightfall many will fly inland to feed undisturbed until the dawn. Teal can be twice as numerous as mallard in winter topping the 500 mark most years with 760 in January 1974, but are absent altogether in summer. Shoveller were much more numerous before the spread of *Spartina* but can still build up to 100 or so during January (only 75 in 1974), though breeding at only one locality in South Gower. Gadwall are rare winter visitors.

Wigeon are much the most numerous of the winter duck, averaging around 3,000 birds most winters rising to an exceptional 4¼ thousand in January 1972 and 3,800 in February 1974, but with only the odd bird or two around in summer. Occasionally they feed alongside the brent geese on the eel grass beds. The deeper-reaching geese pull the plants out of the sand and swallow the creeping stems, letting much of the foliage drift away to by snapped up by the satellite ducks. But not many can feed in

85. Wigeon by the Nether Mill, Llanrhidian

this way for there are only 5-25 brent geese around in some winters, 50-60 in 1974. Barnacle geese are spasmodic visitors first recorded in 1933 and white-fronted geese scarcely more regular.

High tide is the best time to watch the shorebirds proper. From being diffused over thousands of acres of mud and sand, they then merge into flocks and fly to clearly defined roosting areas upshore, where they wait for the ebb, often balanced nonchalantly on one leg—on which they move around unless unduly flurried. Possible upshore refuges are not used indiscriminately, the birds repairing to special sites with which they have become familiar over many generations. The shelduck population, which sometimes rises to nearly 500 birds in February, adjourns to three different high tide roosts—at Whiteford, Llanrhidian and Penclawdd. Curlew will often flight inland to escape the tide.

Oystercatchers, the estuary's most conspicuous waders, are variously known as pied pipers of the shore, sea pies, winkle pickers and mussel scratchers, or as sea magpies in Welsh. They start moving down stream past Salthouse Point to Llanrhidian Sands when the tide approaches the lower *Spartina* beds and are driven further down again to the main high tide roost off Whiteford Point about an hour later, as the grey flood seeps stealthily but inexorably landwards.

There is no diurnal rhythm for birds of the shore. Their habits are governed by the tides and they must learn to feed in the dark as well as the light. Oyster catchers have different modes of feeding in daylight and darkness. By day they use the 'stalk and strike' technique when hunting cockles, striking the sand every few paces and averaging 1 in 3 jabs on target. A man prodding with a stick gets only 1 in 10, so this is no random search. By night a 'sewing machine action' of rapid pecks is employed, the beak slightly open, the jabs very close and the success rate lower. So, when denied the ability to see, the oyster catcher changes from a visual to a tactile method of feeding.

Random probing is ineffective on a rocky substrate, so oyster catchers of rocky shores must retire to roost by night as well as at the peak of daylight tides. Such birds have quite different methods of feeding and are adept at chiselling limpets off rocks and tweaking periwinkles from their shells. Others haul worms from the ground—some 83% of the Skokholm Island birds further West feeding inland, with earthworms and caterpillars their staple fare. Hammerers, chisellers or twisters, oyster catchers are biologically very successful birds with an ability to cope in different ways with different problems.

In the Burry Inlet their chief food consists of bivalve cockles, detected by subtle clues which are hidden from the bird-watcher—the dimple in the sand where the cockle's tubular siphon surfaces for air and food perhaps or the tiniest give-away movement. If the cockle is tardy about clamping its shell shut when hauled to the surface, the oyster catcher can insert its

285

crowbar bill into the gap and force the halves assunder with a brisk twist. If the victim does succeed in closing, it is little better off. The long red bill—a harpoon now—strikes vertically downwards and severs the adductor muscle which controls the hinge, so that the prey is defenceless. The remarkable tool now emulates the opening of a pair of forceps, prising the halves of the shell apart.

Oyster catchers formerly averaged some 16,000 to 18,000 in winter and sometimes reached to 30,000 as in January 1971, but counts in recent years have been confused by culling operations and in 1974 maxima seldom exceeded 10,500. Flock size drops from March to July but can be up again to full winter strength by August, making them far and away the commonest as well as the handsomest of the waders in the Burry Inlet. Next in terms of numbers are the drabber knot and dunlin, which build up gradually from September to January and February peaks of from 4 -7,000; or so of each. These will sometimes consort with ringed plovers, which are present throughout the year but in more modest numbers, rising to little above 250. When an alarm ripples through a mixed flock the knot and dunlin peel off skyward in successive waves to leave the less fearful ringed plovers standing. Similarly a flock of lapwing will rise from the saltmarsh turf screaming their displeasure at an intruder while the accompanying gulls linger on unperturbed. Lapwing numbers approach 800 by February in an average year, but 5,000 congregated under Weobley Castle in the winter of 1974-75. Curlew stay around the 500 mark through much of the year, but can top 1,600 in July, August and September. Their muted banshee wailing has probably inspired as many poets as the song of the lark but the melancholy strains have none of the lark's lilting happiness. Curlew are often loners, stalking sedately along the sides of creeks or making purposeful darts at some telltale movement in the mud, to pounce and withdraw with an indigestible looking shore crab held delicately in the bill tip. When the sensitive, down-curved beak encounters a ragworm or lugworm lurking in a burrow the head is tilted slightly to one side to get better purchase before the several wrigglesome inches are dragged out and swallowed, still squirming. How that multiplicity of bristle feet must tickle! Whimbrel, with their bubbling liquid call, are similar but smaller and seldom occur more than ten at a time, merely passing through on spring and autumn passage, although 45 appeared together in May 1974.

The only waders to approach these two in length of appendages are the godwits, but here the retroussé bill tilts slightly skywards. Bar-tailed godwits are the commoner in the Burry Inlet, sometimes building up to over 800 in January, but no less than 270 black-tailed godwits arrived in September 1971. (The 1974 maximum was 45). Both are passage migrants and winter visitors, but quite a few bar-taileds linger on through the summer. Godwits have a slightly larger than usual nasal gland for the elimination of excess salt as quite a lot of sea water is taken in during the course of feeding.

The long bills of curlew and godwit enable them to tackle shellfish which live deep in the mud—even to 4" down. Peppery furrow shells fall prey to them but the clam or sand gaper skulks at the lower end of a siphon 5" long, enabling it to escape even those probes. Jerks of the head whilst the beak is still buried probably mean that the prey is being torn from its shell below ground. Often, however, it is swallowed shell and all, the crushed shell fragments voided as oval pellets from the crop, via the beak, or passing right through to emerge with the droppings. Ornithologists who spend much time prowling round wader roosts can learn to identify the maker of a pellet by its shape and so discover what the birds have been eating.

One is always conscious of redshanks because they are widely dispersed and highly vocal, but they seldom build up to as many as 800 birds. They are sometimes referred to as the 'wardens of the marshes', their shrill yelping alarm note warning others of danger. The pale-plumaged sanderling skipping over the sand on twinkling feet can rise to 130 or so. Tortoiseshell-patterned turnstones are associated mainly with stony shores but are to be seen in the Burry Inlet the year round. Numbers are low in midsummer but 670 appeared in November 1971 and nearly as many in April 1974. A fair winter average is between 200 and 300 birds. Other waders appear only spasmodically—greenshank and spotted redshank, green sandpiper and common sandpiper, curlew sandpiper and little stint. Watchers at Whiteford on the last day of August 1975 were rewarded by the rare sight of a Baird's sandpiper, which was finally driven off by ringed plover, its long wings taking it vertically into the air.

Much the commonest of the gulls is the species which breeds inland, the black-headed. 1971 saw 2,000 on the estuary in October and only a few short of this number in July, while 2,330 were around in August 1974. Herring gulls come next with close on 1,000 in September and seldom less than 100. Greater black-backs can reach the 100 mark in September (205 in October 1974) but lesser black-backs are surprisingly scarce, with 4 the largest total for any month during the 1971 census, 25 in August and 10 in April 1974. Common gulls, although strictly visiting Gower only in winter from their northern breeding grounds, are actually present throughout the year. From very few in summer they built up to 760 by October 1971 with an August maximum of 440 in 1974. Little gulls were first recorded in 1963 but have been dropping in more frequently since 1969.

Once in a while an Arctic skua swoops in to harry the terns off Whiteford Point and steal their lawfully gained prey, while a long-tailed skua was seen there in 1967. Common and Arctic terns pass through during migration, lingering longer in their more leisurely autumn journey South than when urged northwards in spring by the unquenchable desire to

287

86. Black-headed gulls

breed. Sandwich, little and black terns are rarer but all put in an appearance.

Cormorants, although breeding only on the South side of the peninsula, turn up in large numbers here in the North, rising from a minimum in early Spring to around 100 or to an unusual 160 in Autumn. Three divers visit the estuary in winter, the great northern and red-throated fairly regularly (the latter sometimes in summer too), but the black-throated less often. Small numbers of Slavonian grebes come quite frequently, and there are occasional black-necked, red-necked and less exotic great crested grebes.

33 THE OYSTER CATCHER: COCKLE CONTROVERSY

One could dare to hope, with the recognition of so many ornithological riches at hand, that the Burry Marshes would be regarded as sacrosanct for birds and those who find pleasure in watching them, but not a bit of it. For the last two decades, since the middle fifties, controversy has raged over the oyster catchers, which enjoy eating cockles even more than we do.

Kitchen middens have been found in the western dune slacks at Whiteford containing hordes of cockleshells, along with the odd broken pot or brooch, so we know that Gower families were eating this shellfish as far back as the Iron Age. There is no reason to suppose that oyster catchers were not doing likewise. Certainly they were present in their thousands a century ago, as recorded by the Rev. J. D. Davies in "A History of West Gower" (1877-1894), and numbers have fluctuated very little since regular counts have been made. Yet, for some curious reason, any recent drop in the quantity of cockles available to the commercial cockle industry is blamed on the birds.

Anyone who is aware of the repeated changes in the position of the main channel since 1830 or who has seen the catastrophic advance of the *Spartina* grass over the rising Penclawdd foreshore during the past two decades, will know that many vital features of the cockles' habitat are changing much more fundamentally than the number of oyster catchers feeding on them. Modern industrial effluents and quantities of untreated sewage spewing into the estuary from the Llanelli side cannot fail to have some effect on the food supply and physical environment of the cockles. But the significant lack of well-substantiated environmental data seems to have been totally disregarded in carrying out the government sanctioned slaughter of no less than 11,000 oyster catchers, or half the peak winter population, during the winters of 1973-74 and 1974-75.

At one time the cockle catch was sufficiently modest for the cockle women to walk 8 miles to Swansea Market with the product in baskets on their heads. Until the second world war each plodded down to the sandflats with a donkey or small pony able to carry two bags of cockles on its back and so the catch was limited by the amount it was physically possible to remove before the tide returned. Shortly after the war lorries were brought to the beach, their wheels crushing many of the shellfish which live so close beneath the surface that they can be felt with bare toes. This made gross overfishing possible. Later a happy compromise was reached in the use of light, rubber tyred pony carts which float empty on the water surface as the ponies wade, belly deep, following the tide down. These allow six to eight sacks to be brought off during a single tide.

Cockles from the sandier areas have white shells and are mostly sold whole. Those from the stickier glacial clays have the shells stained black and are more often extracted and bottled or canned. Cockles, oyster catchers and predators of young cockles suffered severe setbacks during the icy winter of 1962-63. Moribund shellfish were slower then in closing their shells so were easier prey for the surviving birds, although of poorer food value.

289

87. Oyster catchers

Very soon after this heavy mortality came an exceptionally good spatfall with infant cockles settling down to grow in untold multitudes. The glut which resulted was more than enough for all and laws were relaxed regarding the number and size of cockles allowed to be removed by the fisherfolk. The cockle women as well as the oyster catchers were taking cockles in their second winter instead of in their third, at a minimum size of 23mm. or a little under an inch long. By the early seventies catches were reverting to normal and, memories being short, the fat years were regarded as average and a scapegoat sought for the decline. Expected harvests lie somewhere between the 1963 "low" of 18,240 cwts. and the 1970 "high" of 80,000 cwts. valued at £80,000.

Scientists know very little of the environmental conditions governing spatfall—only that populations of cockles, like most other animals, are cyclic, with a periodicity of about five years. Short term fluctuations have little or no influence on long term trends. It would seem fruitless to expect great changes until there is another bumper spawning.

Unlike farmers, cockle gatherers invest no money in the land they harvest: they do not cultivate, plant or fertilise it and only 30 rely on cockles for their livelihood although 100 pay the modest licence fee for occasional gathering. Nevertheless, they work hard for their gain whether in a biting wind on the flats or a steamy cockleshed on the shore, and no-one would wish to deny them the fruits of their labours.

The research programmes undertaken so far have not come up with a method of increasing returns beyond the normal expectation and opening

290

the way for the economic growth which would convert a colourful cottage industry into a mechanised input to the Servernside food processing plants. Any large scale mechanisation of gathering could very soon reduce the Burry cockle beds to the status of the now extinct oyster beds off Porteynon and Oystermouth.

Oyster catchers are the obvious scapegoats. They eat large numbers of cockles and they do so conspicuously for all to see. The less obvious facts relating to the fate of the shellfish tend to get overlooked. Millions of infant cockles are consumed by other animals during their free swimming phase, when they form part of the zooplankton which feeds so many marine creatures. More than half of those which settle on the sand and adopt the adult form disappear from one cause or another before they are large enough for the oyster catchers to give them a second glance.

When the tide is in they are gobbled up by flounders and dabs and the taking of these flatfish by fishermen has decreased during recent years because it no longer pays. We know virtually nothing of the planktonic life on which the cockles themselves feed —a life which may well be adversely affected by the industrial and other chemical effluents known to be present. We do know, however, that in some of the beds there are parasites living in the cockles which prevent them from breeding although not actually killing them.

The cockle beds are constantly changing site: a new one appeared off Whiteford Point in 1970 in an area long since evacuated and another off Llanelli. This means that cockling is now carried out less conveniently near to the points of access, but it would be absurd to suggest that the oyster catchers have concentrated their attentions on the more easterly sites, which are close to human habitation and more liable to disturbance. Rather are the cockle gatherers having to withdraw from areas which they themselves have overfished.

It is well known among those concerned that the hydrography and sedimentation of the estuary have changed. The level of the sands is steadily rising—to above the optimum needed by cockles in some instances. Many of the heightened eastern cockle beds, now silted and muddy, have been overrun by *Spartina*. Even if cockles were able to live among the labyrinthine root system at the level of this silt-trapping invader, digging them out would be no fun at all.

And yet, in spite of all this and the preliminary research programme of cannon netting and colour ringing which proved very little, 11,000 oyster catchers were shot in 1973-4-5, with a bounty of 25p on each handsome head. The evidence put forward in favour of this course is hard to accept. A small number of birds were observed over a period and their feeding rate multiplied by the number of birds presumed to be present and the hours during which they would be expected to feed. This on the *Conway* Estuary, not the Burry. Calculations of the weight of cockles taken based

291

on these inevitably approximate figures, took no account of the fact that many of the birds feed away from the commercial cockle beds—nor that many of the cockles taken are those damaged by the cartwheels or moribund from other causes and hence easier to come by. Nor, indeed, did they recognise the fact that individuals do not feed throughout the period that the beds are exposed by the tide.

The main scene of slaughter was off Salthouse Point. Fortunately the chief high water roost is in the Whiteford area, part of which is a national nature reserve and part a national wildfowl refuge established as a sanctuary for all types of birds. Large scale shooting would seem to be indefensible in either.

Rarer species may get frightened away. Some may have contracted lead poisoning as duck, especially, are known to gather up lead shot and add to the grit in the gizzard. Work in America (resulting in a substantial decrease in the amount of lead being put into the shot there) has shown that as few as 8 average pellets are lethal to a duck. Some 2 million pellets were used in the shooting of 7,000 oyster catchers in the 1973-74 winter at an average of three cartridges per bird, and are now lying about in the feeding grounds, along with another million from the following winter—unless already ingested.

And to what purpose? Nature abhors a vacuum and population levels of almost any animal are governed by the amount of food available. In no time at all another 11,000 oyster catchers will have surged in from Scotland, Iceland, the Faroes and Norway to fill the breach. The Norwegians are very angry with "conservation-conscious" Britain for killing so many of the birds which breed on their shores and commit themselves to our care only when driven South by the cold. (Only 2 or 3 pairs breed in the Burry Inlet). The Faeroese, whose national bird this is, are equally displeased.

In the absence of scientific monitoring of all the relevant factors, this unfortunate "cull" can prove nothing. Any fortuitous subsequent increase of cockles may well be attributed to it whatever the cause, and used as an excuse for further culls.

Even if the oyster catcher *were* solely responsible for any supposed decline, can the massacre of what amounts to 10% of all British wintering birds and 4% of those of Western Europe and West Africa be justified in the interests of 100 full time and part time cockle gatherers when they have a value for so many thousands of others, in and out of Britian? Apart from the inevitable return to normal after the 1963 crash, there is no overall increase in numbers of oyster catchers in the Burry Inlet and so no possibility that the number of shellfish taken is any greater than it ever has been.

A publication of the British Trust for Ornithology in March 1974 says what many of the caring public have had on their consciences over

88. Whiteford Point lighthouse and oyster catchers

the years. "It would be a travesty if one of our most popular shore-birds, and one that has a special status for Norwegians, Icelanders and Faeroese alike, were to suffer further, and perhaps unnecessarily, from hasty decisions, especially in Britain—a country otherwise held in high esteem worldwide for its civilised approach to wildlife."

The Burry Estuary is used by many people apart from the cockle gatherers—farmers and fishermen, bait diggers and boat owners, holiday makers and educational parties, ornithologists and research workers. For all of these there are few more awesome spectacles than that of the great piebald hosts winging past across the sands and filling the air with their inimical, evocative piping. Should all of these subordinate their interests to one minority group, however deserving, when there is no proven evidence that the attempt to please the minority will have the desired result?

*   *   *   *   *

It is fitting that we should leave this look at Britain's first "Area of Outstanding Natural Beauty" on a controversial note. The natural beauty of the countryside and its wildlife does not just happen in this age of over population. We must be ever vigilant. There are tremendous pressures on the plants and animals of the land and especially of its seaward fringes.

The charm and diversity of landscape that our ancestors could take for granted must now be husbanded. In the Arcadian world of long ago the plankton wafted up and down the unpolluted inlet to be incorporated into the substance of cockles sufficient to feed all the fish, birds and humans who needed them. But that was before the thoughtless introduction of *Spartina* and irresponsible tipping of waste. From a simple

293

ecosystem able to right itself after minor cyclic setbacks we have 'advanced' to a disturbed ecosystem suffering new types of damage for which it has not yet found the cure. The more we plunder from the natural world the less it has left to offer. Its resilience is enormous, but not inexhaustible.

In this consideration of our natural heritage as it now is, we have run the whole gamut on Gower, from lonely moorland to lonely saltings. We have seen farmlands and waterways man-managed, but with a happy compromise established between the wild and that which we ordain.

On the impregnable cliffs where the human impact is smaller we have witnessed changes not wholly for the worse. Puffins and peregrines have declined but fulmars and kittiwakes have come to fill the breach. The sandy bays and dunes which we wish only to enjoy are being desecrated by sheer weight of numbers.

Clearly all of us who use this exquisite scrap of South Wales must learn to use it with the care we would lavish on our own property. It *is* our property. No other creature has the frightening power to make or mar that is ours. The responsibility cannot be pushed elsewhere. We must discover how to enjoy the present while remaining custodians of a greater future, so that those who come after can enjoy what we have been privileged to enjoy.

Conclusion

Appendices and Index

ALPHABETICAL LIST OF PLANTS MENTIONED IN THE TEXT

This is NOT a complete list of Gower plants.

Scientific names used are those in the second edition of *Flora of the British Isles* by A. R. Clapham, T. G. Tutin and E. F. Warburg (1962) and in the related *Excursion Flora of the British Isles* (second edition) (1968) (Cambridge University Press). Where new names have been adopted subsequently, but have not yet had time to become well known, these are included in brackets after the more familiar scientific name.

English names recommended by the Botanical Society of the British Isles and listed in *English Names of Wild Flowers* by J. G. Dony, C. M. Rob and F. H. Perring (1974) (Butterworths), are also included in brackets if different from those used in the text. The list is heavily cross-referenced for ease of use, but for the many species of rush and sedge see 'rush' and 'sedge'.

The standardisation of English names is essential in the interests of clarity, but it would be the greatest pity if we were no longer able to refer to the wild arum as the well-accepted 'cuckoo-pint' and 'Jack-in-the-pulpit' as well as the now recommended 'lords-and-ladies'. Retention of regional vernacular names, even though these are less widely understood, enriches our language as surely as does the retention in other spheres of Welsh alongside the more widely understood English.

I am grateful to Messrs. Roy Perry and Gwynn Ellis of the National Museum of Wales for checking this list.

Adder's tongue—*Ophioglossum vulgatum*
Agrimony, common—*Agrimonia eupatoria*
  hemp—*Eupatorium cannabinum*
Alder—*Alnus glutinosa*
Alder buckthorn—*Frangula alnus*
Alsike clover—*Trifolium hybridum*
Amphibious bistort—*Polygonum amphibium*
Anemone, wood—*Anemone nemorosa*
Angelica—*Angelica sylvestris*
Annual meadow-grass—*Poa annua*
Archangel, yellow—*Lamiastrum galeobdolon*
Arrow-grass, marsh—*Triglochin palustre*
  sea—*T. maritimum*
Arum, wild (lords-and-ladies)—*Arum maculatum*
Ash—*Fraxinus excelsior*
Asparagus—*Asparagus officinale* subsp. *prostratus*
Aspen—*Populus tremula*

Asphodel—*Narthecium ossifragum*
Aster, sea—*Aster tripolium*
Autumn lady's-tresses—*Spiranthes spiralis*
Autumnal hawkbit—*Leontodon autumnalis*
Avens, water (not present)—*Geum rivale*
  wood—*G. urbanum*
Bartsia, red—*Odontites verna*
Basil, wild—*Clinopodium vulgare*
Basil-thyme—*Acinos arvensis*
Bedstraw, heath—*Galium saxatile*
  lady's—*G. verum*
  marsh—*G. palustre*
  yellow—*G. verum*
Beech—*Fagus sylvatica*
Beet, sea—*Beta vulgaris* subsp. *maritima*
Bell-heather—*Erica cinerea*
Bent-grass, bristle—*Agrostis setacea*
  common—*A. tenuis*
  creeping—*A. stolonifera*

Bilberry—*Vaccinium myrtillus*
Bindweed, field—*Convolvulus arvensis*
  hedge—*Calystegia sepium*
  sea—*C. soldanella*
Birch, downy—*Betula pubescens*
  silver—*B. pendula*
Bird cherry—*Prunus padus*
Bird's foot trefoil, common—*Lotus corniculatus*
  greater—*L. uliginosus*
Bird's nest, yellow—*Monotropa hyphophegea*
Bistort, water—*Polygonum amphibium*
Biting stonecrop—*Sedum acre*
Bitter-cress, hairy—*Cardamine hirsuta*
  wood (wavy)—*C. flexuosa*
Bittersweet—*Solanum dulcamara*
Bitter vetch—*Lathyrus montanus*
Blackberry (bramble)—*Rubus fruticosus* agg.
Black bindweed—*Polygonum (Bilderdykia) convolvulus*
Black bryony—*Tamus communis*
Black horehound—*Ballota nigra*
Black nightshade—*Solanum nigrum*
Black poplar—*Populus* x *canadensis*
Black saltwort (sea milkwort)—*Glaux maritima*
Blackthorn—*Prunus spinosa*
Bladderwort, greater—*Utricularia vulgaris*
  lesser—*U. minor*
Blinks, common—*Montia fontana*
  'western'—*M. fontana* subsp. *amporitana*
Bloody cranesbill—*Geranium sanguineum*
Bluebell—*Endymion non-scriptus*
Blue fleabane—*Erigeron acer*
Bog asphodel—*Narthecium ossifragum*
Bogbean—*Menyanthes trifoliata*
Bog-Cotton (cotton-grass), common—*Eriophorum angustifolium*
  hare's-tail—*E. vaginatum*
Bog myrtle—*Myrica gale*
Bog pimpernel—*Anagallis tenella*
Bog stitchwort—*Stellaria alsine*
Bracken—*Pteridium aquilinum*
Bramble—*Rubus fruticosus* agg.
Brandy-bottle (yellow water-lily)—*Nuphar lutea*
Bristle bent-grass—*Agrostis setacea*
Broad helleborine—*Epipactis helleborine*
Broad-leaved pondweed—*Potamogeton natans*
Brome-grass, soft, common—*Bromus mollis (hordeaceus)*
  least—*B. ferronii*

Brooklime—*Veronica beccabunga*
Brookweed—*Samolus valerandi*
Broom—*Cytisus scoparius*
Broomrape, ivy—*Orobanche hederae*
Bryony, black—*Tamus communis*
  white (extinct)—*Bryonia dioica*
Buckler fern, broad—*Dryopteris dilatata*
  narrow—*D. carthusiana*
Buck's horn plantain—*Plantago coronopus*
Buckthorn, alder—*Frangula alnus*
  purging (common) *Rhamnus catharticus*
  sea—*Hippophaë rhamnoides*
Bugloss, viper's—*Echium vulgare*
Bulbous buttercup—*Ranunculus bulbosus*
Bulrush, greater—*Typha latifolia*
  lesser—*T. angustifolia*
Bur-marigold, trifid—*Bidens tripartita*
Burnet rose—*Rosa pimpinellifolia*
Burnet, salad—*Poterium sanguisorba (Sanguisorba minor* subsp. *minor)*
Burnet-saxifrage—*Pimpinella saxifraga*
Bur-reed, branched—*Sparganium erectum*
  unbranched—*S. emersum*
Bush-grass (wood small-reed)—*Calamagrostis epigejos*
Butcher's-broom—*Ruscus aculeatus*
Buttercup, bulbous—*Ranunculus bulbosus*
  celery-leaved—*R. sceleratus*
  creeping—*R. repens*
Butterfly orchid, greater—*Platanthera chlorantha*
Butterwort (not present)—*Pinguicula vulgaris*
Buxbaum's (common field) speedwell—*Veronica persica*
Calamint, common—*Calamintha sylvatica* (subsp. *ascendens)*
Campion, red—*Silene dioica*
  sea—*S. vulgaris* subsp. *maritima*
Canadian pondweed—*Elodea canadensis*
Caper spurge—*Euphorbia lathyrus*
Caraway, whorled—*Carum verticillatum*
Carline thistle—*Carlina vulgaris*
Carnation sedge—*Carex panicea*
Carrot, wild—*Daucus carota*
Cat's foot (mountain everlasting) (extinct)—*Antennaria dioica*
Celandine, lesser—*Ranunculus ficaria*
Celery, wild—*Apium graveolens*
Celery-leaved buttercup—*Ranunculus sceleratus*
Centaury, common—*Centaurium erythraea*
  lesser—*C. pulchellum*

Charlock—*Sinapis arvensis*
Cherry, bird—*Prunus padus*
  dwarf—*P. cerasus*
  great—*P. avium*
Cherry-laurel—*P. laurocerasus*
Chestnut, horse—*Aesculus hippocastanum*
  sweet—*Castanea sativa*
Chickweed, common—*Stellaria media*
Cinquefoil, creeping—*Potentilla reptans*
  marsh—*P. palustre*
  spring—*P. tabernaemontani*
Clary, wild—*Salvia horminoides*
Cleavers—*Galium aparine*
Clematis (traveller's joy)—*Clematis vitalba*
Clover, alsike—*Trifolium hybridum*
  knotted—*T. striatum*
  least (slender trefoil)—*T. micranthum*
  red—*T. pratense*
  rough—*T. scabrum*
  strawberry—*T. fragiferum*
  white—*T. repens*
  yellow suckling (lesser trefoil)—*T. dubium*
Club-rush, bristle—*Isolepis (Scirpus) setacea*
  grey—*Schoenoplectus (Scirpus)*
    tabernaemontani
  slender—*Isolepis (S.) cernua*
Cocksfoot—*Dactylis glomerata*
Coltsfoot—*Tussilago farfara*
Columbine—*Aquilegia vulgaris*
Cord grass, common—*Spartina anglica*
Corn marigold—*Chrysanthemum segetum*
Cornsalad—*Valerianella* spp.
Corn spurrey—*Spergula arvensis*
Cotoneaster, Himalayan—*Cotoneaster*
  simonsii
  small-leaved—*C. microphyllus*
Cotton-grass, common—*Eriophorum*
  angustifolium
  single-headed (hare's-tail)—*E. vaginatum*
Couch grass, common—*Agropyron repens*
  sand—*A. junceiforme*
  sea—*A. pungens (pycnanthum)*
Cow parsley—*Anthriscus sylvestris*
Cowslip—*Primula veris*
Crab apple—*Malus sylvestris*
Cranberry—*Vaccinium oxycoccus*
Cranesbill, bloody—*Geranium sanguineum*
  cut-leaved—*G. dissectum*
  dove's-foot—*G. molle*
  dusky—*G. phaeum*
  long-stalked—*G. columbinum*
  meadow—*G. pratense*
  shining—*G. lucidum*

Creeping buttercup—*Ranunculus repens*
Creeping cinquefoil—*Potentilla reptans*
Creeping Jenny—*Lysimachia nummularia*
Crested dogstail—*Cynosurus cristatus*
Crested hair-grass—*Koeleria cristata*
Cross-leaved heath—*Erica tetralix*
Crosswort—*Galium cruciata (Cruciata*
  laevipes)
Cuckooflower—*Cardamine pratensis*
Curled dock—*Rumex crispus*
Curled pondweed—*Potamogeton crispus*
Cut-leaved cranesbill—*Geranium dissectum*
Daffodil—*Narcissus pseudonarcissus*
Daisy, field—*Bellis perennis*
  Ox-eye—*Chrysanthemum leucanthemum*
    (Leucanthemum vulgare)
Dame's-violet—*Hesperis matronalis*
Dandelion—*Taraxacum officinale* agg.
Darnel-Poa—*Catapodium marinum*
Deergrass—*Trichophorum caespitosum*
Dewberry—*Rubus caesius*
Dock, curled—*Rumex crispus*
  South American—*R. frutescens*
  water—*R. hydrolapathum*
Dodder (extinct)—*Cuscuta epithymum*
Dogrose—*Rosa canina*
Dog's mercury—*Mercurialis perennis*
Dog-violet, common—*Viola riviniana*
  early—*V. reichenbachiana*
  heath—*V. canina*
Dogwood—*Cornus sanguinea*
Dove's-foot cranesbill—*Geranium molle*
Downy birch—*Betula pubescens*
Downy oat-grass—*Helictotrichon pubescens*
Duckweed, ivy—*Lemna trisulca*
  lesser (common)—*L. minor*
Duke of Argyll's teaplant—*Lycium*
  barbarum
Dune fescue—*Vulpia membranacea*
Durmast (sessile) oak—*Quercus petraea*
Dusky cranesbill—*Geranium phaeum*
Dwarf cherry—*Prunus cerasus*
Dwarf spurge—*Euphorbia exigua*
Eared sallow (willow)—*Salix aurita*
Early hair-grass—*Aira praecox*
Early purple orchid—*Orchis mascula*
Early sand-grass—*Mibora minima*
Eel-grass, narrow-leaved—*Zostera*
  angustifolia
Elder—*Sambucus nigra*
Elecampane—*Inula helenium*
Elm, English—*Ulmus procera*
  wych—*U. glabra*

299

Elm-leaved bramble—*Rubus ulmifolius*
English stonecrop—*Sedum anglicum*
European (common) gorse—*Ulex europaeus*
Evening primrose, large-flowered—*Oenothera erythrosepala*
Everlasting pea, narrow-leaved—*Lathyrus sylvestris*
Eyebright, common—*Euphrasia nemorosa* (dwarf, purple, on Worm)—*E. curta*
Fairy flax—*Linum catharticum*
False fox-sedge—*Carex otrubae*
False oxlip—*Primula veris* x *vulgaris*
Felwort (Autumn gentian)—*Gentianella amarella*
Fennel—*Foeniculum vulgare*
Fennel pondweed—*Potamogeton pectinatus*
Fen orchid—*Liparis loeselii* var. *ovata*
Fescue, dune—*Vulpia membranacea* red—*Festuca rubra* sheep's—*F. ovina*
Field bindweed—*Convolvulus arvensis*
Field madder—*Sherardia arvensis*
Field maple—*Acer campestre*
Figwort, common—*Scrophularia nodosa* water—*S. auriculata*
Fine-leaved heath (bell-heather)—*Erica cinerea*
Fingered (rue-leaved) saxifrage—*Saxifraga tridactylites*
Fiorin (creeping bent)—*Agrostis stolonifera*
Flag, yellow (yellow iris)—*Iris pseudacorus*
Flat-sedge, saltmarsh—*Blysmus rufus*
Flax, fairy—*Linum catharticum* pale—*L. bienne*
Fleabane, blue—*Erigeron acer* common—*Pulicaria dysenterica*
Floating club-rush—*Scirpus fluitans*
Flote-grass (floating sweet-grass)—*Glyceria fluitans*
Flowering rush—*Butomus umbellatus*
Fog-grass (Yorkshire fog)—*Holcus lanatus*
Fool's watercress—*Apium nodiflorum*
Forget-me-not, changing—*Myosotis discolor* early—*M. ramosissima* field—*M. arvensis* water—*M. scorpioides*
Foxglove—*Digitalis purpurea*
Fringed water-lily—*Nymphoides peltata*
Fumitory, white ramping—*Fumaria capreolata*
Garlic, triquetrous (three-cornered leek)— *A. triquetrum*

Garlic, wild (ramsons)—*Allium ursinum*
Garlic-mustard—*Alliaria petiolata*
Gean (great cherry)—*Prunus avium*
Gentian, Autumn—*Gentianella amarella* Welsh (dune)—*G. uliginosa*
Gilliflower (hoary) stock—*Matthiola incana*
Gipsywort—*Lycopus europaeus*
Gladdon (stinking iris)—*Iris foetidissima*
Glasswort, annual—*Salicornia europaea* *S. dolichostachya* *S. ramosissima*
Goat willow—*Salix caprea*
Golden samphire—*Inula crithmoides*
Golden-saxifrage, opposite-leaved— *Chrysosplenium oppositifolium*
Goldilocks-aster—*Aster linosyris*
Gooseberry—*Ribes uva-crispa*
Goosefoot, white (fat-hen)—*Chenopodium album*
Gorse, Spring (common)—*Ulex europaeus* Autumn (Western)—*U. gallii*
Greater bird's-foot trefoil—*Lotus uliginosus*
Greater knapweed—*Centaurea scabiosa*
Greater water-plantain—*Alisma plantago-aquatica*
Great horsetail—*Equisetum telmateia*
Great reedmace (bulrush)—*Typha latifolia*
Great willow-herb—*Epilobium hirsutum*
Green hellebore—*Helleborus viridis*
Green-winged orchid—*Orchis morio*
Grey willow—*Salix cinerea*
Gromwell, common—*Lithospermum officinale* purple—*L. (Buglossoides) purpurocaeruleum*
Ground-ivy—*Glechoma hederacea*
Groundsel, common—*Senecio vulgaris* heath—*S. sylvaticus*
Guelder-rose—*Viburnum opulus*
Hair-grass, annual—*Aira praecox* crested—*Koeleria cristata* silver—*Aira caryophyllea*
Hard-grass, common—*Parapholis strigosa* curved—*P. incurva*
Hard-Poa—*Catapodium rigidum*
Harebell—*Campanula rotundifolia*
Hare's-foot clover—*Trifolium arvense*
Hart's-tongue—*Phyllitis scolopendrium* (*Asplenium phyllitis*)
Hawkbit, Autumn—*Leontodon autumnalis*
Hawkweed, mouse-ear—*Hieracium pilosella* (*Pilosella officinarum*)

Hawthorn—*Crataegus monogyna*
Hazel—*Corylus avellana*
Heath, cross-leaved—*Erica tetralix*
  fine-leaved (bell-heather)—*E. cinerea*
Heath bedstraw—*Galium saxatile*
Heather—*Calluna vulgaris*
Heath-grass—*Sieglingia decumbens*
Heath dog violet—*Viola canina*
Hedge garlic (garlic-mustard)—*Alliaria petiolata*
Hedge-parsley, knotted—*Torilis nodosa*
Hellebore, green—*Helleborus viridis*
  stinking—*H. foetidus*
Helleborine, broad-leaved—*Epipactis helleborine*
  marsh—*E. palustris*
Hemlock—*Conium maculatum*
Hemlock water-dropwort—*Oenanthe crocata*
Hemp-agrimony—*Eupatorium cannabinum*
Hemp-nettle, narrow-leaved—*Galeopsis angustifolium*
Herb-Paris—*Paris quadrifolia*
Herb-Robert—*Geranium robertianum*
Hoary plantain—*Plantago media*
Holly—*Ilex aquifolium*
Honeysuckle—*Lonicera periclymenum*
Hop trefoil—*Trifolium campestre*
Horehound, black—*Ballota nigra*
  white—*Marrubium vulgare*
Hornbeam—*Carpinus betulus*
Horned pondweed—*Zannichellia palustris*
Horned poppy, yellow—*Glaucium flavum*
Hornwort, soft—*Ceratophyllum submersum*
Horse-chestnut—*Aesculus hippocastanum*
Horse-radish—*Armoracia rusticana*
Horsetail, great—*Equisetum telmateia*
  variegated—*E. variegatum*
  water—*E. fluviatile*
  wood—*E. sylvaticum*
Hound's-tongue—*Cynoglossum officinale*
Hutchinsia—*Hornungia petraea*
Iris, stinking—*Iris foetidissima*
  yellow—*I. pseudacorus*
Isle-of-Man cabbage—*Rhynchosinapis monensis*
Italian poplar—*Populus serotina*
Ivy—*Hedera helix*
Ivy broomrape—*Orobanche hederae*
Ivy duckweed—*Lemna trisulca*
Ivy-leaved crowfoot—*Ranunculus hederaceus*
Ivy-leaved speedwell—*Veronica hederifolia*
Ivy-leaved toadflax—*Cymbalaria muralis*

Jack-by-the-hedge (garlic-mustard)—*Alliaria petiolata*
Jointed rush—*Juncus articulatus*
Juniper—*Juniperus communis*
Kidney vetch—*Anthyllis vulneraria*
Kingcup (marsh-marigold)—*Caltha palustris*
Knapweed, common—*Centaurea nigra*
  greater—*C. scabiosa*
  slender—*C. nemoralis*
Knotgrass—*Polygonum aviculare* agg.
Knotted hedge-parsley—*Torilis nodosa*
Knotted pearlwort—*Sagina nodosa*
Lady-fern—*Athyrium filix-femina*
Lady's bedstraw—*Galium verum*
Lady's fingers (kidney vetch)—*Anthyllis vulneraria*
Lady's-tresses, Autumn—*Spiranthes spiralis*
Lamb's-lettuce (cornsalad)—*Valerianella* spp.
Lamb's-tongue (hoary) plantain—*Plantago media*
Larch, European—*Larix decidua*
  Japanese—*L. leptolepis* (*Kaempferi*)
Lavender (sea-lavender), common—*Limonium vulgare*
  rock—*L. binervosum*
Lemon-scented fern—*Thelypteris limbosperma*
Lesser celandine—*Ranunculus ficaria*
Lesser (common) duckweed—*Lemna minor*
Lesser reedmace (bulrush)—*Typha angustifolia*
Lesser water-parsnip—*Berula erecta*
Lesser water plantain—*Baldellia ranunculoides*
Lettuce, wall—*Mycelis muralis*
Lilac—*Syringa vulgaris*
Lime, small-leaved—*Tilia cordata*
Ling (heather)—*Calluna vulgaris*
Live-long (orpine)—*Sedum telephium*
Loosestrife, purple—*Lythrum salicaria*
  woodland (yellow pimpernel)—*Lysimachia nemorum*
  yellow—*L. vulgaris*
Lords-and-ladies—*Arum maculatum*
Lousewort—*Pedicularis sylvatica*
Lundy cabbage (not present)—*Rhynchosinapis wrightii*
Lyme-grass—*Elymus arenarius*
Madder, field—*Sherardia arvensis*
  wild—*Rubia peregrina*
Maidenhair fern—*Adiantum capillus-veneris*
Maidenhair spleenwort—*Asplenium trichomanes*

Male fern—*Dryopteris filix-mas*
Mallow, common—*Malva sylvestris*
   marsh—*Althaea officinalis*
   musk—*Malva moschata*
   tree—*Lavatera arborea*
Mare's tail—*Hippuris vulgaris*
Marigold, bur—*Bidens tripartita*
   corn—*Chrysanthemum segetum*
Marjoram—*Origanum vulgare*
Marram—*Ammophila arenaria*
Marsh arrow-grass—*Triglochin palustre*
Marsh bedstraw—*Galium palustre*
Marsh cinquefoil—*Potentilla palustris*
Marsh foxtail—*Alopecurus geniculatus*
Marsh helleborine—*Epipactis palustris*
Marsh lousewort—*Pedicularis palustris*
Marsh-mallow—*Althaea officinalis*
Marsh-marigold—*Caltha palustris*
Marsh-orchid, early—*Dactylorhiza incarnata*
   southern—*D. praetermissa*
Marsh pennywort—*Hydrocotyle vulgaris*
Marsh St. John's-wort—*Hypericum elodes*
Marsh violet—*Viola palustris*
Marsh willow-herb—*Epilobium palustre*
Mat-grass—*Nardus stricta*
Mayweed, scentless—*Tripleurospermum*
   maritimum subsp. *inodorum*
Meadow-grass, annual—*Poa annua*
   common (smooth)—*P. pratensis*
   tall (rough)—*P. trivialis*
Meadow-rue, lesser—*Thalictrum minus*
Meadow saxifrage—*Saxifraga granulata*
Meadowsweet—*Filipendula ulmaria*
Mercury, dog's—*Mercurialis perennis*
Milfoil (yarrow)—*Achillea millefolium*
Milfoil, water-, alternate—*Myriophyllum*
   alterniflorum
   spiked—*M. spicatum*
Milkmaid (cuckooflower)—*Cardamine*
   pratensis
Milkwort, common—*Polygala vulgaris*
   heath—*P. serpyllifolia*
   sea—*Glaux maritima*
Mimulus (monkeyflower)—*Mimulus guttatus*
Mind your-own-business—*Soleirolia*
   soleirolii
Mint, corn—*Mentha arvensis*
   round-leaved—*M. rotundifolia* (*suaveolens*)
   water—*M. aquatica*
Mistletoe—*Viscum album*
Monkeyflower—*Mimulus guttatus*
Monk's-hood—*Aconitum napellus*
Montbretia—*Crocosmia* x *crocosmiflora*

Moonwort—*Botrychium lunaria*
Moor-grass, purple—*Molinia caerulea*
Moschatel—*Adoxa moschatellina*
Mountain-everlasting (extinct)—*Antennaria*
   dioica
Mouse-ear, common—*Cerastium holosteoides*
   (*fontanum* subsp. *triviale*)
   little—*C. semidecandrum*
   starwort—*C. atrovirens* (*diffusum* subsp.
   diffusum)
   sticky—*C. viscosum* (*glomeratum*)
Mouse-ear hawkweed—*Hieracium pilosella*
   (*Pilosella officinarum*)
Musk (monkeyflower)—*Mimulus guttatus*
Myrtle, bog—*Myrica gale*
Narcissus—*Narcissus pseudonarcissus*
Narrow buckler-fern—*Dryopteris carthusiana*
Navelwort—*Umbilicus rupestris*
Nettle, common—*Urtica dioica*
Nightshade, black—*Solanum nigrum*
   enchanter's—*Circaea lutetiana*
   woody (bittersweet)—*Solanum dulcamara*
Nitella (stonewort)—*Nitella flexilis*? (an
   alga)
Oak, holm—*Quercus ilex*
   pedunculate—*Q. robur*
   sessile—*Q. petraea*
Oat-grass, downy—*Helictotrichon pubescens*
   false—*Arrhenatherum elatius*
   yellow—*Trisetum flavescens*
Old-man's beard (traveller's-joy)—*Clematis*
   vitalba
Orache, Babington's—*Atriplex glabriuscula*
   common—*A. patula*
   spear-leaved—*A. hastata*
Orchid, Autumn lady's-tresses—*Spiranthes*
   spiralis
   bee—*Ophrys apifera*
   common spotted—*Dactylorhiza fuchsii*
   early marsh—*D. incarnata* subsp.
   incarnata and subsp. *coccinea*
   early purple—*Orchis mascula*
   fen—*Liparis loeselii* var. *ovata*
   greater butterfly—*Platanthera chlorantha*
   heath spotted—*Dactylorhiza maculata*
   subsp. *ericetorum*
   marsh helleborine—*Epipactis palustris*
   southern marsh—*Dactylorhiza*
   praetermissa
   pyramidal—*Anamcamptis pyramidalis*
   twayblade—*Listera ovata*
Orpine—*Sedum telephium*
Osier—*Salix viminalis*

Oxalis (wood-sorrel)—*Oxalis acetosella*
Oxlip, false—*Primula veris* x *vulgaris*
Oxtongue, bristly—*Picris echioides*
Pansy, wild—*Viola tricolor* subsp. *curtisii*
Parsley-piert—*Aphanes arvensis*
Parsley water-dropwort—*Oenanthe lachenalii*
Parsnip, water, lesser—*Berula erecta*
Pathfinder (slender) rush—*Juncus tenuis*
Pea, marsh—*Lathyrus palustris*
   narrow-leaved everlasting—*L. sylvestris*
   yellow (meadow vetchling)—*L. pratensis*
Pearlwort, knotted—*Sagina nodosa*
   sea—*S. maritima*
Pellitory-of-the-wall—*Parietaria judaica*
Pennywort, marsh—*Hydrocotyle vulgaris*
   wall (navelwort)—*Umbilicus rupestris*
Pepper, wall (biting stonecrop)—*Sedum acre*
   water—*Polygonum hydropiper*
Perennial rye-grass—*Lolium perenne*
Perforate St. John's-wort—*Hypericum perforatum*
Petty whin—*Genista anglica*
Pick-a-back plant—*Tolmiea menziesii*
Pignut—*Conopodium majus*
Pimpernel, blue—*A. arvensis* subsp. *caerulea*
    (*A. foemina*)
   bog—*Anagallis tenella*
   scarlet—*A. arvensis*
   yellow—*Lysimachia nemorum*
Pine, Corsican—*Pinus nigra*
   Scots—*P. sylvestris*
Pineappleweed—*Matricaria matricarioides*
Plantain, buck's-horn—*Plantago coronopus*
   hoary—*P. media*
   ribwort—*P. lanceolata*
   sea—*P. maritima*
Ploughman's-spikenard—*Inula conyza*
Polypody—*Polypodium interjectum* and *P. vulgare*
Pondweed, bog—*Potamogeton polygonifolius*
   broad-leaved—*P. natans*
   Canadian—*Elodea canadensis*
   curled—*Potamogeton crispus*
   fennel—*P. pectinatus*
   horned—*Zannichellia palustris*
   tasselled (beaked tasselweed)—*Ruppia maritima*
Poplar, black—*Populus* x *canadensis*
   grey—*P. canescens*
   Italian—*P. serotina*
   white—*P. alba*
Poppy, yellow-horned —*Glaucium flavum*
Portland spurge—*Euphorbia portlandica*

Prickly saltwort—*Salsola kali*
Primrose—*Primula vulgaris*
Privet—*Ligustrum vulgare*
Purging buckthorn—*Rhamnus catharticus*
Purging (fairy) flax—*Linum catharticum*
Purple gromwell—*Lithospermum (Buglossoides) purpurocaeruleum*
Purple loosestrife—*Lythrum salicaria*
Purple moor-grass—*Molinia caerulea*
Purslane, sea—*Halimione portulacoides*
   sea (sea sandwort)—*Honkenya peploides*
   water—*Peplis (Lythrum) portula*
Pyramidal orchid—*Anacamptis pyramidalis*
Quaking-grass—*Briza media*
Ragged-robin—*Lychnis flos-cuculi*
Ragwort—*Senecio jacobaea*
Ramping fumitory, white—*Fumaria capreolata*
Ramsons—*Allium ursinum*
Raspberry—*Rubus idaeus*
Rattle, red (marsh lousewort)—*Pedicularis palustris*
   yellow—*Rhinanthus minor*
Red bartsia—*Odontites verna*
Red campion—*Silene dioica*
Red fescue—*Festuca rubra*
Red-rattle (marsh lousewort)—*Pedicularis palustris*
Red valerian—*Centranthus ruber*
Reed—*Phragmites australis*
Reed-canary-grass—*Phalaris arundinacea*
Reedmace (bulrush), great—*Typha latifolia*
   lesser—*T. angustifolia*
Restharrow, common—*Ononis repens*
   small—*O. reclinata*
Rhododendron—*Rhododendron ponticum*
Ribwort—*Plantago lanceolata*
Rice-grass (cord-grass)—*Spartina anglica*
Rock-cress, hairy—*Arabis hirsuta*
Rock-rose, common—*Helianthemum nummularium*
   hoary—*H. canum*
   white—*H. appeninum*
Rock samphire—*Crithmum maritimum*
Rock spurrey—*Spergularia rupicola*
Rock whitebeam—*Sorbus rupicola*
Rose, burnet—*Rosa pimpinellifolia*
   dog—*R. canina*
   field—*R. arvensis*
Roseroot—*Sedum (Rhodiola) rosea*
Round-leaved mint—*Mentha rotundifolia (suaveolens)*

Rowan—*Sorbus aucuparia*
Royal fern—*Osmunda regalis*
Rue-leaved saxifrage—*Saxifraga tridactylites*
Rush, blunt-flowered—*Juncus subnodulosus*
    bulbous—*J. bulbosus* agg. (incl. *J. kochii*)
    club, bristle —*Isolepis (Scirpus) setaceus*
      grey —*Schoenoplectus (Scirpus)*
        tabernaemontani
      slender—*Isolepis (Scirpus) cernua*
    flowering—*Butomus umbellatus*
    hard—*Juncus inflexus*
    heath—*J. squarrosus*
    jointed—*J. articulatus*
    pathfinder (slender)—*J. tenuis*
    saltmarsh—*J. gerardii*
    sea—*J. maritimus*
    sharp—*J. acutus*
    sharp-flowered—*J. acutiformis*
    slender—*J. tenuis*
    soft —*J. effusus*
    spike, common—*Eleocharis palustris*
    toad—*J. bufonius*
Rustyback fern—*Ceterach officinarum*
    (*Asplenium ceterach*)
Rye-grass, perennial—*Lolium perenne*
Sage, wood—*Teucrium scorodonia*
St. John's wort, marsh—*Hypericum elodes*
    perforate—*H. perforatum*
    slender—*H. pulchrum*
    trailing—*H. humifusum*
Salad burnet—*Poterium sanguisorba*
    (*Sanguisorba minor* subsp. *minor*)
Sallow (willow), eared— *Salix aurita*
    goat—*S. caprea*
    grey—*S. cinerea*
Saltmarsh flat-sedge—*Blysmus rufus*
Saltmarsh-grass—*Puccinellia maritima*
Saltwort, prickly—*Salsola kali*
    (glasswort)—*Salicornia* spp.
Samphire, golden—*Inula crithmoides*
    rock—*Crithmum maritimum*
Sand cat's-tail-grass—*Phleum arenarium*
Sand couch—*Agropyron junceiforme*
Sand-grass, early—*Mibora minima*
Sandwort, sea—*Honkenya peploides*
    thyme-leaved—*Arenaria serpyllifolia*
Saw-wort —*Serratula tinctoria*
Saxifrage, meadow—*Saxifraga granulata*
    rue-leaved—*S. tridactylites*
Scabious, devil's-bit—*Succisa pratensis*
    sheep's-bit—*Jasione montana*
    small—*Scabiosa columbaria*
Scots pine—*Pinus sylvestris*

Scurvy-grass, common—*Cochlearia*
    officinalis
    Danish—*C. danica*
    English—*C. anglica*
Sea arrow-grass—*Triglochin maritimum*
Sea aster—*Aster tripolium*
Sea beet—*Beta vulgaris* subsp. *maritima*
Sea bindweed—*Calystegia soldanella*
Sea blite, annual—*Suaeda maritima*
Sea buckthorn—*Hippophaë rhamnoides*
Sea campion—*Silene maritima* (*S. vulgaris*
    subsp. *maritima*)
Sea couch—*Agropyron pungens* (*pycnanthum*)
Sea-holly—*Eryngium maritimum*
Sea-lavender, common—*Limonium vulgare*
    rock—*L. binervosum*
Sea mayweed—*Tripleurospermum maritimum*
Sea-milkwort—*Glaux maritima*
Sea pearlwort—*Sagina maritima*
Sea pink (thrift)—*Armeria maritima*
Sea plantain—*Plantago maritima*
Sea purslane—*Halimione portulacoides*
Sea rocket—*Cakile maritima*
Sea rush—*Juncus maritimus*
Sea sandwort—*Honkenya peploides*
Sea sedge —*Scirpus maritimus*
Sea spleenwort—*Asplenium marinum*
Sea spurge—*Euphorbia paralias*
Sea spurrey, greater—*Spergularia marginata*
    (*S. media*)
    lesser—*S. salina* (*S. marina*)
    rock—*S. rupicola*
Sea stock—*Matthiola sinuata*
Sea storksbill—*Erodium maritimum*
Sea wormwood—*Artemisia maritima*
Sedge, bristle (clubrush) —*Isolepis (Scirpus)*
    setacea
    carnation—*Carex panicea*
    common—*C. nigra*
    cyperus—*C. pseudocyperus*
    false fox—*C. otrubae*
    flea—*C. pulicaris*
    glaucous—*C. flacca*
    greater tussock—*C. paniculata*
    great pond—*C. riparia*
    lesser pond—*C. acutiformis*
    long-bracted —*C. extensa*
    pill—*C. pilulifera*
    remote— *C. remota*
    sea—*Scirpus maritimus*
    slender (clubrush) —*Isolepis (Scirpus)*
      cernua
    star—*Carex echinata*

Sedge, yellow, common—*C. demissa*
  small-fruited —*C. serotina*
Self heal—*Prunella vulgaris*
Service tree—*Sorbus torminalis*
Sessile oak—*Quercus petraea*
Sheep's bit—*Jasione montana*
Sheep's fescue—*Festuca ovina*
Sheep's sorrel—*Rumex acetosella*
Shepherd's needle—*Scandix pecten-veneris*
Shield-fern, soft—*Polystichum setiferum*
Shining cranesbill—*Geranium lucidum*
Silver hair grass—*Aira caryophyllea*
Silverweed—*Potentilla anserina*
Skullcap, greater —*Scutellaria galericulata*
  lesser—*S. minor*
Slender thistle—*Carduus tenuiflorus*
Sloe (blackthorn)—*Prunus spinosa*
Small-reed, wood—*Calamagrostis epigejos*
Snow-in-summer—*Cerastium tomentosum*
Soapwort—*Saponaria officinalis*
Soft-brome, common—*Bromus mollis*
  least—*B. ferronii*
Soft-grass, creeping—*Holcus mollis*
Solomon's-seal—*Polygonatum multiflorum*
Sorrel, common—*Rumex acetosa*
  sheep's—*R. acetosella*
  wood—*Oxalis acetosella*
Sow-thistle, common—*Sonchus oleraceus*
  perennial—*S. arvensis*
  prickly—*S. asper*
Spearwort, lesser—*Ranunculus flammula*
Speedwell, Buxbaum's (common field)—
  Veronica persica
  germander—*V. chamaedrys*
  heath—*V. officinalis*
  ivy-leaved—*V. hederifolia*
  slender—*V. filiformis*
  spiked—*V. spicata* subsp. *hybrida*
  thyme-leaved—*V. serpyllifolia*
  wall—*V. arvensis*
  water, pink—*V. catenata*
  wood—*V. montana*
Spiked water-milfoil—*Myriophyllum spicatum*
Spike-rush, common—*Eleocharis palustris*
Spindle, common—*Euonymus europaeus*
  Japanese—*E. japonicus*
Spleenwort, black—*Asplenium adiantum-nigrum*
  maidenhair—*A. trichomanes*
  sea—*A. marinum*
Spotted-orchid, common—*Dactylorhiza fuchsii*
  heath—*D. maculata* subsp. *ericetorum*

Spring squill—*Scilla verna*
Spring whitlow-grass—*Erophila verna*
Spurge, caper—*Euphorbia lathyrus*
  dwarf—*E. exigua*
  Portland—*E. portlandica*
  sea—*E. paralias*
  sun—*E. helioscopia*
  wood —*E. amygdaloides*
Spurge-laurel—*Daphne laureola*
Spurrey, lesser—*S. salina* (*S. marina*)
  rock—*Spergularia rupicola*
  sand—*S. rubra*
  sea, greater —*S. marginata* (*S. media*)
Squill—*Scilla verna*
Squinancywort—*Asperula cynanchica*
Starwort, water, common—*Callitriche stagnalis*
  intermediate—*C. intermedia*
Stinging nettle, common—*Urtica dioica*
Stinking hellebore—*Helleborus foetidus*
Stinking iris—*Iris foetidissima*
Stitchwort, bog—*Stellaria alsine*
Stock, hoary—*Matthiola incana*
  sea—*M. sinuata*
Stonecrop, biting—*Sedum acre*
  English—*S. anglicum*
  white—*S. album*
  yellow (biting)—*S. acre*
Stoneworts—*Chara vulgaris* }
  Nitella flexilis } Algae
Stork'sbill, common—*Erodium cicutarium*
  musk—*E. moschatum*
  sea —*E. maritimum*
  sticky —*E. cicutarium* subsp. *bipinnatum* (*dunense*)
Strawberry, barren—*Potentilla sterilis*
  wild —*Fragaria vesca*
Strawberry-tree —*Arbutus unedo*
Sundew, great—*Drosera anglica*
  oblong-leaved—*D. intermedia*
  round-leaved—*D. rotundifolia*
Sweet chestnut—*Castanea sativa*
Sweet vernal-grass—*Anthoxanthum odoratum*
Sweet violet—*Viola odorata*
Sweet woodruff—*Asperula odorata* (*Galium odoratum*)
Sycamore—*Acer pseudoplatanus*
Tansy—*Tanacetum vulgare*
Tasselweed, beaked —*Ruppia maritima*
Teaplant, Duke-of-Argyll's—*Lycium barbarum*
Teasel—*Dipsacus fullonum*

Thistle, carline—*Carlina vulgaris*
   dwarf—*Cirsium acaule*
   nodding (musk)—*Carduus nutans*
   slender—*C. tenuiflorus*
   stemless (dwarf)—*Cirsium acaule*
Thrift—*Armeria maritima*
Thyme, basil—*Acinos arvensis*
   wild—*Thymus drucei*
Thyme-leaved sandwort—*Arenaria serpyllifolia*
Thyme-leaved speedwell—*Veronica serpyllifolia*
Toadflax, common—*Linaria vulgaris*
   ivy-leaved—*Cymbalaria muralis*
   pale—*Linaria repens*
   small—*Chaenorhinum minus*
Toothwort—*Lathraea squamaria*
Tormentil—*Potentilla erecta*
Tree lupin—*Lupinus arboreus*
Tree-mallow—*Lavatera arborea*
Trefoil, hop—*Trifolium campestre*
   lesser—*T. dubium*
   slender—*T. micranthum*
Turret (hair rock) cress—*Arabis hirsuta*
Tussock-sedge, greater—*Carex paniculata*
Twayblade, common—*Listera ovata*
Valerian, common—*Valeriana officinalis*
   marsh—*V. dioica*
   red—*Centranthus ruber*
Vernal-grass, sweet—*Anthoxanthum odoratum*
Veronicas (see speedwells)
Vervain—*Verbena officinalis*
Vetch, bitter—*Lathyrus montanus*
Violet, dame's—*Hesperis matronalis*
   dog, common—*Viola riviniana*
      early—*V. reichenbachiana*
      heath—*V. canina*
   hairy—*V. hirta*
   marsh—*V. palustre*
   sweet—*V. odorata*
Viper's bugloss—*Echium vulgare*
Wallflower—*Cheiranthus cheiri*
Wallflower cabbage—*Rhynchosinapis cheiranthos*
Wall lettuce—*Mycelis muralis*
Wall pellitory (pellitory of the wall)—*Parietaria judaica*
Wall pennywort (navelwort)—*Umbilicus rupestris*
Wall pepper (biting stonecrop)—*Sedum acre*
Wall-rue—*Asplenium ruta-muraria*

Wall speedwell—*Veronica arvensis*
Water avens (not present)—*Geum rivale*
Water (amphibious) bistort—*Polygonum amphibium*
Water blinks, common—*Montia fontana*
   western—*M. fontana* subsp. *amporitana*
Water-cress, common—*Rorippa nasturtium-aquaticum*
   fool's—*Apium nodiflorum*
   lesser—*Rorippa microphyllum*
Water-crowfoot, brackish—*Ranunculus baudotii*
   common—*R. aquatilis* agg.
   ivy-leaved—*R. hederaceus*
   round-leaved—*R. peltatus*
Water dock—*Rumex hydrolapathum*
Water dropwort, hemlock—*Oenanthe crocata*
   parsley—*O. lachenalii*
   tubular—*O. fistulosa*
Water figwort—*Scrophularia auriculata*
Water forget-me-not—*Myosotis scorpioides*
Water lily, fringed—*Nymphoides peltata*
   white—*Nymphaea alba*
   yellow—*Nuphar lutea*
Water-milfoil, alternate—*Myriophyllum alterniflorum*
   spiked—*M. spicatum*
Water mint—*Mentha aquatica*
Water parsnip, lesser—*Berula erecta*
Water pepper—*Polygonum hydropiper*
Water-plantain, greater—*Alisma plantago-aquatica*
   lesser—*Baldellia ranunculoides*
Water purslane—*Peplis (Lythrum) portula*
Water-speedwell, pink—*Veronica catenata*
Water starwort, common—*Callitriche stagnalis*
   intermediate—*C. intermedia*
Wavy hair-grass—*Deschampsia flexuosa*
Wayfaring tree—*Viburnum lantana*
Welsh (dune) gentian—*Gentianella uliginosa*
Western gorse—*Ulex gallii*
Whitebeam, rock—*Sorbus rupicola*
White clover—*Trifolium repens*
White horehound—*Marrubium vulgare*
White stonecrop—*Sedum album*
White water lily—*Nymphaea alba*
Whitlow-grass, spring—*Erophila verna*
   yellow—*Draba aizoides*
Whorled caraway—*Carum verticillatum*
Wild celery—*Apium graveolens*
Wild service tree—*Sorbus torminalis*

Willow, almond (extinct)—*Salix triandra*
  crack—*S. fragilis*
  creeping—*S. repens*
  goat—*S. caprea*
  grey—*S. cinerea*
  osier—*S. viminalis*
  white —*S. alba*
Willowherb, great—*Epilobium hirsutum*
  marsh—*E. palustre*
  rosebay—*E. angustifolium*
Winter-cress—*Barbarea vulgaris*
Wintergreen, round-leaved—*Pyrola rotundifolia* subsp. *maritima*
Wood anemone—*Anemone nemorosa*
Wood avens—*Geum urbanum*
Wood (wavy) bitter-cress—*Cardamine flexuosa*
Wood horsetail—*Equisetum sylvaticum*
Woodland loosestrife (yellow pimpernel)—*Lysimachia nemorum*
Wood millet—*Milium effusum*
Woodruff, sweet—*Asperula odorata (Galium odoratum)*

Wood sage—*Teucrium scorodonia*
Wood sanicle—*Sanicula europaea*
Wood small-reed—*Calamagrostis epigejos*
Wood soft-grass—*Holcus mollis*
Wood sorrel—*Oxalis acetosella*
Wood spurge—*Euphorbia amygdaloides*
Woody nightshade (bittersweet)—*Solanum dulcamara*
Wormwood, sea—*Artemisia maritima*
Yarrow—*Achillea millefolium*
Yellow archangel—*Lamiastrum galeobdolon*
Yellow bird's-nest—*Monotropa hyphophegea*
Yellow horned-poppy—*Glaucium flavum*
Yellow loosestrife—*Lysimachia vulgaris*
Yellow pimpernel—*L. nemorum*
Yellow rattle—*Rhinanthus minor*
Yellow water lily—*Nuphar lutea*
Yellow whitlow-grass—*Draba aizoides*
Yellow-wort—*Blackstonia perfoliata*
Yew—*Taxus baccata*
Yorkshire-fog—*Holcus lanatus*

ALPHABETICAL LIST OF BUTTERFLIES MENTIONED IN THE TEXT

Argus, brown—*Aricia agestis*
Blue, common—*Polyommatus icarus*
  holly—*Celastrina argiolus*
  small—*Cupido minimus*
Brimstone—*Gonepteryx rhamni*
Brown, hedge (gatekeeper)—*Maniola tithonus*
  meadow—*M. jurtina*
Comma—*Polygonia c-album*
Fritillary, dark green—*Argynnis aglaia*
  heath—*Melitaea athalia*
  pearl-bordered—*Argynnis euphrosyne*
  silver-washed—*A. paphia*
  Small pearl-bordered—*A. selene*
Gatekepper (see hedge brown)
Grayling—*Eumenis semele*
Green hairstreak—*Callophrys rubi*
Marbled white—*Melanargia galathea*

Orange-tip—*Anthocharis cardamines*
Painted lady—*Vanessa cardui*
Peacock—*Nymphalis io*
Red admiral—*Vanessa atalanta*
Ringlet—*Aphantopus hyperanthus*
Skipper, dingy—*Erynnis tages*
  grizzled—*Pyrgus malvae*
  large—*Ochlodes venata*
  small—*Thymelicus sylvestris*
Small copper—*Lycaena phlaeas*
Small heath—*Coenonympha pamphilus*
Small tortoiseshell—*Aglais urticae*
Speckled wood—*Pararge aegeria*
Wall brown—*P. megera*
White, green-veined—*Pieris napi*
  large—*P. brassicae*
  small—*P. rapae*

BIBLIOGRAPHY

BALCHIN, W. G. V. *et al* (1971). *Swansea and Its Region*. Swansea. (Published on the occasion of the British Association meeting in Swansea, Sept. 1971).

BEYNON, T. G. (1968). Some notes on the dragonflies of Broad Pool, Gower. *Glam. Nats. Trust Bull.*, *7*, 14-20.

COAD, B. W. (1973). On the food of three species of littoral fish from the Gower Peninsula. *Nature in Wales*, *13*, 3, 186-193.

CONDER, P. (1974). Ministerial ignorance (Kill of 11,000 oyster catchers). *Birds*, 5, 1, 6.

COOKE, J. A. L. & COTTON, M. J. (1962). Some observations on the ecology of spiders on sand dunes at Whiteford Burrows, Gower. *The Entomologist*, *xcvii*, 183-187.

COOKE, J. A. L., DUFFEY, E. & MERRETT, P. (1968). The male of *Lasiargus gowerensis* (Araneae, Linyphiidae), a recently discovered British spider. *Jour. Zool. Lond.*, *154*, 165-172.

DUFFEY, E. (1968). An ecological analysis of the spider fauna of sand dunes. *Jour. Animal Ecol.*, *37*, 641-674.

ELIAS, D. (1976). A South Gower Breeding Census in 1976. *Gower Birds*, 2, 4.

EMERY, F. V. (1964). A note on the age of Broad Pool, Cilibion, Gower. *Glam. Nats. Trust Bull.*, *3*, 12-13.

EVANS, J. G. & JONES, H. (1973). Sub-fossil and modern land snail faunas from rock rubble habitats. *Jour. Conch.*, *28*, 103-129.

GILLHAM, M. E. (1964). The vegetation of local coastal gull colonies. *Trans. Cardiff Nats.* (1961-63) *XCI*, 23-33.

GOODMAN, G. T. (1961) *Plant Life on Gower*. Swansea. (Gower Society booklet).

GOODMAN, G. T. (1968). Whiteford Burrows. *Glam. Nats. Trust Bull.*, 7, 7-9.

GOWER SOCIETY (1965). *A Guide to Gower*. Swansea. (Gower Society booklet).

GRIFFITHS, H. (1971). The Gower Woodland Survey, 1966-1970. *Gower Birds*, *1*, 4, 39-43.

HAMBURY, H. J. (1960's). Newspaper articles on Gower Wildlife as Thomas Heron.

HAMBURY, H. J. (1968). Whiteford. An object lesson of principles and practice of county trust work. *Glam. Nats. Trust Bull.*, 7.

HANFORD, D. M. (1971). A survey of breeding birds on the South Gower cliffland, 1967-1970. *Gower Birds*, *1*, 4, 46-50.

HARDING, Paul T. (1967). *Armadillidium album* Dollfus, Isopoda, Oniscoidea (White woodlouse). *Glam. Nats. Trust Bull.*, *6*, 11-12.

HATTON, R. H. S. (1969). Broad Pool. *Glam. Nats. Trust Bull.*, *8*, 30.

HATTON, R. H. S. (1972). *Saltmarshes of Gower*. Swansea. (Glam. Nats. Trust Booklet).

HOPE-JONES, P. (1974). Welsh Whales. *Nature in Wales*, *14*, 2, 115-116.

HOWELLS, R. J. (1972). Birds in the Burry Inlet in 1971. *Gower Birds*, *1*, 5, 37-39.

HOWELLS, R. J. (1975). Birds in the Burry Inlet in 1974. *Gower Birds*, 2, 3, 150-152.

KAY, Q. O. N. & WOODELL, S. R. J. (1976). The vegetation of anthills in West Glamorgan salt-marshes. *Nature in Wales*, *15*, 2, 81-87.

311

KING, P. E. (1968). Beetles of Gower. *Gower, 19*, 75-79.

KING, P. E. (1969). Sea spiders on Gower shores. *Gower, 20*, 19-22.

KING, P. E. (1970). Sea spiders in Glamorgan. *Nature in Wales, 12*, 124-131.

KING, P. E. (1971). Pseudoscorpions. *Gower, 22*, 20-22.

KING, P. E. & OSBORN, A. (1969). Oyster dredging. *Gower, 20*, 76-81.

KING, P. E. & RATCLIFFE, N. A. (1970). The surface structure of the cuticle of an intertidal Hemipteran, *Aepophilus bonnairei. Entomol. Monthly Mag., 106*, 1-2.

KING, P. E. & RYLAND, J. S. (1972). Fish on and around the shores of Gower. *Gower, 23*, 62-68.

KING, P. E. & STABINS, V. (1971). Aspects of the biology of a strand-living beetle, *Eurynebria complanata*(L). *Journ. Nat. Hist., 5*, 17-28.

MACFAYDEN, A. (1964). Broad Pool. *Glam. Nats. Trust Bull., 3*, 7-12.

McLEAN, R. C. (1935). An ungrazed grassland on limestone in Wales with a note on plant dominions. *Jour. Ecol., 23*, 436-442.

MORGAN, C. I. & KING, P. E. (1970). Water bears on Gower. *Gower, 21*, 63-65.

NELSON-SMITH, A. (1975). Death on the Sands. *Birds*, 37.

PRATER, T. (1974). Oyster catchers veisus cockles. *B.T.O. News, 64*, March.

THOMAS, D. (1976). Wintering blackcaps (at Mumbles). *Nature in Wales, 15*, 2, 90.

THOMAS, D. K. (1975). A breeding bird survey of Nicholaston Wood, Gower. *Gower Birds, 2*, 3, 153-156.

TROW, A. H. (1911). *The Flora of Glamorgan*, Cardiff.

TUCKER, H. M. (1951). *Gower Gleanings*. Swansea. (A Gower Society Booklet).

WALSER, A. R. (1968). First record of the white-sided dolphin, *Lagenorhynchus acutus*, on the Welsh coast. *Glam. Nats. Trust Bull., 7*, 22.

WARREN, R. G. (1972). Butterflies in Glamorgan. *Glam. Nats. Trust Bull, 11*, 21-22.

WARREN, R. G. (1973). Butterflies and moths in some Gower reserves. *Glam. Nats. Trust Bull., 12*, 28-31.

WEBB, J. A. (1953 & 1954). The trees and shrubs of Gower. *Jour. Gower Soc., VII & VIII*, 12-16 & 37-40.

WEBB, J. A. (1958). Ferns and fern allies of Gower Wallica. *Jour. Gower Soc., XI*, 47-48.

WILLIAMS, A. T. (1974). Sand movement at Fall Bay, Gower. *Nature in Wales, 14*, 2, 106-108.

WOODS, R. W. (1969). A preliminary survey of reed and sedge warblers at Oxwich Marsh, Gower in 1968. *Gower Birds, 1*, 2, 6-8.

Unpublished Sources of Material

BURNS, A. (1959). Report of a botanical survey of the Gower Coast National Nature Reserve during August 1959.

COWLEY, J. (1952). List of insects collected in Gower in June, 1952.

DUFFEY, E. (1964 & 1965). Lists of spiders on Whiteford National Nature Reserve.

FONSECA, A. E. (1972). Lists of Diptera collected between June 1952 and June 1972.

GOODMAN, G. T. (c. 1954). The vegetation of Oxwich and Nicholaston.

GOODMAN, G. T. (c. 1964). The vegetation of Pwll Du Head and Bishopston Valley.

HAGUE, D. B. (1966 & 1967). Burry Holms Archeological excavations in 1965-6-7. Typed report to Royal Commission on Ancient Monuments, Wales & Mon.

MACFAYDEN, A., LLEWELLYN, L. C. & LEWIS, J. O. (1959). Gower Coast nature reserve: report on zoological survey, August, 1959.

MACHAN, S. P. & BLACKBURN, R. O. (1972). Freshwater Molluscs in Gower.

MAKINGS, P. & HATTON, R. H. S. (1968). Report on the fauna found during experimental weed clearance in part of Broad Pool, Gower, Oct. 28th, 1968.

MORRIS, M. G. (1965). List of insects at Whiteford Burrows, Sept. 1965.

NATURE CONSERVANCY COUNCIL. Management plan for Oxwich national nature reserve.

NATURE CONSERVANCY COUNCIL. Management plan for Whiteford national nature reserve.

NATURE CONSERVANCY COUNCIL. Management plan for Gower Coast national nature reserve.

NELSON-SMITH, A. Marine life in Oxwich Bay. (Lecture &c. to E.M. weekend course).

NELSON-SMITH, A. The ecology of rocky shores around Swansea Bay. 1. Gower.

NIEDZWIEDZKI, P. Beetles and other invertebrates of Whiteford Burrows Reserve.

RANWELL, D. (1955). Notes on the vegetation of Worm's Head, Inner region, 1949 Report by King's College, London Biol. Soc.

RIDDELSDELL, REV. H. J. (1911). Flora of Worm's Head and nativity of certain disputed species in 1910.

SMITH, K. G. V. (1960). List of Diptera and other insects and woodlice collected at Oxwich and South Gower cliffs in Sept. 1960.

THOMAS, D. (1976). Recent counts of reed warblers and sedge warblers at Oxwich.

WARREN, R. G. (1971). List of Lepidoptera at Whiteford Burrows in July, 1971.

Information regarding most of the above typescripts can be obtained from the Nature Conservancy Council Information Centre at Oxwich or the Zoology Department, University College, Swansea.

INDEX

Plants and butterflies are entered under their scientific names; for common names see the appendices. Page numbers in heavy type refer to colour plates and those in italics to monochrome plates.

315

Burry Estuary

Whiteford Point   Berges I

Llanrhidian Sands

Llandimore Marsh

Cwm Ivy

Broughton Bay   Tor gro   Llanrhidia Mars

Bluepool Corner   Llanmadog   Cheriton   Landimore

Burry Head   Llanmadog Hill   Weobley Castle

Spaniard Rocks   Ryers Down   R. Burry   Llanrid

Llangennith   Kennex·stone

Hillend   Hardings Down   Arthur's Stor

Rhossili Bay   White Moor

Rhossili Down   Burry   Reynoldston

Llanddewi

Rhossili   Penrice Castle

Worm's Head   Kitchen Corner   Pilton Green   Scurlage Castle

Tears Point   Fall Bay   Mewslade   Berry

Thurba   Hangman's cross

Red Chamber

The Knave   Deborah's Hole   Horton   Eastern Slade

Paviland Cave   Paviland Manor   Port Eynon

Foxhole Slade   Overton   Port Eynon Bay   Holy Wash

Longhole   Overton Mere   Sedgers Bank

Culver Hole